The Sumi Baptist Church Mission

Christian Heritage Rediscovered

The Series, as the name suggests, is meant to focus on Christian Faith & Living vis-à-vis topics like Literature & Poetry, Indigenous Philosophizing, Ethical response towards Agriculture, Health & Healing, Science & Technology, Ecofeminist Theology, Sociological approach towards Human Rights, Law & Politics, Arts, History of Ideas, Ancient Civilizations, Cultural Contiguity, Religious Cosmologies & Mysticism, Footsteps of famous Theologians, World Peace & Harmony, Global Capitalism, Network Marketing, Cybertheology, Population & Demographics, Epigraphic Studies, Contextualized Education, and many others. We welcome a Mss. on any topic/s mentioned, whether they are original works, scholarly monographs, collections of conference papers, revised dissertations, or translations of historical documents. Through the Series we, the Publishers, are striving to put forward published works that may help Institutions, Academic Bodies, Researchers, Scholars and the World at large in furthering their respective knowledge and understanding on the concerned subject. We welcome your comments on our efforts and further suggestions on how we can foster the upcoming thoughtful theologically grounded books.

Christian Heritage Rediscovered - 33

The Sumi Baptist Church Mission

Towards the Emerging Socio-Economic Context of Nagaland

Hetoni Swu

CWI

Christian World Imprints(TM)

First Published in 2016 by

Christian World Imprints(TM)
Christian Publishing & Books from India
H-12 Bali Nagar, **New Delhi-110015**
info@christianworldimprints.com
www.ChristianWorldImprints.com
Phone: +91 11 25465925

ISBN: 978-93-5148-110-2 (HB) ISBN: 978-93-5148-111-9 (PB)

Cataloging in Publication Data--DK
Courtesy: D.K. Agencies (P) Ltd. <docinfo@dkagencies.com>

Swu, Hetoni, author.
The Sumi Baptist Church Mission : towards the emerging socio-economic context of Nagaland / Hetoni Swu.
pages cm. -- (Christian heritage rediscovered ; 33)
Includes bibliographical references.
ISBN 9789351481102 (HB)
ISBN 9789351481119 (PB)

1. Home missions--India--Nāgāland. 2. Sumi Baptist Church.--Missions. 3. Naga (South Asian people)--Missions--India--Nāgāland. 4. Naga (South Asian people)--India--Nāgāland--Religion. 5. Nāgāland (India)--Church history. 6. Naga (South Asian people)--India--Nāgāland--Social conditions. 7. Naga (South Asian people)--India--Nāgāland--Economic conditions. 8. Nāgāland (India)--Social conditions. 9. Nāgāland (India)--Economic conditions. I. Title. II. Series: Christian heritage rediscovered ; 33.

BV2653.S98 2016 DDC 266.0220954165 23

Printed at D. K. Fine Art Press Pvt. Ltd.

THE BOOK

The book presents the locus standi of the Sumi Baptist Church in Nagaland. It also proposes the future course of action the Church should employ along with various non-governmental organizations, churches and the government organizations for the betterment of the society in socio-economic context. It suggests the Church to look seriously into biblical teachings and reflect theologically on the present problems for mission direction.

This scholarly work recommends for transformational development that allows establishment of God's desire in human society and in the rest of the creation for total life. It addresses the challenges being faced by the Sumi Baptist Church in the process of transformational development of the Naga society. The work is a treat for readers as it reconsiders four vital impediments in the quest of Naga Spirituality and their transformational development: Stewardship and socio-economic development, Justice in the midst of injustice and division among the Naga community, Liberative mission towards the oppressive socio-economic and political structures, Upholding kingdom community amid Naga society where the social and moral values are corrupted and spiritually bankrupt.

To eradicate the said impediments the author has provided well-researched suggestions like: Strengthening Naga traditional institution of customary laws and acts; Co-operative community development; Reviving community work culture; Human potential - Resource development, Educational development; and Job creation coupled with Project development.

The book is meant to fight against all the social odds that Nagas and society at large are facing. It paves the path for their transformational development so that in future the society can become a God's Intended Society.

THE AUTHOR

Dr. Hetoni Swu, hailing from the Sumi Community of Dimapur (Nagaland), is an active member of the Sumi Baptist Church.

She began her theological voyage by doing B.Th from Clark Theological College, Aolijen, Mokokchung; B.D from Bishop's College, Kolkatta; M.Th in Missiology from Serampore College, Serampore; and Ph.D under the Consortium from Indian Missiological Education (CIME), Bangalore. She had been on various positions at different renowned institutions and colleges. Since 2012, she is a teaching faculty at the Servanthood Bible College, Dimapur. She has also contributed numerous articles in various leading journals.

FOREWORD-I

The Latin term *Missio Dei* can be translated as the "mission of God," or the "sending of God." Thus, *Missio Dei* is seen as a movement from God to the world; and the church is viewed as an instrument for that mission. As David Bosch has said, " To participate in mission is to participate in the movement of God's love toward people, since God is a fountain of sending love." As God's instrument, the mission of the church is directed to the whole inhabited world. In the recent past, the term mission has been applied usually to foreign missionary activities. Now, the mission of the church is perceived as the task of the church wherever it is found, which includes building and strengthening Christian communities. It involves crossing all human boundaries for the purpose of witnessing, proclaiming and serving a lost humanity. As followers of Christ we do mission as a loving response to the triune God who suffers for humanity and who calls us to do mission together with Him. The challenge of mission is inescapable.

The church in Nagaland was established in 1872 when an American Baptist Missionary settled in a small village in Mokokchung district to evangelize the tribes. From that time onwards churches were established everywhere in the Naga Hills. Whatever has happened in Nagaland Church History since 1872 is phenomenal. Today, Nagaland claims that apart from the immigrants, the tribal population is 99% Christians. This is also true for the other hill states such as Mizoram, Meghalaya, and Manipur. The Naga Church is growing not only in terms of quantity but also in terms of quality.

It has zeal for doing missions more than what has happened before. In such a context where there is much interest about doing missions, questions are often raised as to what entails missions? There are many questions before the Naga Church which must be answered if the work of missions is to bear fruit in the near future. This book is an attempt to answer the question of the mission of the Sumi Baptist Church in the context of the emerging socio-economic scenario in Nagaland.

The author challenges the Sumi Baptist Church to be an agent in the transformational development of the Naga society. In this mission of the church, she identifies several issues which need the attention of the church such as stewardship and socio-economic development, justice, the need to uphold the kingdom ethics in the midst of a society where the social and moral values are corrupted and spiritually bankrupt. Further, the author challenges the church to get involved in Christian educational ministry for the purpose of building people's critical consciousness of the socio-economic and political realities of Nagaland and help them to act responsibly towards social injustice so that awareness is created and all human beings are able to enjoy the fullness of life.

I am happy that the author has touched upon a subject that is relevant and has much significance for the church in Nagaland. I hope that the book will be a source of blessing for the church and the mission agencies and especially for all those who are interested in the subject of missions.

Rev. Dr. Takatemjen
Principal
Clark Theological College

FOREWORD-II

How do we view the mission of God in the present context in India? Is mission limited to evangelisation and preaching or does it has socio-economic dimensions? In the midst of human cries for justice and social equality, how does the church view its roles and responsibilities for the world, which is created by God. The word of God is crystal clear that it is biblical mandate to "preach the good news to the poor ... to proclaim freedom for the prisoners and recovery of sight to the blind, to release the oppressed, to proclaim the year of the Lord's favour." (Mt. 4:18-19)

This book by Swu, Hetoni is indeed an eye opener for the Churches in North East India and particularly for the Church in Nagaland. The Church in North East India must play a great role to influence the larger issues faced by the society. The emerging socio-economic issues in North East India are throwing greater challenges to churches in fulfilling the mission of God. The Church cannot be silent spectator of emerging socio-economic context, where the rich are becoming richer and the poor are becoming poorer.

The Church has been often involved in its own issues and organizational matters and has ignored the issues of justice, stewardship, kingdom values and equality for all irrespective of caste, class and gender. These omissions have resulted into problem of leadership, power politics, few becoming wealthier, increasing unemployment, poverty, lack of health care and human rights violation.

It is essential that the Church must respond positively to these contextual issues and help the society to know that the Kingdom of God is at hand. The researcher has rightly pointed out that in the midst of emerging socio-economic context the Sumi Church has an obligation towards society and has to fulfil God's mission. The Church must find its sure foundation in biblical teaching and through theological reflection to respond to the needs of the society which will not only revive Naga spirituality but also bring transformation in Naga society.

This is very important research done by Dr. Hetoni Swu and now she is bringing out these important findings in the book form for the wider readership. Those who will read this book will truly appreciate the hard work done by her and find ways and means to do transformational mission in India.

Once again I want to congratulate the author for her excellent contributions in the field of Mission and making her research work available in a book form.

Rev. Dr. Shekhar Singh
Principal
Union Biblical Seminary

FOREWORD-III

It is often the case that Church does not think that 'worldly' activities like socio-economic activities are to be considered as a mission area. Forgetting that Jesus was concerned about the physical aspects of a person's life as well as his or her spiritual life, the Church neglects working to bring the reign or rule of God in all areas of social, political and economic life concentrating only spiritual activities. In this context, it is extremely gratifying to note that Hentoni Swu is bringing out a book that focuses on what should be the Mission of the Sumi Baptist Church in the emerging socio-economic situation of Nagaland. This book reminds us that God has called us to be co-creators with God in the holistic salvation of the world. We are called to be the stewards of God's creation. The book shows us how there is a biblical and theological basis for Mission to be carried out by the Church in the socio-economic context. It proposes transformational development as being the key to the kind of Mission that should be employed by the Sumi Baptist Church in Nagaland.

This is a book that contains some very detailed analysis of the socio-economic situation of the people of Nagaland, pointing out the various areas in which there are problems. There are relevant and practical suggestions for the conduct of mission in the context of Nagaland today. Among them are strengthening traditional Naga institutions, reviving community work culture, developing human resource potential, educating Naga people for development and job creation.

I would recommend this book to all who are interested in Mission practice, especially those who are looking for models of Mission practice relevant to the North East Indian context. They will certainly gain insight into ways of doing things for the extension of the Kingdom of God in their own area.

Rev. Dr. Sunil M. Caleb
Principal
Bishop's College

PREFACE

The focal point of the book is to investigate the ways in which the Sumi Baptist Church can participate in missions with regard to the socio-economic context of Nagaland.

The discussion provides a critical analysis of the past and the recent developments of the socio-economic situation. The economy of the people, once subsistence with credibility of their work culture, is hardly noticed. The following are the observed findings: leadership, recognition, power, possessions, political differences, money, unemployment, underemployment, lack of resources and management for survival. In this situation, people aspire for social integrity, political freedom, economic progress, and development which lie far behind in reality.

There are a few social and non-governmental organizations and the government that work for the upliftment of the society. They play an important role among the Naga people by bringing a spirit of renaissance in the form of health care, socio-political struggles, care for women and underprivileged people, moral and community building and economic awareness through developing creatively the human power and potentiality. All these issues challenge the Nagas, to relate to the experiences and realities of life.

Besides, Nagaland Baptist Church Council (NBCC), Nagaland Development Outreach (NDO), Council of Naga Baptist Churches (CNBC) and particularly Sumi Baptist Church have religious flavour and interpretations in their approach and commitment to build Naga society. They contribute to the political peace process, social integrity and economic development. The church also directly involves in health concerns through seminars and trainings, especially on HIV/AIDS, protection against social evils in the form of liquor and educational concerns both formal and informal.

God being the creator and manager holds together all His creation: sustaining and liberating human beings and the whole creation. In this sense, the whole concept of divine 'economy' of God is to provide a holistic salvation to human beings to become a community of God as witnessed in Trinitarian relationships. All these teach humankind to execute perfect stewardship as co-creators with Him.

The issues of Stewardship, Justice, Wealth, Kingdom, Community, and Human rights are considered as a pertinent message for the quest of Naga spirituality and transformation of the society. Therefore, Sumi Church has an obligation to seriously look into biblical teaching and reflect theologically on the problems for mission direction.

The researcher proposes the introduction of transformational development that allows God's intended will to be established in human society and in the rest of the creation for total life.

The Naga context calls the Sumi Baptist Church in the transformational development of the Naga society. As such the four relevant issues reconsidered are: Stewardship and socio-economic development, Justice in the midst of injustice and division among the Naga community, Liberative mission to address the oppressive socio-economic and political structures. Finally, to Uphold kingdom community amid Nagas society where the social and moral values are corrupted and spiritually bankrupt.

Practical suggestions are brought out in six points for the church to participate- Strengthening Naga traditional institution of customary laws and acts; Co-operative community development; Reviving community work culture; Human potential- Resource development; Education for development; and Job creation coupled with Project development.

It is imperative that Sumi Church takes a serious reflection on theological vision of mission and broadens its horizon to the socio-economic context of Nagaland. Sumi Church as prophetic church should involve in Christian educational ministry directing towards liberating, denouncing what is wrong and announcing God's will for the world that is to be more humane, just and loving. In doing so, the researcher believes that Sumi Church can build people's critical consciousness of the socio-economic and political realities of Nagaland and help them to act critically and responsibly towards social injustices creating awareness and making all human beings enjoy the fullness of life.

ACKNOWLEDGMENTS

I would like to acknowledge my special thanks to Dr. Bonita Aleaz and Dr. Viggo Sogaard who guided me in preparing my interview guide and survey questionnaire, for further correcting, commenting and advising me for improvement on my research writing. Special thanks to my guides, Dr. Takatemjen and Dr. Sunil Caleb for their valuable time, guidance and contributions towards my research writing so as to enable me to bring out my best within the given time.

I extend my heartfelt thanks to the Board of Consortium for Indian Missiological Education (CIME), Union Biblical Seminary and Dr. Shekhar Singh for allowing me to publish my doctoral research done during the period 2002-2005. Also, I am responsible for the changed title, contents and the opinions expressed in it with all the due permissions required. My special thanks to Dr. Leaderwell, former Principal who gave me this opportunity for research studies and to all faculty members and staff who supported me in their prayers. I am grateful to Dr. Siga Arles who has been a source of encouragement and inspiration through out my studies.

My thanks and gratitude to Miss Jessica Demeny who took pains and spared her valuable time in editing my work. Not forgetting my dear friends and loved ones who helped me in distributing and collecting questionnaires, for conducting interviews, and helping out in computer work.

I am indebted to my parents who stood besides me all these years in spite of their struggles and pains. They were faithful in their prayers and gave me strength to accomplish my studies. Above all, I honour God for letting me accomplish my research writing for His grace was sufficient for me to endure the pain and struggles I underwent during my writing.

ABBREVIATIONS

AASU	-	All Assam Students' Union
APO	-	Assistant Project Officer
BDO	-	Block Development Officer
CADPs	-	Command Area Development Projects
CASA	-	Church Auxiliary for Social Action
CNBC	–	Council of Naga Baptist Churches
CRDS	-	Comprehensive Rural Development Services
DWCRA	-	Development of Women and Children in Rural Area
EA	-	Entrepreneurs Associates
EAMF	-	Entrepreneurs Associates Micro Finance
ETCs	-	Extension Training Centers
GB	-	Gaon Buras
ILP	-	Inner Line Permit
IRDP	-	Integrated Rural Development Project
JRY	-	Jawahar Rozgar Yojana
KVIC	-	Khadi and Village Industries Commission
MORD	-	Ministry of Rural Development
NBCC	-	Nagaland Baptist Church Council
NDO	-	Nagaland Development Outreach

NEHU	-	North East Hill University
NGOs	-	Non-Governmental Organisations
NIRD	-	National Institute of Rural Development
NIV	-	New International Version
NMA	-	Naga Mothers Association
NMM	-	Nagaland Missionary Movement
NPCC	-	Nagaland Pradesh Congress Committee (Indira)
NPMHR	-	Naga People's Movement for Human Rights
NSCN-IM	-	Nationalist Socialist Council of Nagaland (Isaac – Muivah)
NSF	-	Naga Students' Federation
NWUM	-	Naga Women's Union Manipur
OI	-	Opportunity International
RD	-	Rural Development
REGP	-	Rural Employment Generation Programme
SABAK	-	Sumi Aphuye Baptist Akukuhou Kuqhakulu
SBAK	-	Sumi Baptist Akukuhou Kuqhakul
SBCC	-	Sumi Baptist Church Council
SHGs	-	Self Help Groups
SIRD	-	State Institute of Rural Development
SN	-	Sisterhood Network
SSIF	-	Self-Sustainable Integrated Farming
URF	-	United Revival Fellowship
VDB	-	Village Development Board
WSBAK	-	Western Sumi Baptist Akukuhou Kuqhakulu
WVI	-	World Vision of India

CONTENTS

Chapter 1

INTRODUCTION

This chapter first introduces the people and the setting of Nagaland, and later presents the research problem and statement, importance of the problem, objectives, scope and limitations, definition of the terms related to the purpose, previous research and reviews, methodology and chapter divisions of the book.

The word 'Naga' can originally be traced back to the following theories. First, the Burmese word for '*Naka*' means people with pierced ears, considering the fact that all Nagas in the earlier days had pierced ears.[1] Second, from the Assamese word '*Noga*' which meant 'mountaineer' or 'mountain man', with the consideration that Nagas lived in mountainous places. There are other views that the word Naga might have come from the word '*Nok*' or '*Noka*' meaning 'folk' or 'people' in some tribal languages.[2] Others agree that it might have come from the Sanskrit word '*Nanga*' which means 'naked'.[3]

---

1 Also in some of the Naga languages like those of the Konyaks 'inter alia' meaning pierced ears as the Nagas had the tradition of making holes in the ears for ear decorations.

2 Wezote Khutsoh, *Tourism Scenario and its Potentiality in Nagaland* (Guwahati: Marg Advertising, 2000), 14.

3 Vasum, R. *Nagas' Right to Self-Determination: An Anthropological Historical Perspective*. New Delhi: Mittal Publications, 2000.

Whatever might be the origin of the word, Nagas are popularly known by this name today. The term 'Naga' covers a group of people geographically widespread and culturally diverse. They are found in the North Eastern States of India, namely, Arunachal Pradesh, Assam, Manipur & Nagaland, and the North Western regions of Myanmar (Burma).[4] They trace their origin to the Indo-Mongoloid stock by race.[5] Nagas consists of (ethnic) tribal groups, of which 16 are major tribes and other sub tribes included.[6] There are hosts of other migrants from all over India and neighbouring countries mainly for commercial reasons. These groups of people also work as officials, administrators, teachers, farmers and domestic workers. This culturally mixed setting has a wide influence on both the Nagas and the outsiders settled in Nagaland.

Nagaland attained its statehood on 1st December 1963. It is the sixteenth state of the Indian Union and has 11 Districts.[7] According to 2001 census the total population of Nagaland was shown as 1,988,636 with 67.11% literacy rate (exclusively aged 7 and above).[8]

Nagas have lived their life in isolation, untouched by social problems like caste, dowry and other social inequalities.[9] From times immemorial, Nagas have been living independently in their self-contained Village-Republics democratically.[10] According to Murkot Ramunny, Nagas were hard working, self-sufficient, lived a satisfied

---

4 An introduction to the Ethnic Problem in Manipur / A Reportage on the Naga-Kuki Clash: A Prose in Counter-Insurgency, *A Booklet* Reproduced by NSF, Kohima, Nagaland. 8. This is a combination of two titles originally contributed by Gam a Shimray, Shimreichon Luithui and Tapan Bose (the first Title) and Sanjay Kumar Singh (the second title).

5 Khutsoh, Wezote. *Tourism Scenario And Its Potentiality in Nagaland*. Guwahati: Marg Advertising, 2000.

6 Sumi tribe is one of the major tribes of Nagaland.

7 The 11 districts are: Kohima, Mokokchung, Phek, Tuensang, Mon, Wokha, Zunheboto, Dimapur, Longleng, Kiphiri, and Paren.

8 *Statistical Hand Book of Nagaland 2001* (Kohima: Directorate of Economics & Statistics Government of Nagaland, 2002), 44.

9 Negating this, there is a gradual emergence of class distinction, which was unheard of earlier (discussion follows in the later section).

10 *A Brief Account on Nagaland,* Prepared by Federal Government of Nagaland (Kohima: Nagaland, June, 2000), 1.

life, and their village administration left nothing to be desired.[11] For Nagas, nature was their main provider. With the coming of British colonisation in 1832 and the Christianity in 1876, which was followed by a full-fledged statehood in 1963 in India gave the Nagas a new outlook on common life and its socio-economic dispensation. However, the hope and aspiration of a new era of progress and prosperity did not follow suit.[12]

Today, Nagaland like many other North Eastern tribal states of India is facing a seemingly intractable problem of uneven development and rising 'impoverishment of dependency'.[13] In addition, the unstable political system, the insurgency and the lack of industrial infrastructure in the region have led to a socio-economic crisis.[14] To cope with the problem, the central government has responded to the cry of the tribals by pouring money irrationally. However, the benefit goes only to a handful of privileged and powerful who are able to grab the central subsidy.[15]

The new middle class in Northeast India is found to be a special characteristic of social structure.[16] The growth of the middle class in

---

11 Murkot Ramunny, *The World of Nagas* (New Delhi: Northern Book Center, 1988), 6.

12 Ibid., 1. On the eve of Nagaland statehood, Nehru proclaimed, "Our policy has always been to give the fullest autonomy and opportunity of self-development to the Naga people, without interfering in any way in their internal affairs or way of life". Ramunny added, "Nagas are as independent as any other Indian citizens."

13 Keval J. Kumar, "Communication Approaches to Participation and Development: Challenging the Assumptions and perspectives," in *Participatory Communication: Working for Change and Development,* edited by Shirly A. White (New Delhi: Sage Publication 1994), 84. The original theory of dependency comes from Paul Baran (1967) and Andre Guder Frank (1967). According to their theory, Third World nations become dependent on first world countries because of economic and industrial backwardness.

14 D. B. Shekatkar, "Resolving Conflict in North East," *The North East Frontier Magazine* (Feb. 2004), 9-14. Insurgency is observed as a common hindrance to development.

15 K. Thanzauva, "Theology of Human Development," *NCCR,* CX/7 (August, 1990), 399.

16 Middle class comprises of the bureaucrats, businessmen (contractors to shopkeepers), and those belonging to independent professions, such as law and

Nagaland is intimately linked up with the spread of education and is not based either on a landed aristocracy, which never existed, or on commercial activity, which came only with the introduction of English education.[17] The activities of both the urban and rural areas are controlled and influenced by the urban people who are from the middle class. They control the entire socio-economic and political activities of the State.[18]

I. The Research Problem

1. Statement of the Problem

The book investigates the ways in which the Sumi Baptist Church can participate in missions in relation to the socio-economic context of Nagaland.

2. Elaboration of the Problem

The motivation to explore the role of the Sumi Baptist Church mission in the socio-economic context of Nagaland has arisen from its own context. The researcher being from this particular context has much experience of the people's needs and struggles for survival. There is no scene of people literally begging on the corners of the streets but somehow it seems to take place in other forms. When the researcher makes this statement, she does acknowledge the positive aspects of the on going socio-economic developments.

The government facilitates socio-economic development programs under the Central Schemes and projects it to be delivered at Local, State and District levels such as; Prime Minister's fund; the Chief Minister's Corpus Fund for unemployment candidates;

---

medicine. The migrant middle class is a product of the massive expenditure on development schemes dating back to the 1960s and consists of contractors, shopkeepers, food grain dealers, from North India and others. These types of people mostly occupy Dimapur town and many local people have taken to profession of letting out houses for earning income from rents.

17 B. P. Singh, *The Problem of Change: A Study of Northeast India* (Delhi: Oxford University Press, 1987), 67.

18 B. B. Ghosh, "Emergence and Role of Middle Class in Nagaland," in *The Emergence and Role of Middle Class in Northeast India,* edited by B. Datta Ray (New Delhi: Uppal Publishing House, 1983), 220.

and Child Welfare Programmes. There are several other Command Area Development Projects (CADPs); the National Schemes, viz., Integrated Rural Development Project (IRDP), Village Development Board (VDB), Development of Women and Children in Rural Area (DWCRA) and Jawahar Rozgar Yojana (JRY) for unemployment and underemployment in rural areas.[19] The Khadi and Village Industries Commission (KVIC), Dimapur has been implementing the Rural Employment Generation Programme (REGP) through Public sector banks since 2001[20], State Institute of Rural Development (SIRD) and many others.

On the other hand, the NGOs and other social organizations such as the Nagaland Development Outreach (NDO), a developmental wing of the Nagaland Baptist Church Council (NBCC) initiates a socio-economic development programme for fostering a holistic change in the Naga society; it's mission is to empower the under-privileged and marginalized through awareness program, capacity building, and assimilation of information, advocacy, lobbying and networking.[21] There are Comprehensive Rural Development Services (CRDS) providing vocational training, where the trainees are selected through church, and then they are motivated to take up leadership. It also undertakes certain development activities and small-scale projects in the field of industries. World Vision of India (WVI) works in Nagaland with the active co-operation of Nagaland Baptist Church Council, NBCC

---

19 G. N. Bag, *Rural Transformation in Tribal Areas* (New Delhi: Akansha Publishing House, 2001), 140-143. Cf. D. D. Mali, "TRYSEM and Development of Rural Entrepreneurship in North-Eastern Region" in *Development Planning of North East India,* edited by P. C. Barua (New Delhi: Mittal Publications, 1990), 311-316; P. C. Barua, "Employment Survey: Need for Changed Emphasis," in *Development Planning of North East India,* edited by P. C. Barua (New Delhi: Mittal Publications, 1990), 317-326.

20 Sanen Pongen, "KVIC Scheme on Employment Generation," *Nagaland Post,* Dimapur 25 March 2005, 3.

21 *A Profile of Nagaland Development Outreach,* Prepared by NDO Office, Chumukedima: Nagaland. cf. NDO *Brochure*; Annual Report of NDO Submitted at Triennial Convention Nagaland Baptist Church Council, CBLT on Jan. 30-Feb. 1, 2004.

and Church Auxiliary for Social Action (CASA) for community development, education and health.[22]

The Entrepreneurs Associate (EA) seeks to create economic awareness through seminars and writings of individual's experience, success and attempts; it has such programmes that arouse interest of young people by highlighting to them the present realities.[23] The Mother's Hope, Sisterhood Network and Morung at Dimapur give importance to uplifting socio-economic situations of Naga mothers, women and young respectively. There are individuals who write articles in the local Newspapers raising awareness, forming groups and meetings in regard to these issues.[24]

Social organizations such as rehabilitation and counseling centers, Hohos, Mother's Association and Student Unions are visible bodies towards the social awareness of development.[25] On the other hand, social organizations like Hohos deal mainly with issues and

---

22 Bag, *Rural Transformation*, 150-151.

23 Lecture by Neichute Doulo at UBS, Pune on 22 April 2004, organized by Center for North East Studies and Policy Research. cf. Neichute Doulo (co-editor), *Katalyst* (A bi-monthly newsletter of the Entrepreneurs Associates) published by Entrepreneurs Associates, Kohima: Nagaland; Interview with Neichute Doulo, EA, at Pune on 22 April 2004.

24 Dodo Savi, "The Naga Youth and the Naga Economy," in *Nagaland Post,* 27 September 2004, 6. cf. another article by Atou Liezietsu, "Confusion over advertisement for CM's Corpus Fund," *Nagaland Post*, 1 October 2004,1.

25 The Naga Mothers Association empowers women through conducting programmes such as seminars, workshops and self help groups. Cf. Interview with Khevili Aye, Associate women Pastor, 6 September 2004. Dimapur Sumi Baptist Akukuhou (DSBA), Women Department (a local church under WSBAK) conducts occasional Seminars and Workshops for women. For instance, Special Workshop on "Self Help", "Horticulture", "Health and Cookery" was organized on 20th May 2004. Individual Sumi women are involved in this ministry, e.g., Mrs. Phutoli at Tuensang District runs rehabilitation center cum SHG in that particular area among the women. Cf. *Dimapur Sumi Baptist Akukuhou Totimi Sutsa*, 8 May 2005 produced by Women Department, Dimapur Sumi Baptist Church, 8. Some of the individual who are leading examples among the Sumi women are: T. Hukheli the first women designer among the Sumi; Ghukhuli the first Sumi lady who opened flower Nursery; Hovili is known for growing flower among the Sumi women; Pitoli who has won 5 times award in the field of knitting excellence gives training to many women in this field; S. Hokhuli is the proprietor of Faith Hospital Dimapur

decision-making at higher levels in the society. Groups of student leaders participate in meeting students' needs and problems, and protest in any other social evils.

The Western Sumi Baptist Akukuhou Kuqhakulu (WSBAK) women department has a project since 2002, i.e., Samaritan Home project which empowers women through counseling, spiritual nourishment and vocational training, sharing the burden with the victims of the society, the poor, the orphans, the widows and the helpless. More specifically, it seeks to rescue the commercial sex workers and women substance abusers.[26]

Despite these efforts the socio-economic scenario in Nagaland as a whole has not been encouraging. We find many disorganized structures at all levels of administration. The funds provided for projects and facilities are rarely utilized for the welfare of the common people. Thus, the prevailing system fails to provide truth, freedom, rights, trust, honesty, responsibility and development in the Community. The educated few remain unemployed; one of the reasons could be due to the failure of learning and less emphasis given on practical skills and developments within the system. There are some wealthy people who do not properly utilize their wealth or share with others. Rich natural resources are laid unused simply because the people are less motivated to work or are ignorant of utilizing it.

Therefore, we observe a decline of stewardship and responsibility, which extend the gap between the rich and poor. Thus, the related issue of diminishing work ethics among the Naga community is revealed today. The influx of migrants from outside Nagaland is observed as hampering agents towards economic productivity of the local people and not utilizing available human resources. Finally, the insurgency in Nagaland contributes a negative impact on the socio-economic condition of the people in general.

---

and also member of Confederation of Indian Industry and she herself is an industrious woman through her service many women have employment.

26 Interview with Kanili Aye, Women Secretary, WSBAK on 6 October 2004. cf. WSBAK Women Department *Brochure* on *Samaritan Home Project* (Networking with Priscilla Center Guwahati), which aims at empowering women.

There seems to be increased rate of divorce, dependence on family and parents, dropouts, drug addicts, bribing, extortion, gambling, unemployment, infidelity and other problems in relation to marriage, threat and rampant killings. The economic instability may be one of the reasons contributing to the disintegration of moral values and promoting these social evils.

The Nagas, being predominantly Christians, have the twin advantage and obligation, both from the religious and social sphere, for the well being of the society. Inspite of this, the Nagas suffer from lack of proper leadership, commitment & responsibility, and uneven growth in development of the society.

These challenges force Naga Christians to be concerned citizens and responsible members of the society. Therefore, it is imperative for the Sumi Baptist Church today to rethink "Spirituality" from becoming monotonous and ritualistic. Rather attempts should be to solve socio-economic problems, theologically and missiologically.

In this situation, the following questions would be raised and explored- What is the socio-economic situation in Nagaland and problems identified? What are the roles played by the NGO'S and other social organizations in addressing the problems in the context? What are the roles played by the Government/politics? What are the roles played by the Naga Churches and particularly Sumi Baptist Church in addressing the problems in the context? What would be the biblical and theological basis for the mission of the church? In what ways the Sumi Baptist Church can contribute for the transformational socio-economic development of the Naga Society? In the light of all these questions the church can work towards the interconnectedness of the expressions of faith and socio-economic prospects as one entity for the transformational development of the Naga society.

II. Importance of the Problem

The research problem is proposed for a number of reasons. First, the previous research on Sumi community focuses on subjects like Christianity and its impact on Sumi Culture; Revival movement; Role of Mission in general and Evaluation on recent Mission works. A handful of research done at a secular university (North East Hill

University, Shillong) has different approaches, such as, Agriculture, Education in government schools, teachers' attitudes on education, emergence of middle class in Nagaland, unemployment problems and development in Nagaland (a review of the above areas of research is seen in the following sections). There are a few studies done on Naga theological reflections on church, politics and culture. However, as far as the researcher is aware, there is no missiological reflection done particularly on socio-economic area.

Therefore, the book by giving due consideration to the role of the Sumi Baptist Church mission in the socio-economic context of Nagaland, has the potential to contribute to a fuller understanding of the mission. Second, the analysis of the present mission role of Sumi Baptist Church brings into focus the need of envisioning and integrating the mission focus in the future. Finally present book attempts to provide the Sumi Baptist Church with genuine insights for transformational development of Sumi Naga community in particular and the Nagas in general.

III. Purpose Statement

The purpose of this research is to analyse factors that influence the mission of the Sumi Baptist Church in the socio-economic context of Nagaland with a view to enhance the role of the church's mission.

IV. Research Objectives

1. To study the socio-economic situation of Nagaland and identify factors leading to the problems.
2. To review the role of the Government, NGOs, Social Organizations and the Naga Church.
3. To describe the role of the Sumi Baptist Church and its impact in the context.
4. To explore the Biblical and Theological basis for the mission of the church.
5. To identify the possible ways in which the Sumi Baptist Church can theologically and missiologically contribute to the transformational development of the socio-economic situation.

V. Scope and Limitations

The research work focuses on the Western Sumi Baptist Akukuhou Kuqhakulu (WSBAK), Dimapur. It would be difficult to research all the four Associations at different districts or to include the other Naga tribes due to the size of population and geographical differences. However, the experience and reality of the people is pertinent to all Naga people. Therefore, based on the Sumi tribe the research would attempt to justify and substantiate the findings for the future role of the church mission.

The study will depend on the published and unpublished documentation, reports, and articles from the Sumi Baptist church/es' perspective, various individuals, Governmental and social organisations. It will also utilize data from field research carried out through personal interviews and survey research to compensate for the lack of literature relevant to this subject.

VI. Definitions

1. Socio-economic

The word economics is derived from *oikos* (house) and *nomos* (law), means literally managing a household, which relates to the concerns of the production, distribution and use of income, wealth and commodities.[27] The Concise Oxford Dictionary gives a similar idea of the term economics dealing with the production, distribution and consumption of material goods and services, for profit on business footing, paying expenses high enough to compensate builder, owner, connected with industrial arts, also the condition of a country as to material prosperity.[28] Thus, it implies the concept of the responsible society, which plays a major role as a criterion for the assessment of economic progress.

Social economics may be defined as the socio-economic analysis of human behaviour within a broad economic, social, and political context for the purpose of improving the quality of life and

---

27 J. E. M. Arputhamurthy, "Ecology, Economics and Ecumenics," *TBT Journal* 2/1 (2000), 42.

28 H. W. Fowler, *et al.*, *The Concise Oxford Dictionary of Current English*, 3rd Edition (Oxford: Oxford University Press, 1934), 361.

enhancing human welfare. Social economists have been especially concerned with impoverished people who have been denied the opportunities and the privileges that have been so easily available to the more affluent component of the population. Social economics is an applied policy science that seeks to solve problems of social justice and economic privation.[29]

Similarly a glance at the biblical material that bears (however tangentially) on economic matters is much concerned with covenantal stipulations and other moral exhortation. It deals with ethical norms typically giving a theological justification. In the discussions of the biblical material, certain key passages regularly appear, though their interpretation varies from author to author. The creation narratives are used to mandate the creation of wealth and responsible stewardship through work. The teaching of law concerning economic and social life can be found at three places, Exodus 20: 22-23:19; Leviticus 25 and Leviticus chapters 5 - 26 beginning with a restatement of the Decalogue and going on to detailed commands, which are broadly divided between those relating to worship and ritual purity; and those related to social and economic relationships.[30]

In summing up the above discussion the ultimate goal of economics is human welfare, which involves a considerable role of

---

29 Lewis E. Hill, "Economic History as A Source of Socioeconomic Normative Value," *Social Economics: Premise, Finding, and Policies,* edited by J. O' Boyle (London: Routledge, 1996), 9.

30 Donald A. Hay, *Economics Today: A Christian Critique* (Leicester: Intervarsity Press, 1991), 31. "Biblically derived institutional norms not only show us how we are meant to live, how institutions such as the state, the family, the corporation, and the financial system should be shaped, but also provide a way of understanding pathological economic outcomes. Economic crises are to be understood as failures to adhere to the normative principles. For example, poverty is to be understood as a deviation from scriptural principles. Whatever view is taken on the correct way to utilize the biblical records in economic prescription, there still remains the crucial questions, so far unaddressed, of what precisely is the character of the (prescriptive) biblical witness on matters of economics. The failure to observe the law in its social and economic aspects is an important theme in the proclamation of the prophets from the eight century onwards that concentrates on three elements, which are frequently linked: the accumulation of wealth by the rich, the oppression of the poor and the failure to help them, and the perversion of justice."

wealth for development and growth. To attain welfare, one must strive for social justice and an equitable distribution of wealth. According to S. Radhakrishna, welfare signifies 'wholeness of being' and it 'is not a matter of the goods we consume.'[31] He maintains that since a human being acquires wealth only with the help of the community, no person can have an absolute say in its disposal. Finally 'the acquisition of wealth is contingent on the fulfilment of our social obligations.'[32] Thus, the implication for the Christian economist in his or her professional capacity is that Christian witness does not manifest itself in the economic analysis but rather in the excellence of personal conduct and moral character.[33]

Thus, the implication of the term socio-economic in this research refers to the Naga context where these two words cannot be separated. Socio-economics seeks to improve the economic sphere of life by giving people a better living standard and taking measures to empower people, drawing their potentialities and resourcing progress in their life. Naga Christians being majority are responsible for the social upliftment and development of the Naga society. Thus, fulfilling the tasks becomes complete in God's intended purpose.

2. Sumi Baptist Church/es

Sumi Baptist Church basically refers to the Western Sumi Baptist Akukuhou Kuqhakulu (WSBAK), which covers roughly around 150 local churches. It also refers to Sumi Baptist Town Church (DSBA).[34]

Generally, the Sumi Baptist Church is one of the biggest churches in Nagaland and it comprises of total over 400 hundred local churches. Sumi Baptist Church has four different Associations situated at different districts: two at Zunheboto District Sumi Baptist Akukuhou Kuqhakulu (SBAK, Aizuto and SBAK, Nito Mount);

31 Clarissa Rodrigues, *The Social and Political Thought of Dr. S. Radhakhrisnan: An Evaluation* (New Delhi: Sterling Publishers, 1992), 52-54.

32 Ibid.

33 Hill, *Economic History,* 166.

34 DSBA/ Sumi Baptist Town Church is one and the same (a local church under WSBAK and one of the backbone churches to WSBAK which has 2500-3000 membership).

two others at Kohima Sumi Aphuye Baptist Akukuhou Kuqhakulu (SABAK) & Western Sumi Baptist Akukuhou Kuqhakulu (WSBAK) at Dimapur District. The research is concentrated on WSBAK at Dimapur District. The Sumi Baptist Church Council (SBCC) is an apex body over all these Sumi Baptist Churches' Associations although these organizational associations have their independent structures, administrations and functions.

3. Transformational Development[35]

The English word "development" comes from the root word "envelop" in French, which was considered to be a military word.[36] "Development," thus means to de-envelop, to unseal, to open, to free, or to remove what was prevented from moving out for freedom and advancement."[37]

Similarly, Webster's Dictionary defines development as unfolding, the unravelling of a plot, a gradual growth or advancement through progressive changes.[38] It means to bring out or make visible what is hidden through progressive involvement that entails social, cultural, political and economic transformation. Development, therefore, is more than economic growth. It is a systematic effort to improve the quality of life, especially of those marginalized, deprived, and exploited due to social, cultural and political imbalances. It aims at enabling them to become persons who can freely use their innate faculties of decision-making, goal orientation and goal achievement.[39]

Transformation is a value-loaded concept and as such there is no absolute definition. As with many development concepts the

---

35 Bryant Myers, *Walking with the Poor: Principles and Practices of Transformational Development* (New York: Orbis Books, 1999). This term is borrowed from Bryant Myers of World Vision who has offered a comprehensive analysis and definition of the concept of 'transformational development.'

36 M. Rongsen, *Development and Ecology* (Delhi: Cambridge Press, 1999), 1.

37 Ibid.

38 *New Webster's Dictionary of the English Language*, 6th edition (New Delhi: Surjeet Publications, 1995), 430.

39 Desmond A. D'Abreo, *Voice to the People: Communication for Social Change* (Madras: Culture and Communication, 1990), 14.

variations of definition are numerous as the people tries to define it in the manner they feel. In trying to be specific, "transformation is a process that knows no end-point. Although external factors play an important role, transformation is an inside-out phenomenon. It is fundamentally internal and happens all the time."[40]

Opportunity International's (OI) current working definition of transformation can be summed up as 'a deeply rooted change in people's economic, social, political, spiritual and behavioural conditions resulting in their enjoyment of wholeness of life under God's ordinances.'[41] The crux of this definition is the intrinsic assumption that transformation is about the whole person's (holistic) development. Contrary to the world's conception of development as materialistic, OI's approach pertinently takes human development in its entirety including behavioural considerations. OI's all encompassing definition treats all sides of human life, suggesting two critical components of transformational development, i.e., 'having and being.' Its twin goals of transformational development are financial excellence and biblical transformation that result in the establishment of all types of freedom, the creation of opportunities and the shaping of healthy character among the poor. These two (freedom and character) are intertwined essentials of transformational development.[42]

As understood from the above discussion, the author's aim is not to analyse various development theories but taking the literal understanding of the word and meaning, to seek the relevance of the concept of development for the Naga society. She also aims to educate the Sumi Baptist Church as they involve in mission and

40 Makonen Getu, "Measuring Transformation: Conceptual framework and indicators," *Transformation*, 19/2 (April, 2002), 92.

41 Ibid. Since OI was established in 1971, it has become one of the major micro finance institutions in the world. Ol seeks to run micro finance programmes that will help the poor not only to create employment and generate income but also to transform their lives in such a way that they become freer and better people. Cf. Samuel Jayakumar, *Mission Reader: Historical Models for Wholistic Mission in the Indian Context* (Delhi: ISPCK, 2002), 24-25

42 Makonen Getu, "Measuring Transformation: Conceptual framework and indicators," *Transformation*, 19/2 (April, 2002), 93.

the Naga people in general on the understanding of the concept of development from a missiological perspective. Since, the Sumi Baptist Church mission at present lacks the social aspect of mission, the author would like to bring to an awareness of the need of the people. Therefore, this book aims to take socio-economic issues as one of the approach and incorporate it in the mission of the Sumi Baptist Church towards fulfilling the holistic dimension of God's mission. Thus, the implication of the term is to indicate transformational development in Nagaland.

4. Holistic Mission

The Latin word *mitto*, which translates in Greek as *aposetello* (to send) corresponds with the English term "mission". The term "mission", with no direct biblical equivalent, has a broad range of acceptable meanings. The Contemporary secular definition of mission is simply "sending someone forth with a specific purpose". Thus, the purpose may be defined broadly to represent the interests of the sender or very narrowly to hand- deliver a message written by the sender.

With the broadness of the term, our concept of the mission of the church will to a large degree depends on our theological orientation rather than an etymological analysis.

The evangelicals understood missions as evangelism and the evidence of successful missions was the extension of the church through the crossing of cultural, geographic and linguistic boundaries, at least until the IMC Willingen Conference in 1952. The missiological term *Missio Dei* was coined by Karl Hartenstein in 1934 and was thus used in 1952 to mean that mission is God's and not of the church.[43] Later, George Vicedom popularised in Mexico City Conference in 1963.[44] Thus, the themes such as "let the world

43 Cited in A. Scott Moreau, Harold Notland and Charles Van Engen, *Evangelical Dictionary of World Mission* (Grand Rapids: Baker Books, 2000), 637. Cf. David J. Bosch, *Transforming Mission* (Mary Knoll: Orbis Books, 1991), 389-392.

44 Cited in Moreau, Notland and Engen, *Evangelical Dictionary of World Mission,* 637. His textbook, *The Mission of God* (*1965 – Mission Dei*) focuses on everything God does in His task of establishing His Kingdom in all its fullness in the entire world.

set the Agenda" were driven by a recognition that God is not limited to His work in and through the church and that His mission is seen wherever kingdom values especially justice and mercy are being promoted, fought for, or instituted.

By 1972, George Peters wrote that mission, in contrast to missions was "a comphrensive term including the upward, inward and outward ministries of the church. It is the church a 'sent' (a pilgrim, stranger, witness, prophets, servant, as salt, as light in the world)".[45] He maintains that missions on the other hand are the actual work and the practical realization of the mission of the church.

Evangelical approaches for defining mission have not been unified. Some evangelicals have varied concerns that dropping the "s" might lead to the loss of commitment to, and action for, world evangelization and church planting. Since Laussane three streams have solidified with evangelicalism. First, the focus remains at the development of thriving church movements among people groups around the world. Second, focus on integrating a holistic approach to mission, incorporating evangelism and issues of social justice and reconciliation. Third, no priority is given to either social justice or evangelism, in other words the focus is on both as the one and the same.[46]

Along this line of thought holistic mission is concerned with ministry to the whole person through the transforming power of the gospel. While holistic mission affirms the functional uniqueness of evangelism and social responsibility it views them as inseparable from

---

45 Cited in Moreau, Notland and Engen, *Evangelical Dictionary of World Mission,* 638. George Peter is an evangelical teaching at Dallas Theological Seminary.

46 Moreau, Notland and Engen, *Evangelical Dictionary of World Mission,* 638. The first stream emphasizes the historic orientation of mission on evangelism and carried on in meetings organized in 1989, 1995 and 1997 on the "Global Consultations on World Evangelization (GCOWE). This second stream followed Stott. The Wheaton Consultation in 1983 laid a sound theological basis for the mission of the church with no dichotomy between evangelism and social responsibility. The third stream followed people like Ron Sider, Rene Pedilla and Samuel Escobar. Sometimes, this group is referred as radical discipleship group. Cf. John Stott, *Christian Mission in the Modern World* (Bombay: Gospel Literature Service, 1975), 25-28.

the ministry of the Kingdom of God.[47] Therefore, holistic mission is the intentional integration of building the church and transforming society. This Scripturally holistic mission begins with creation of perfect harmony under the Lordship of God (Gen 1-2) and human in relationship with creator as stewards of His creation (Gen 1:27-30). The church as the community of God's redeemed people is called to fulfill the mission of Christ in Creation.[48] Therefore, mission is the commitment to all that the church is called to which includes the great commission (Mtt 28:18-20) and the great commandment (Mtt 22:37-40).

Central to the concerns of holistic mission is the relationship between evangelism and social responsibility. The contemporary concern arose out of the fundamentalist and liberal movements of the early twentieth century. The liberal movement moved toward a conciliar position with other religions and away from the issue of conversion, emphasizing cooperation on issues of social gospel, evangelical missions emphasizing the Uniqueness of Christ as the only way of Salvation and making evangelism the primary emphasis of the missionary task.[49]

The researcher does not intend to analyze or draw a conclusion on the understanding of mission or missions and holistic mission. The purpose of the discussion is to bring into light the contemporary issues from various wavelengths, which still remains debatable.

---

47 Chris Sugden, *Gospel, Culture and Transformation* (New Delhi: Regnum Books International, 2000), 20-22.

48 Mtt 18:20; Rom 12:5-8; I Cor 12; Eph 4:1-16; I Peter 4:10-1; Eph 1:20-23; 3:10-11.

49 Moreau, Notland and Engen, *Evangelical Dictionary of World Mission,* 449. The dichotomy has been reflected in the traditional evangelism and church planting despite their widespread involvement in education, health and development growing out of the concerns for social needs evangelical relief and development organization have multiplied. Unlike traditional missions, the relief and development groups have concentrated on physical and social needs, cooperating with other groups in their efforts. Thus, the internationalization of missions and the increased cooperation among organizations have functionally expanded the view of the church's role in the world and the necessity for a greater understanding of holistic mission.

Therefore, it will be obscure to simplify into one concrete definition on each.

However, for the sake of this book necessary to understand that the researcher believes that mission as *Missio Dei* (Mission of God) and church's participation in this mission fulfills God's intended purpose.[50] Hence, whatever the Sumi Baptist Church does is participation in God's mission and is definitely calls for holistic mission. Therefore, present book on socio-economic issues is one of the aspects of holistic mission as understood by the author. Although there is no mention of holistic mission from the title of the book the research is directly concern with this line of thought. It has certainly an implicit understanding of the core approach of mission in holistic perspective in the author's mind and approach in the book.

VII. Previous Research and Reviews

Some of the important writings from the recent past are noted in the following:

Rongsenrenla Tali studies socio-economic development particularly from educational approach. Her overall argument lies in the weakness of high school education in Nagaland, which means the negligence in preparing the learners for active participation in the socio-economic development of the state.[51]

Lanu Aier attempts to look into the growth of urban centres and new occupations that have altered the traditional system. He argues that these changes have resulted in class development particularly an emergence of middle class in the Naga society.[52]

N. Myanbemo Kikon compares the rest of Nagaland to Wokha District. The Wokha district being in the western part of Nagaland, borders with the plains of Assam, therefore got exposed to the neighbouring areas where some people carried out trade through

---

50 For further understanding of *Mission Dei*, see; J. Andrew Kirk, *What Is Mission? Theological Explorations* (Minneapolis: Fortress Press, 2000), 29-37.

51 Rongsenrenla Tali, "A Study of the Problems Faced by High School Teachers and their Attitudes Towards Teaching Profession in Nagaland," (Ph.D. Dissertation, North Eastern Hill University, 1984).

52 I. Lanu Aier, "The Emerging Middle Class in Naga Society," (M.Phil. Thesis, North Eastern Hill University, 1982).

barter system with the people in the plains. On the other hand, the rest of Nagaland being isolated remained unaffected by economic development. His overall argument is on account of the development process and modernization in terms of the living standard of the people in the region has improved.[53]

Kape Loli focuses mainly on the changing economic trend in Dimapur district of Nagaland. Looking to the recent development and clashes in the nature and function of economy, he examines the growing scene of the town itself into a large commercial center with tremendous changes in the recent years. In the phase of this changing process he looks for an alternative that provides better living where he analyses the moral and social integrity of the people in the context.[54]

Hokishe Sema gives a background study on development of Naga life and history, extensively from the socio-economic and political struggles of the people. He then proposes the need for a fresh look at development, safeguarding culture and social values, re-orientation of administration, relevant education; which prepares an individual for life and livelihood and implementation of development programmes.[55]

M. M. Thomas argues that the establishment of the state of Nagaland within the Indian Union has led to political, social and economic development of the people. The transition from tribal mores to modern systems of polity and economy has created imbalances. He emphasizes on social relations, which are to be humanised by undergirding economics, and politics by values embedded in culture. Education, he propounds, is always training for participation in the

---

53 Myanbemo Kikon Lotha N., "Social and Cultural Implications of Agricultural Development: A Case Study of Two Villages in Wokha District" (M.Phil. Thesis, North Eastern Hill University, 1987).

54 Loli Kape, "A Christian Ethical Analysis of and Response to Contemporary Economic Trend in Dimapur," (M.Th Thesis, United Theological College, 1999).

55 Hokishe Sema, *Emergence of Nagaland: Socio-economic and Political Transformation and the Future* (Uttar Pradesh: Vikas Publishing House, 1986). Previously, he was the Governor of Himachal Pradesh and later the Chief Minister of Nagaland.

larger society. Religion and spirituality for him must get involved not only in subjective emotional experiences and private morality but also in the creation of a new public morality and discipline of people and leaders within its framework, which will enhance better development of the human potential.[56]

Cynthia explores the implications of Amartya Sen's ideas, expressed in his book *Development as Freedom*, for the church in development. The author appreciates Sen's perspective on development as freedom, and suggests that the Christian focus on the freedom that Christ has given us, provides a way of working with Sen's ideas. Thus, she brings out three key themes: the church as an agent of freedom, advocate of freedom and empowering of people.[57]

Charles Elliot points out that development is inevitably a slow process, an unhurried ripening of society, a steady maturation and integration of diverse growing points and a progress towards social goals. Development cannot be defined only in measurable/physical terms. Speaking from a broader sense, Elliot writes that development is to make people more human: to lift them out of degrading, inhumane and dehumanizing conditions of poverty, unemployment, ill-health, disease and ignorance and give them back a chance to be fully human. Development must be at the same time economic, healthful, educative and cultural, psychological, sociological and political.[58]

Denis Goulet expresses development processes as both cruel and a necessary choice. People are faced with cruel choices because

---

56 M. M. Thomas, *The Nagas Towards, A.D. 2000* (Madras: Center for Research on New International Economic Order, 1992), 64.
M. M. Thomas, a person who devoted his whole life to study and research on the relevance of religion and culture, society and politics in rapid change, served as the Governor of Nagaland from May 1990 to April 1992. This book is an outcome of that period. He deals with his attempts to understand the current problems faced by the Nagas as they move from their traditional tribal patterns waking up to modernity, self-identity and self-realization as he calls it. He has expressed his genuine interest in the awakening and the Nagas' search for identity in the context of the Modern world.

57 Holder-rich, "Cynthia: Development as freedom or freedom as development?" *Journal of Theology for Southern Africa*, 110 (July, 2001), 89-96.

58 Charles Elliott, *The Development Debate* (Great Britain: SCM Press LTD, 1971).

development benefits are obtained only at a great price. He insists that first priority must go to the satisfaction of life sustenance needs of all; the second to provide goods, which enhance human expression and creativity; and the third to provide luxury goods. He refers to the degree of freedom and responsibility of human beings from the ethical point of view. Insisting on development, one must accept endless risk-taking and a maximum commitment to liberation of the oppressed and responsibility for all.[59]

According to Amartya Sen, the whole thrust of development promotes the end and not the means, i.e., Justice comes only when freedom is enhanced and concentration is on the 'means' to uphold unfreedom.[60] This is exemplified by John Rawls' theory of "the priority of liberty" and whole arguments that contrast to the well being with the utilitarian perspective.[61] Thus, democracy is praised as a conductive attitude towards freedom and importantly an individual commitment to freedom.

Thus, the above research and reviews have brought us to the light of different approaches to development and its impact focusing ultimately on socio-economic context at large (and particularly the research on Naga socio-economic context). Further, proposing the importance of development in all aspects of life: social, political, economic, educational, psychological, and ecological, that incorporates cultural values (which are now less apparent in the processes of development) for the reality of development in future. The book refers the background knowledge from the research mentioned above. Yet, it

---

59 Denis Goulet, *The Cruel Choice: A New Concept in the Theory of Development* (Cambridge: Center for the Study of Development and Social Change, 1973).

60 Amartya Sen, *Development as Freedom* (New York: Anchor Books, 1999). Amartya Sen's book *Development as Freedom* was based on his five lectures as a Presidential Fellow at the World Bank during 1996. The book centers on the analysis of political, economic, social, transparency guarantees and protective security realities of freedom, that is, as an "instrumental" perspective. The book covers the social need to understand *freedom* but also it spirals down to the individual commitment to it.

61 Cited in Sen, *Development as Freedom*. The elements such as income, poverty, markets, values, tradition, culture and democracy are all analyzed on how they hinder or promote freedom.

proposes to look into the roles of different organisations that contribute positive factors to the existing effects of the socio-economic situation as seen from various angles. On the basis of that, the present research would take a different route updating the research information and focusing specifically on Sumi Baptist Church mission role for wider transformational development of the Naga society bringing out the reflections from theological and missiological perspectives.

VIII. Research Methodology

The research is descriptive and interdisciplinary in approach; that includes the Socio-economic and Cultural dimensions, Biblical/Theological and Missiological perspectives.

The research data collection is based on four approaches:

1. Library Research

Existing studies and relevant literature were studied in order to meet the needs of Objective: 1. This also gave background information to Objectives 2 – 4. The library research was done from various libraries, including, Nagaland University library, Lumami; Nagaland library of Arts and Culture, Kohima; Theological Colleges and Institutional libraries and Tribal Research Center, Pune.

2. Personal Interviews

Personal interviews were conducted with 34 people representing different groups of people such as: Government Officials and Naga Political leaders, missionaries and full time church workers, different leaders and members of NGO's and social organizations. For each group of people a different interview guide (that helped the researcher to be specific in conducting interview) was prepared according to the information needed. This selection of the people helped to receive varied opinions, which provided the researcher a whole picture representing particular bodies to the field of subject sought.

Personal interviews were required in order to receive accurate, personal and confidential data needed for exposing the reality of the context. This was from their personal experiences, participation and observations of the present socio-economic situation, which helped to fulfil the requirements of objectives 2, 3 and 4.

3. Survey Research

The questionnaires were distributed to 100 people in Dimapur Town representing different groups of people. The reason for this selection was to receive varied opinions so as to bring out their observations, experiences and aspirations in the context. 50% of questionnaires were distributed personally, and certain friends and people who could personally distribute them helped with the other half.

The questionnaire was constructed in such a way that it fitted all groups of people. It was prepared to receive the observation experiences, feedbacks and aspirations on socio-economic, political, religious and cultural life of the people. Thus, the data received from the survey helped the researcher to construct and furnish background information for the research structure and findings. The questionnaire included both fixed-alternative and open-ended questions in different sections. This provided information needed for Objectives 2 and 3.

4. Sampling: Rationale Behind

A sample of 100 people was taken for quantitative findings on the Sumi Tribe.

The first reason for this selection was mainly because the Naga tribal population as a whole would be too large.

Second, the researcher selected the Western Sumi Community of Dimapur Town, as the area for the research work because a large number of Sumis have moved from the Zunheboto District and have concentrated in and around Dimapur Town for various reasons like: easier life and communication, children's education, officials and business, establishing their land and settlement.

Finally, the researcher selected a significant number of representatives and people with different interests, experiences and aspirations. The targeted groups were basically- 10 business people aged between 30 and above, 15 Government employees aged ranges from mid twenties, 20 young people (employed and unemployed) aged from 20–30, 10 women both single and married aged 20 and above, 20 social and religious activists aged 28 and above, and 25 common people of mixed group and age. The questionnaire was accordingly dispatched and collected at different section (ward-wise) in Dimapur town. The sampling procedure followed in this research is convenience sampling within a non-probability sampling process.[62] This being quantitative analysis, general trends can be deduced through the responses.

IX. The Structure of the Book

The first chapter deals with the Introduction on 'Naga' tribe, people, Sumi Baptist Church and the presentation of the subjected issue as discussed above.

The second chapter studies the past and present socio-economic situation of the people.

The third chapter (Section-A) explores the different organisations involved in socio-economic upliftment of the Nagas in Nagaland, which includes some Social Organisations, NGOs, Government and Naga Church.

The fourth chapter (Section-B) is the continuation of the third chapter but focusing on Naga churches- NBCC and CNBC.

The fifth chapter studies the present role of the Sumi Baptist Church in particular taking into consideration the overall mission of the church.

The sixth chapter deals with a biblical - theological basis for church mission in the socio-economic context of Nagaland and includes an overview study from Old Testament to New Testament thematically and bringing out the relevance to the context.

The seventh chapter proposes the transformational development mission of the Sumi Baptist Church in the emerging socio-economic context of Nagaland with a few practical suggestions.

---

62 Viggo Sogaard, *Research in Church and Mission* (Pasadena: William Carey Library, 1996), 112-119. In sampling procedures, probability sampling and non probability sampling are the two basic categories. Probability sampling category has three types: simple random sample, stratified sample and cluster sample. Non probability sample also has three types: convenience sample, judgment sample and quota sample.

Chapter 2

THE SOCIO-ECONOMIC SITUATION OF THE NAGA PEOPLE IN NAGALAND

Introduction

Nagaland is one of the hill states in Northeast India, famous for its numerous tribes and rich culture. Each tribe has its own unique traditionally designed attire. The important festivals are *Sekrenyi* for Angamis, *Moatsu* for Aos, *Tuluni* for Sumis,[63] and many more.

Nagas are very sociable and community oriented people by nature. Village polity includes every individual in decision-making. Economically independent and self-subsistent, the Nagas meet their day-to-day needs through their hard work and professionalism in natural skills and arts. Traditionally, Nagas were headhunters, which add prestige and fame to men's life. By religion they were known as animists (although Nagas had a belief of life after death). For them, nature is seen to be alive with invisible forces, minor deities

---

63 *The Main/Important Festivals of Sema Naga*, A booklet produced by K. David Sema in 2001. '*Tulini*' is a festival which is observed and celebrated by the Sumi tribe of Nagaland every year immediately after the second round of weeding in the field (*Mozaqhi*) and the first part of (*Aniqhi*). It is mainly observed to enable paddy crops in the field to grow luxuriantly and to bear grain plentifully, which continues for 7 days. This is a traditional festival celebrated by the Sumi forefathers and handed down to generations.

and spirits. With the advent of the British rule in the 19th century, Christianity was introduced, and Baptist missionaries became active in this region. As a result, the population now is predominantly Christian.[64]

Nagas once lived by themselves in a shell of isolation. They viewed with hostility and suspicion anything coming from outside. Today, Nagas are reaching out for the benefits of modern life. Since the desire for social progress is intense, the people are enthusiastically cooperating with the Government in its many programs of development. The common people's desire for peace is directly linked with their desire for progress and development.[65]

Looking back into history, despite the British policy to keep the Nagas in isolation, it was the Japanese invasion in 1944,[66] which opened a new pattern of trade and commerce to the Nagas. Kohima became crowded with a multitude of troops, machines and contemporary weapons. Dimapur became a military station and local stores and resources were also mobilized. The Nagas hitherto excluded from contact with the other world, people witnessed new activities and life, which affected their culture and attitudes.

The discussion in the following section provides a critical analysis of the past and the recent developments of the socio-economic situation. We shall avoid studying the details and general background information of the people since much research has been published in this area.[67]

---

64 "Nagaland a profile and map," published by the *Nagaland Pradesh Congress Committeee (I),* www.mapsofindia.com/stateprofiles/nagaland/ *(25 March 2003).*

65 K. S. Singh, ed., *Tribal Situation in India* (Simla: Indian Institute of Advanced Study, 1972), 121-127.
In the name of education, trade and commerce people are moving from rural places to urban settings. Urban growth ushered new forms of occupation for livelihood other than traditional rural occupation of cultivation. Social differentiation in terms of occupation and the trend of migration resulted in greater social and economic mobility.

66 V. H. Zhimomi, *British Policy and Administration in Nagaland* (M.Phil. Dissertation, Northeastern Hill University, 1981), 94-95.

67 For immediate reference see the series of writings on "Nagas" by J. H. Hutton. He has dealt with some major Naga tribes such as Aos, Angami, Sema (Sumis),

I. The Past Situation

1. Village Administration

The Naga government by and large is democratic in principle, and republic or monarchical in nature. Every tribe has a chief who is also the head of the village. In most of the tribes, chieftainship is hereditary. Nagas are patrilineal and patriarchal society.[68] The village is composed of various clans where each of them has representatives as leaders. A small clan usually joins a big clan in exercising its right for choosing a representative. With the advent of British Administration, these selected representatives were designated as *Gaon Buras* (GB), meaning village elders. The choice of representative is based on the integrity, honesty and sense of justice of the person and not on his wealth, prosperity or education.[69] The clan members looked upon them as people who could serve them justly and protect them from exploitation and defend them when abused.

At first, the British Government made all GBs their agents for collecting house tax from the clans as well as from the villages. They were traditionally persons entrusted with many other responsibilities. There were no written principles governing functions of GBs, but they were responsible for the administration of the village on various counts like: judiciary, political, social and economic development.

---

etc. See also Yepthomi, Najekhu "Early History of the Naga" in *From Darkness to Light,* ed. by P. Along Aier (Publication of the Nagaland Baptist Church Council on the Occasion of the Celebration of 125 years of Christianity in Nagaland. 1997); Bendangyabang A. Ao, *History of Christianity in Nagaland: The Ao Naga Tribal Christian Missionaries, 1872-1972* (Mokokchung: Shalom Ministry Publication, 200); N.Toshi Ao, *Mission to the Nagas: A Tryst with the Aos* (NP, 1995). The above two references are particularly of Ao tribe's concerns but it also gives us insights on the origin of the first Naga church and beginnings of Christianity in Nagaland since they were the first tribe to be touched by the gospel in Nagaland; see also, Puthenpurakal, *Baptist Missions in Nagaland* (Shillong: Vendrame Missiological Institute, 1984).

68 Vasum, Nagas' Right to Self- Determination, p.14.

69 Vamuzo, *Develop Your Own Village: An Approach to Grass Root Planning and Development,* (Kohima: Author,1978, 2. (He was the then Minister for Finance, Industry, Commerce, Revenue and Election, Nagaland).

Now, GBs are responsible for execution of all kinds of development work in the village. They take all kinds of cases and settle them according to the traditional customs and laws. They are also responsible for settlement of inter-village land dispute.[70] In order to strengthen and refuel this institution of the village, the State Government has designated it as 'Village Council.' It is instituted on the traditional pattern to facilitate the village people to function better both socially and economically and to live in their traditional way. The Village and Area Council Act was passed in the year 1973, and subsequently amended in the year 1978.[71]

Thus, GBs are the direct responsible persons whose role is expected to be the communicator or mediator and act on behalf of a village community for the welfare of its community by giving positive impact to the social, economic and political life of the people. However in many instances, the responsibility is not properly executed for community.

2. Village Community and Common People

The traditional system gives every family in a village the right to own land. Such system emerged most probably from the necessity of warding off exploitation, though class antagonism as such was not prominent yet. Involvement in manual work and earning wages in common was a traditional practice among the Naga villages. Equal distribution of the amount commonly earned among the members regardless of strength, sex and age was an exceptional characteristic of their social practice. Socialism of this kind was practiced. For centuries, such system enabled the Nagas to live virtually free from the ruthless exploitation and domination found in other societies of the world. Fair distribution of wealth and the sanction of security to a great extent solved the problem of law and order, which has now changed. The complicated modern setting might make the practicability of the traditional system tough in the present times. The latest trend of the economic superpowers towards "integrated

70 Vamuzo, *Develop Your Own Village: An Approach to Grass Root Planning and Development,* 3-4. The customary laws are mostly based on natural justice and equity.

71 Ibid., 5.

global economy" has to be critically viewed as it has the greatest advantage to exploit the conditions of total free market system.[72]

The very essence of relationship in Naga Society prevalent in former days was the principle of 'give and take'. People's standard of dealing in everyday affairs was mutual giving and mutual taking. Their consciousness of the nature of society being interdependent was high and practically wholesome. There is a Naga saying, "Where is the pleasure of taste if it is not in the common sharing"?[73] This speaks of the noble standard of the society in general. Poverty and security were in the long run, the concern of the society as a whole. Discrimination was almost non-existent though the elders and rich were respected. By and large, all citizens lived in peace and harmony. Such high values of system were found in Naga Society.

For instance, the practice of the Nagas of having 'collective communal provision' or 'paddy store house or room' of paddy for the poor and needy, the village guests and visitors is a unique indeed. The poor and the needy would be provided paddy according to their needs. The individual families voluntarily contribute according to their produce. Usually, families who harvest more paddies contribute more for the community.[74] The community possessions usually included the whole of forest areas, mineral resources, rivers, ponds and lakes. Everyone was entitled to the use of public land and other communal properties. Any entry made into the public properties was regarded as violations.

There was a social system called '*morung*' (youth dormitory), which played a vital role in Naga society. 'Morung' is not a Naga word. It is probably said to be of Assamese origin. Each Naga tribe has a specific name for the term. For example, the Sumi termed as '*Illiki/Apuki*.' Every boy and girl who had attained the age of puberty generally became an active member of it. It is in this male and female

---

72 "Christian Socialism in the Naga Context" In *Manifesto of the National Socialist Council of Nagalim: National Socialism*, 2. www.nscnonline.org/webpage/manifesto/national-socialism.htm (15 March 2003).

73 "Christian Socialism in the Naga Context," *Manifesto of the National Socialist Council of Nagalim: National Socialism*, 1.

74 Vashum, *Nagas' Right to Self Determination: An Anthropoligical Historical Perspective*, 18.

dormitory where a sense of social responsibility was intensively inculcated in the young people and practiced. Social problems were discussed and tackled though it was not a law making body. The obligation youth had towards the people naturally served much of the need of the society. To defend the village was always their honoured responsibility.

They worked in groups by rotation and feasted themselves in the field and at home, group hunting and fishing were their favourites. Diligence was much appreciated and those who could prove themselves better were praised and respected. A spirit of competition was always there among the members of the *morung* and also between different *morungs*. Their thoughts and deeds were mostly in terms of social benefits. They were the mainstays of the society.[75] It was one common and very important socio-cultural institution of the Nagas. In the modern sense, the nearest equivalent would be 'educational institution.'[76]

Feasts of merit were traditionally celebrated in the Naga community with great splendour and honour. It bestowed so much distinction on their donors and shows that it was the distribution of wealth rather than its possession that was important. These feasts include everybody, not merely one's relations and rich friends, but the poorest and least important.[77] Takatemjen writes that there were three basic beliefs behind this (1) It was believed that the giver would

75 "Christian Socialism in the Naga Context," 2. cf. K. Thanzauva, "Tribal Ecclesiology: 'Community House' as the Basis of Tribal Ecclesiology," in *Tribal Theology: A Reader*, edited by Shimreingam Shimray (Jorhat: Tribal Study Center, 2003), 122, 126ff. Thanzauva has developed the understanding of *Morung* in his own tribal Mizo term as *Zawlbuk* translated into English as 'Community Home', which was an institution for *tlawngaihna* (means theoretically taught and practically demonstrated in all activities) in the Mizo society (one of the North eastern tribal communities). The researcher has keen interests to note this to show the similarities operating among the tribals of the North East.

76 Vashum, *Nagas' Right to Self Determination: An Anthropoligical Historical Perspective,* 15, 24. But *Morung* certainly would mean more than educational institution.

77 Verrier Elwin, *Nagaland* (Shillong: P. Dutta for the research Development, 1961), 104.

gain honour for himself by giving these feasts, in this life and hereafter, the right of wearing certain clothes and ornaments, also to decorate the house colourfully. (2) The skulls of the sacrificed animals hung in the outer room of the house were believed to bring prosperity to the person and to his heirs. (3) The feast was an act of charity in its best form for it was a means of feeding the poor and sharing wealth with the entire population.[78] The Naga feasts of merit involved much labour, time and wealth. This great day was remembered by both rich and poor in the village. The accumulated resources were assured for social ends. Feasts of Merit were liberative in character that involved sharing of goods with the poor.[79] Hence by the process of giving the feasts, the rich committed themselves to the cause of the poor and the powerless and became their defender.

Today, the individual Naga lives in a liberal atmosphere and he has the opportunity for free personality growth and greater self-expression. But the other side of the picture is that the old values of community solidarity and corporate action are disappearing. There is no doubt the trend is towards an atomised society of the modern type. Our task is to guide the social change so that there will be a healthy balance between individual freedom and community.

The modern life and culture has a strong influence on Nagas. The average Naga has become individualistic and concerned for the individual's advancement and welfare. Formerly, the Naga villages were well-knit units with strong social cohesion. Hekali comments that the village unit was the strongest unit and basis of community strength.[80] Today, there is loosening of the community structure and the individual is more and more on his/her own. One has to be reminded that the whole ethos of community life and sharing has direct socio-economic implications, which stands out true and relevant to the present Naga context.[81]

---

78 Takatemjen, *Studies on Theology and Naga Culture* (Delhi: ISPCK, 1998), 75.

79 Liberative because they enjoyed the freedom of being in a community.

80 Interview with Hekali, Deputy Commissioner of Dimapur, 4 May 2005.

81 This discussion will be further taken into consideration in the later stage of discussion. In the midst of these problem faced by the Nagas there is a ray of light in the form of cultural renaissance in ideology (politically) and values. Further, the emergence of the whole concept of 'communitization' covers the

3. Subsistence Economy

The Nagas were quite self-reliant people. This was particularly true in the context of the villages as every village was a self-sufficient unit. They did everything for themselves, constructed their inter-village paths, built their bridges and gave relief to one another in time of need. They made their clothing and prepared their medicines, cooking vessels, crockery, cosmetic and the like.[82] Dignity of labour was highly valued. Any person who neglects work was shunned or not respected by the community. The Nagas have deep rooted attachment to the value of action-oriented way of living. The Nagas have the attitude that one lives by the sweat of one's brow.[83] The issue on the 'dignity of labour' has to be re-examined in the present context. Although in theory the nature of work culture still remains among the Nagas but in practice it is diminished.[84]

Their main economy was based on agriculture and animal husbandry, bamboo, cane, spear making and weaving. The Naga work force is mainly agricultural with around 73% of the people engaged in different types of agricultural practices, Jhum or shifting cultivation being the main one. Traditional village industries based on local forest product form the backbone of this sector.

In the past, trade and commerce was not much in vogue. Thus, whenever there was the necessity of any article, it was obtained through barter system. The anomaly of such a system was that it was the necessity and not the intrinsic value of the commodity that determined the price. There were no fixed market centres. The different tribes practised different primitive systems of currency. For instance, salt was used as the currency in some Sumi areas.[85]

---

over all aspect of community life, such as, Health, education and economic concerns. These perspectives are seen as positive developments but are slow in process.

82 Elwin, *Nagaland,* 103.

83 Vashum, *Nagas' Right to Self Determination: An Anthropoligical Historical Perspective,* 17.

84 This point will be elaborated in a later section.

85 Imnayongdang, *Levels of Rural Development in Nagaland: A Spatial Analysis* (Meerut: S. K. Mittal, 1990), 53-54.

However, the Japanese invasion of Nagaland during World War II brought the Nagas into greater contact with the outside world and their economy changed to some extent. The change was in respect of earning wage as daily labourers by supplying men and materials for the war efforts. Nagaland entered into contract with the government for various constructions and supply of materials.[86]

The researcher's concern on this discussion has come up with the question on how the Nagas today can live without depending on others, which does not necessarily mean to return back to self-subsistence economy or currency. With the change of time the individual needs are increased challenging their very survival, which should be seriously checked.

II. The Present Situation

The situation in Nagaland has undergone an enormous metamorphosis compared to the past situation. Some dominant aspects of the new emerging situation in Nagaland are mentioned below:

1. Socio-Cultural Bankruptcy

The socio-cultural setting at a moment is complex and the whole socio- cultural ethos is disturbed at a deep level.

The Naga political situation has left common people with false promises and delayed hope leading to identity crisis. The young people join the Naga militant without much education and firm decision, which affects not only their career but also become problem to the family and society as well. In many instances these are the groups of people that spoil the reputation of the land. Hekali observes that many people those involved in this movement are dropouts, frustrated young people in relation to employment and relationships. Although the goal of the political movement is right, the approach sometimes ends up in wrong means.[87]

The uneducated young people, dropouts and unemployed youths are influenced by the social evils of the day. The growth of

---

86 Imnayongdang, *Levels of Rural Development in Nagaland: A Spatial Analysis*, 54.

87 Interview with Hekali.

frustrated educated unemployed also leads to social problems. For instance, there are problems like drug addicts and drug peddlers, the illegal search for earning money through extortion and taxation, and even a good part of the spirit of insurgency.[88] The crime rate at Dimapur continues to be very high compared to the rest of Nagaland. Surprisingly Hekali said to have discovered 60 illegal organisations of taxation on traders and commercial people.[89]

Table no. 1

The following table gives the figures of various social evils that exist and the height of its seriousness according to the opinion of respondents during field research.[90]

	Very Serious	A little Serious	Not a Serious	No Problem	No Response	Total Respondents
Drug addiction	63	27	7	0	3	100
HIV/AIDS	57	33	6	0	4	100
Intoxicating drinks	35	46	17	0	2	100
Division/classes	27	49	10	1	3	100
Illegal marriage	13	31	37	10	3	100
Prostitution	26	39	29	4	2	100
Divorce	13	28	45	10	4	100
Infidelity	16	31	29	13	11	100
Abortion	27	42	19	10	2	100
Killing/murder	48	34	14	0	4	100
Indulge in criminal cases	34	43	19	0	4	100
Theft	19	39	37	4	1	100
Easy money	59	26	9	5	1	100
Threat	31	47	19	3	0	100
Injustice	49	36	9	2	4	100

88 M. M. Thomas, *The Nagas*, p. 65.

89 Interview with Hekali.

90 Source: Questionnaire. Questions, 35-49.

The table above shows that 63% of the respondents expressed drug addiction as very serious problem; the other 59% of them opined easy money as very serious social evils that exist; 57% of the respondents expressed HIV/AIDS as very serious; 49% of them expressed injustice and finally 48% of the respondents expressed killing/murder to be very serious social evils in the Naga society. Of all the social evils that are indicated in the table accordingly with the percentage against each problem, we find that the above mention few are seen as very serious problems in the Naga society today. The rest of the problems are expressed to be at a lesser degree although they are visibly destructive and contribute to disintegration of the social values of Nagas.

The following paragraph gives the respondents' opinion on why the social evils exist today?

35% of the respondents reported that economic constraints in various forms lead the young people to indulge in social evils; namely the problems of unemployment, social injustice, corruption, division, lack of basic needs for survival and vocational avenues, and the government's inability to take up the responsibility strictly for the welfare and development of the people. 20% of the respondents expressed that these social evils are because of the people's mental desire for wealth and riches, and their poverty, educational background, ignorance and lack of integrity force them to indulge in social evils. Another 13% agree that insurgency and its influence results in free flow of easy money and self-centeredness. 20% of the respondents propose as a reason for decline the diminishing work culture where people have lost their motivation to work and the space for recreation is devalued. 12% of the respondents agree that the lack of spiritual orientation and teaching at home and in the churches becomes a failure and root cause for the problem. The remaining 7% remain silent to the reasons.[91]

Nagas have lost a sense of their cultural and traditional values. The traditional Naga pre-Christian beliefs and practices need to be evaluated in the light of the revealed word of God. It will be wrong to label everything as having no value or practical purpose. In

91 Source: Questionnaire. Question, 50.

other words, it serves the very practical purpose of giving continuity and meaning to life, which are absent in many "civilized" societies today.[92]

For instance, particularly among the Sumi Naga, marriage was treated with great respect. A long process took place before the marriage ceremony. The cost of the bride was considered high according to the worth in regards to her moral, potential and capability of taking responsibility. Therefore, the marriage remained safe from immorality and separation. This traditional value in marriage is diminishing gradually. The findings below give a picture to this issue.

Surprisingly, 95% of the respondents oppose the present expensive nature of marriage, which involves material expenses, cash, physical labour and time. It has become a 'showbiz' and luxurious beyond one's capacity exclusive of the rich. Marriage has become a burden to the parents and compulsion to the family to reproduce the trends of marriage that exist. Despite the expensive marriage people face marriage failure and divorce. Generally, when a couple cannot afford the people's expectation or under go frustration they opt for illegal marriage.[93]

The community life of the Nagas has undergone a tremendous change. 15% of the respondents give a positive description of Nagas as peace loving Christians who have attained better living standards and increased literacy; all these make Nagas proud of their community life at present. 36% gives a balanced and optimistic opinion pointing both to the negative and positive aspects. Despite of these changes one cannot generalize the whole issue. They commented on the possibility of future improvement of the situation through proper guidance though the positive developments may seem slow. The other 45% of the respondent, which is also majority in percentage, express their grief and concern on the Naga community life, citing the degradation of moral values, which has affected the ethos of cultural and traditional value in everyday life, the division among

---

92 Ricky Medom Noulezhalie, *The Relevance of the Theological Motif of Exile to the Naga's Struggle for Sovereignty as a People* (Delhi: ISPCK, 2002), 92.

93 Source: Questionnaire. Questions, 51.

Nagas in the form of tribalism, clanism, leadership crisis and factional problems; the evils like, nepotism, corruption, injustice, dishonesty, disunity, hatred, robbery, rape cases and so forth. The rest 4% did not respond to the specific question.[94]

On the basis of the realities discussed above the author is of the opinion that the present state cannot be blamed solely on the sociological theories of change. In fact the changes take place in every society and what the Nagas are facing is simply a part of that change. However, Wati Aier writes that in the Naga context, from a sociological and historical vantage, the introduction to these changes point to the weakness of the established authority and to the exhaustion of institutionalised tradition.[95]

Further he points out that Nagas has lost both the capacity and the will to confront the difficulties facing people constructively. Truth is painful for many, while a few may shun the reality and disseminate the facts and happenings as fiction and distortion. The seriousness of the situation calls for a theological reflection and response. Finally, the Biblical dictum calls for radical allegiance to Christ that is totally opposed to the "principalities and powers" which have enslaved and dehumanised the people.

Thus, the commitment towards Christ calls for a radical change and demands justice/ righteousness acknowledging Christ calls for a new relationship to persons and especially to the poor, the outcast, the "rebels," and the marginalized of the exploitative systems. The Sumi Church has a wide opportunity and responsibility for God's mission in transforming and liberating the Naga society from all social evils that exploit the cultural and traditional ethos of Naga community.

2. Educational Concerns

British Administration was introduced in the Naga Hills, not as a policy of aggrandizement, but in response to the appeal from some villages for protection against raids of others. Naturally the first duty

94 Source: Questionnaire. Questions, 32, 52, 59.

95 Wati Aier, "Nagas At Present: From a Theological Perspective," in *From Darkness to Light,* edited by Alongla P. Aier (Kohima: NBCC, 1997), 169.

of the first administrations was to stop raids and headhunting. When a group of villages came under administration it enjoyed peace and security. Other villages saw its benefit and appreciated it and so they also came forward for introduction of administration in their area. Thus, gradually the whole of the present Nagaland came under the influence of administration.

One good aspect of the British administration was the spread of western education and its humanizing influences. The whole of India along with the tribal areas owe considerably to the British government and western Christian missions for the development of their diverse literature and languages, which went together with the spread of education.[96] Although the schools were opened on request to the British administration, the Christian missionaries were already in the area since 1870s.

Education was valued as a means of social and economic ascent, which implied a sense of reward in terms of status and other benefits, particularly a salaried profession as opposed to traditional occupation. It provided an opportunity for any aspirant of making a better life, free from the constraints and limitations of tradition and customs.[97]

In the wake of administration and education there came the opportunity of Government service and small contract works. So we see that the most important contribution introduced by administration in this area is stoppage of headhunting, introduction of education and of monetary economy.

Therefore, everybody could get higher education and earn money, but poor people could not avail the opportunities due to their financial limitations. The disparity continued between the rich and the poor. Today, by middle class we understand a certain educated class of people who earn their bread by employing their brain, i.e., by

96 M. M. Thomas, *Tribal Awakening* (Bangalore: Christian Institution for the study of religion and society, 1965), 99.

97 Aier, "The Emerging Middle Class," *From Darkness to Light,* 79-80. He cites J. P. Mills' view of Naga attitudes towards education that other than making one fit for ordinary life, an educated Naga expects a ready made govt. post, described as a 'sitting and eating job.' Such were the effects of western education that explains the attitude of educated Nagas.

themselves; and do not depend on the interest of the money invested or on other's labour, neither on physical labour as most of the lower class people depend on.[98] On the other hand, the poor people remain illiterate and unfortunate.

In regard to the educational field the Nagas have rapidly progressed during these recent decades. A massive adult education programme was launched in 1978 in an effort to educate the illiterate adult population in the age group of 15-35 years in a period of five years. To encourage young people to take up higher studies, Government assistance in the form of grants and scholarships is made available to deserving students.[99]

People go out of the state and the region to achieve higher goals. It is evident that even at the national level there are a few who serve as high Government officials in various departments. But the story is not always the same on the other side. The government schools and colleges in Nagaland, particularly in Dimapur, do not exhibit quality education. People fall into the trap of commercialisation. In this sense, the preparatory and competent education is not achieved.

In the past, about 90% of educational institutions in Nagaland were in the hands of the Christian Mission. Many of the teachers were not qualified yet they were dedicated and could produce very disciplined and responsible citizens in the society. Today the government runs 90% of the educational institutions, which have not been able to produce 20% socially productive citizen in the society.[100] V. K. Nuh states that Nagas are highly literate but less educated. Nagaland figures the highest per capita expenditure in the education sector in India spending on average 30-35 crores of rupees mainly outside the state for children' education alone.[101]

The majority of the school going pupils in Nagaland leaves the system after acquiring high school education. This is commonly

---

98 B. Datta Ray, *The Emergence and Role of Middle Class in North-East India* (New Delhi: Uppal Publishing House, 1983), 215-218.

99 Milada Ganguli, *A Pilgrimage to the Nagas* (New Delhi: Mohan Primlani, 1984), 271.

100 V. K. Nuh "Education from Christian Point of View," Unpublished paper, 2005. 1.

101 Ibid.. 2.

due to factors like poor economic status, poor academic achievement and failure to find any link between their education and actual life activities, they remain unemployed or go back to their traditional life style and become cultivators, while a few likely become delinquent.[102] Therefore, most of the Naga young people stop their education on the way and their vocational aspirations remain unrealistic. This may be due to improper planning of academic program and also lack of practical knowledge on the part of educationists in the state.[103]

Findings from the questionnaire[104] show that 14% of the respondents expressed the costs of education being very high. People from poor background and those having many children at home cannot afford this type of education. The private schools and institutions have made education a business and are money oriented. 25% of respondents opined that with the changing time, the spirit of competitiveness has crept in. Therefore, serious need arises for reconsidering the education system by providing practical knowledge with career orientation. 50% of the respondents give similar opinion that the education system, does not meet the needs of the Naga society today. Further, 50% raised concern on the teachers' sincerity, commitment and qualification. 11% of them did not respond to the particular question at all. This could be simply out of their ignorance or hesitancy.

In regard to the discussion on education the researcher points out that Nagas have to develop a right motivation and correct understanding towards education. Although the establishment of the educational institutions is very common at high school and college levels the need for development of relevant education is now crucial. Following this the indigenous and traditional teaching forms, language and cultural elements along with the western education could be of high value in producing competent and responsible citizens.

The above discussion, points to the management of educational institutions as business centres. Thus, the researcher strongly felt that

102 Tali, "Special Role of High School," 11.
103 Tali, "Special Role of High School," 10.
104 Source: Questionnaire. Questions, 16-17.

such system need to be confronted so that people will value education for future socio-economic prospects of the young generation and the state at large. The Naga Baptist Church could be recommended to take into serious consideration through awareness, teaching and reforming the educational structure and system for betterment of Naga society.

3. Wealthy vs Common people

The integrated social life from a family unit to a larger community is now replaced with division and hatred in every bit of life. The elders and village chiefs were a help to the common people in all circumstances and they were very highly respected in return. People were quite faithful in their approach to one another. Animistic religion helped them to cope with life's uncertainties. People sincerely performed various forms of sacrifices and feasts to the spirits.

The following analysis from the questionnaire shows the present degradation of community life, specifically concerning the poor, orphans and widows.[105]

15% of the respondents are convinced that there is provision for the poor and orphans, yet less has been utilized. Another 25% realize that the provision is supplied in the form of material needs through the government, NGOs, VDB Schemes and from groups of believers in the churches. 32% are unaware or uninformed about the facilities and provisions. 33% of the respondents do not agree to the above statements. It is not because they are unaware of the situation but they are positively convinced that the present Naga community does not give room to such consciousness. The community is more on the side of self-accumulation and monopoly by a handful of people. Therefore, the provisions that are already there do not benefit the expected beneficiaries. 5% of the respondents did not respond to the question.

As the Naga society emerges from the traditional tribal form and moves into the modern agro-industrial phase, disparities developing between the different sections of the population and between the urban and the rural sectors can be visibly seen. A few have become

---

105 Source: Questionnaire. Questions, 34.

very rich whereas the bulk of the population still remains poor. A few educated and wealthy middle class people get hold of all the possible facilities at the government level, with regards to employment or on any competitive examination. There are other similar forces, which manipulate the rights of the people in the name of Naga political movement that disturb the people.

The following findings from the questionnaire analysis will show the figures in percentage against the poor and rich.

Table no. 2

The percentage suggested by the respondents on poor and rich:[106]

% Poor	90%	85%	80%	75%	70%	65%	60%	40%	No Response	Total %
	4	5	10	18	11	15	22	5	5	100

% Rich	60%	50%	40%	44%	35%	30%	25%	20%	15%	10%	No Response	Total%
	2	4	21	9	15	10	16	7	3	8	5	100

22% of the respondents suggested that 60% of the Naga people fall under the category of the poor. On the other 21% of the respondents suggested 40% of the Naga people to be rich. The figures show clearly from the table that majority of the respondents weigh equally against the suggested percentage respectively. The following opinion from the respondents gives the reasons for becoming rich.

44% of the respondents commented that people have simply become richer through selfish ends and accumulation of public wealth and poor poorer. Another 25% responded that people solely depend on government funds and salary despite this money being manipulated by the higher ups. There are an other 15% who said the rich rely on bribing, corruption, dishonesty, easy money and self-centeredness. 10% of them expressed the need for infrastructures and proper development where people can look for survival. Further comments were made on the irresponsibility of the political and

106 Source: Questionnaire, Question, 33. The bold figures are the proposed percentages against the Poor and the Rich respectively.

social leaders who could appropriately look into the welfare of the common people. The rest 6% respondents did not respond to the question. [107]

The other picture of the analysis reveals the economic imbalance among the people due to the present political movement. Unfortunately 27% of the respondents did not answer the question. The reason could be either that they were uncomfortable or were hesitant to respond. 25% of the respondents felt quite balanced in their response. They appreciate the present movement, which gives them a sense of identity and common goal in spite of the awkward situation they face. They are optimistic about the movement provided the leaders' determination is taken forward and properly guided with unity. The other 48% of the respondents showed disagreement with this present movement, which has done a lot of damage to the people's consciousness, hampered development in the state and imposed taxation over common people's income resources. Some have accumulated wealth for themselves for selfish ends in the name of political purpose, which has resulted into a big gap economically among the people. [108]

Hence, not only in respect of financial emoluments and physical facilities, but also in other respects such as cultural standards and ways of living, great disparities are highly a concern. And as these disparities go beyond a certain limit, the social tensions are bound to arise. But the time is not far off when they will. It will be wise and farsighted to guide the course of economic growth and social development so that the new Naga society will have a reasonable measure of equality and integration even as the old Naga society used to have.[109]

The corruption and irresponsibility of the able, powerful and authoritative Naga people affects the common peoples' pride. On the other hand, few of the people enjoy wealth to the fullest. It is observed both at the Governmental level and private sector or village

---

107 Source: Questionnaire. Questions, 53.

108 Source: Questionnaire. Question, 81, 85.

109 Singh, *Tribal Situation in India,* 121-127.

community that the rights of the people have been absorbed. These in return have remained underdeveloped for many years.

While some poor of the village do not get enough of their share of land to survive, these people go on laboring for day wages, which is not sufficient for the family. All this clearly reveals the double privileges and advantage held by the upper levels of people in the Naga society. At this end, the Naga Baptist Church has full responsibility to play a prophetic role breaking the barriers of injustice and projecting the rights of an individual and all human being bringing them at peace and right relationship in the Naga society.

4. Decline of Dignity of Labour

In the recent past, Naga community's life and work covered the whole ethos of cultural and traditional life. People devoted their life together for the cause of common good. Accountability and contribution towards community life was expected from one and all. Today, Nagas have lost the sense of being in a community both in belief and practice. The important part of nature and worship, which is in the form of hardwork, is diminishing especially among the young people.

The table below shows the opinions and analysis of the present status of work culture prevalent among the Naga community during the field research.

Table no. 3

The working hours per day spent by respondents:[110]

% of respondents	2-3hrs	4-5hrs	6-8hrs	9 & above	No Response	Not working	Total Respondents
	35	25	13	7	2	18	100%

As indicated in the table only 7% of the respondents work for nine hours. The maximum 35% work for two to three hours, which shows a big difference between the two. 25% still shows very short duration of four to five working hours. 13% of the

110 Source: Questionnaire. Question, 13.

respondents work for six to eight hours, which could be considered as normal. Surprisingly 18% do not engage in any work (this could be understood in the sense of any permanent jobs). Finally 2% gave no response to the question.

However, the working hours are spent mostly on domestic works such as cooking, washing, cleaning and gardening. There are others who attend the office, personal business, private appointments, voluntary engagements, teaching, agricultural work and the like. These depict the ignorance of the people's attitude towards work, which greatly affects one's socio-economic survival. In relation to this the table below shows the level of people's attitude towards work.

Table no. 4

The general attitude of the Nagas to work as observed and indicated by the respondents:[111]

	Mostly	Commonly	Very Rare	Not At All	No Response	Total Respondents
Feel embarrass	22	54	15	5	4	100
Afraid	15	35	27	18	5	100
Lazy	43	38	12	2	5	100
Active	16	17	51	10	6	100
Not motivated	45	31	11	9	4	100
Energetic	15	22	46	14	3	100
Sincere	13	20	45	18	4	100
Do not give importance	38	32	25	3	2	100
Ignorant about work	23	43	9	5	3	100
Find hard	45	35	13	4	3	100
Graceful	8	22	45	20	5	100
Keep distant	35	39	15	7	4	100
Not bothered	35	46	10	8	1	100

111 Source: Questionnaire. Question, 18-30.

45% of the respondents expressed as 'no motivation' and 'find hard' on general attitude to work among the Nagas. On the other majority 54% of the respondents expressed as 'feel embarrass' to work. The rest of the percentages against the particulars are at lesser degree comparing to the two mentioned. However, all of these indications shown in the table are visible strength and weaknesses that contributes to the attitude of the Nagas to work.

The problem of their attitude could be an influence of modern culture, psychological complexities, physical, educational background, and the kind of environment one is brought up or motivated. The findings on attitude to work do not help the individual or community to improve the socio-economic status. Young people look for higher jobs, government facilities and employment. Therefore, any lower job without designation or well-paid salary is abandoned. The people who are at work or employed in government offices spend less time working. Although in general senses, the Nagas have that instinct and inherent nature of work; practically it is an outdated concern today.[112]

In book of genesis God has exhibited himself as a Creator, Sustainer and Liberator. The Naga Baptist church has a very urgent relational calling to carry out to the Naga society. Thus, the church needs to be encouraged to educate and help them practically in developing the value and reviving work culture in near future.

The analysis below supplements the above discussion idea on work culture. Thus, the following analysis is the findings from the respondents on work environment at their homes:[113]

Generally 60% of the parents encourage their children to work apart from their studies. Usually they are asked to help in domestic or household works such as cleaning, washing, ironing, gardening, mopping, sweeping and shopping. In spite of the parents' encouragement and force on children to work it still remains doubtful whether the children take up the responsibility. 30% of them do not give a serious thought to let the children work. Domestic helpers

---

112 However, there is a renaissance among the Nagas on socio-cultural values and tradition, which we would take up in the next chapter for discussion.

113 Source: Questionnaire. Questions, 31, 14 and 15.

either do this or parent themselves. 10% did not respond to the question.

Turning to the children or young people at home the analysis on the other hand shows a different picture. School and college goers spend 30-40% time in study, 10% for domestic helping and the rest 50% time is spent in recreation, playing, gambling, watching television and idling away. The analysis does not show an equal picture of time division and amount of work done.

The analysis of the children and young people who do not attend school or college shows that 22-30% are engaged in domestic work, 20% are involved in small earnings, private tuitions, business, offices and voluntary work in a community, and the rest 50% do not do anything specific. Most of the people from the last group are into gambling, playing, roaming, visiting friends, watching television and the like. These are the groups of people observed to be most likely influenced into unwanted social evils.

The traditional and cultural value of work that was once honoured is not seen among the Naga community. Although much is being said and done the integrated life style of the past is left far behind. Particularly the dignity of labour in the form of manual labour, hunting, and arts and crafts, lifting of community socio-economic status through common labour and sharing is now drowned in modern forms and culture. This has led people into the influence of free flow of easy money, corruption, bribery, dependency, and all other kinds of social evils.[114]

5. Migrant Influx

The integration of Naga Hills with the British Indian Empire and the subsequent development of roads and towns also pushed the markets in to the hill areas. As a result, the border market did not remain as the only trading station. Money economy and the merchants' community penetrated in to the Naga Hills replacing the barter economy. The entire trade at Kohima was now in the hands of a small number of merchants. For instance, there were altogether

114 Refer the discussion back to the first point of the same section (Socio-cultural bankruptcy).

18 shops in Kohima, out of which the *Marwari* merchants kept 13 shops.[115] Foreign goods and finished products began to appear in the markets. Indigenous goods were neglected and people began to develop a fancy for foreign goods. Currency was made available to the local people. Payments for labourers' salaries and commercial transaction were now made through the medium of currency.

The non-locals coming from outside the land extract wealth from Nagas. The fact is that more than 50% of the shopping centres, hotels and restaurants and any other businesses in Dimapur are run by non- Nagas. For instance in 2005 there were over four thousand trade licenses issued and among those, only 5-10% Nagas involved.[116]

The findings below will give a further picture of the people's opinion from the questionnaire on the influx of outsiders and its effect on the socio-economic situation of the local people. 47% of the respondents opined that the presence of these people has affected the economy of the local people. Since outsiders can earn money easily without much difficulty and that they are ready for any type of opportunity and job. For this reason Nagas are dependent on them from domestic help to economic affair which is direct implication on the lost sense of self-reliance. This group of migrants are considered a threat to Naga economy at present and in the future bringing in the influence of social evils like, threat, crime, and extortion. Politically these people become vote banks to the political leaders in the state.

25% felt that these people should be allowed to stay within the local boundary under certain terms and conditions. Since the influx continues their presence needs to be checked strictly. 21% opined that the local people are reluctant to take advantage of the opportunities and lack motivation to work hard and earn their livelihood. Therefore, one should not condemn the outsiders for being dominant over them. This group of people shows concern about the rapid population growth in the land. However, they appreciate the

---

115 V. H. Zhimomi, *British Policy and Administration in Nagaland* (M.Phil. Dissertation, Northeastern Hill University, 1981), 94-95.

116 Interview with Vikheho, Chairman, Municipal (Town Committee) Dimapur, 4 April 2005.

outsiders' helpfulness in manual work and labour force in various areas of life. In spite of the differences and difficulty, this group felt that a mixed culture society is the best way to live and suggest rather the Nagas need to learn from these outsiders. There are Nagas who have taken advantage of outsiders going to the extent of robbing and causing destruction. This is one of the hindrances that discourage the non-locals to run a business in Nagaland, which is also partly hampering the development of the land. 7% of the respondents failed to respond to the particular question.[117]

An issue related to the influx is cultural intermarriage with the outsiders. These are the findings during the field research. 56% of the respondents give negative response expressing that intermarriage should not be encouraged because the outsiders take advantage of marrying the local girls, specifically to receive the support from that particular background for the purpose of business and economic benefits. The second reason is because they belong to a different race, culture, religious background, which does not correspond with local cultures (and customary law which is practiced even today to some extent). Therefore, it is a threat to the economy of the people and produces another race that suffers from identity crisis.

28% felt open in their opinion. Many of them accept intercultural marriage because it leaves room for free exchange of learning from each other and maintaining wider relationships with people, thus bridging the gap which results with better socio-economic development provided that they guard their identity.

18% of them gave a paradoxical opinion giving choice to couple's that considers their values of religion, culture and children's identity. On the other hand they also opined the importance of maintaining a relationship with outsiders. However, a person being a Naga should be encouraged to remain as Naga. 8% did not respond to this particular question.[118]

The analysis above shows that people are now conscious of this problem. With the incoming of illegal immigrants and the great number of business people from neighboring states there is

117 Source: Questionnaire. Question, 60 and 61.

118 Source: Questionnaire. Question, 62.

the practical threat of a socio-economic bankruptcy. It has not only disturbed the socio-cultural values but economically Nagas have given advantage to them. It is partly because of the lack of people's motivation to work and exercise legal disciplines. This is a crucial problem that the Nagas face today because it has devalued the Naga image as a full human. Their potentiality and capability given by God remains unutilized. The Church could be quick in tackling these problems through the initiatives of social organizations and government administrators. Thus in doing so, the church will demonstrate a transforming participation and fulfilling God's mission in Naga society.

6. Economic Disparities

The basic reasons for backwardness as Hokishe stated way back in 1986 was ignorance of utilization of the available resources; the soil is fertile, climate is moderate but the land utilization is not on scientific lines; institutional credit facilities are poor; banking assistance is almost negligible and the state is simply depending on central assistance.[119]

However, in order to begin with all the development activities from the grass root level, the Government of Nagaland had adopted a new policy to form Village Development Board. The Government have been trying its best to penetrate the most backward and interior villages with various schemes and plans of development, but in spite of attempts of all sorts, these have not succeeded and it is an admitted fact that whatever fund is allotted for the village and rural development, some or the other villages never got any help from the Government and remain neglected.[120] Therefore, the idea to form Village Development Board came into existence to bring about a balanced development of rural areas with proportionate fund investment with maximum opportunity and initiative for the villagers themselves to develop their own villages with fund available at their disposal. A special development programme was introduced

---

119 Sema, *Emergence of Nagaland*, 174.

120 Vamuzo, *Develop Your Own Village: An Approach to Grass Root Planning and Development*, 7.

only after 1963, when the area attained statehood and the local people took initiative in the political arena and structure for all round development.[121]

Formal Statehood initially brought in opportunities of employment in government services, contract, and supply-work. People left cultivation work in favour of business and educated people entered into government service. All these brought in money in an unprecedented amount. However, the easy money has led to easy life changing standards of living, with many people now gradually becoming averse to hard work and indulging in a life of pleasure.[122]

Due to the armed hostilities in Nagaland, the first three Five-year Plans could not effect infrastructural developments; even the benefits of the Fourth Five- Year Plan affected Nagaland marginally; The fifth and sixth Five- Year Plans could not be fully implemented because there was political instability and the political leadership could not devote their full time and energy for any comprehensive economic development programme for the whole of Nagaland.[123]

M. M. Thomas agreed in 1990s that the instability of Naga Government is one of the major causes of lack of economic development in the land. Thus, he recommends the necessity of political stability for economic and social development.[124] The argument still goes on as Iralu states that the 'underdevelopment is not the cause of insurgency in Nagaland.'[125] Therefore, we need development in an environment of freedom and liberty and not under political and military oppression. This is possible only when political solution finally dawns on the battle scarred lands of Nagaland.

There is hardly a shop or office in Kohima that is exempted from extortion. There has been no progress worth the name. The Nagaland University, in the process of taking shape, reeks of with

121 Jogamaya Saikia, "People's Participation in Rural Development: A Study in Nagaland," in *Rural Development in North-East India: Perspectives, Issues and Experiences*, edited by R. K Samanta, (New Delhi: Uppal Publishing House, 1991), 187.

122 Imnayongdang, *Levels of Rural Development*, 55.

123 Sema, *Emegence of Nagaland*, 174.

124 Thomas, *The Nagas*, 63.

125 Iralu, Kaka D. *How Then Shall We Live?* Kohima: Kaka D. Iralu, 2001, p. 111

corruption.[126] The referral Hospital at Dimapur, Nagaland, which involves a multi crore amount of money lays abandoned due to mismanagement and corruption.

Another pressing problem facing the youth of the state is unemployment.[127] Unemployment in Nagaland has reached an alarming stage with a recent report indicating that 34,755 educated youths were jobless on March-31st, 2003. Nagaland has one of the highest unemployment rates in the Asian sub-continent.[128] Injustice at the administrative level is obvious especially when one is educated but denied to provide his or her right to serve the people at the governmental level.

The pervasive nature of unemployment is also attributed to the complete non-existence of private sector and the domination of a strong public sector.[129] Further, with the coming of new cultural settings, the fresh young graduates are less or not at all skilful in other areas of arts and thus, are simply getting employment in the government offices.[130]

Generally there are people who opt for timber business, *jhum* cultivation, hunting wild animals and farms for survival, which is partly seen as ecological devastation on environment in which the people live. The analysis on ecological concerns highlights that majority 75% of the respondents agree to the fact that the growing damage on natural resources, endangers life in future. On the

---

126 Kuldip Nayar, "Nagaland: Too Distant and Too Alienated," www.radicalparty.org//humanrights/nagaland.htm (24 October 2004).

127 Thomas, *The Nagas Towards, 2000 A.D*, 64.

128 Sunup Naga, "Unemployment," *Eastern Mirror*, Dimapur, 8 August 2003, 2.

129 Ibid.

130 Researcher points out that the discussion above also implies quality education system in the land. The education that is invested in youngsters today is all imported education system once received from the Missionaries and Britishers. We do not deny its value or usefulness when it comes to competing with people at national and international level. Yet the urgent quest for our situation today is to revise the importance of relevant integrated education, which one can opt for that our next generation may not suffer of survival and leadership. The following section provides more discussion to this point. See also Hokishe Sema, *Emergence of Nagaland: Socio-Economic and Political Transforming and the Future* (Delhi: Vikas Publishing House, 1986), 174-175.

other hand, 20% expressed that ban of timber business has caused disadvantage for people who completely depended on this resource as main occupation for survival. Thus, the sudden setback of income resource has resulted in economic disparities in many homes because of the lack of the government with no alternatives provided for these people to survive. 5% of the respondents did not respond to the question.[131]

Though there is ecological concern on the majority side the researcher is of the opinion that these 20% are equally valid and genuine. Because of the lack of employment avenues and resource income facilities people are forced to take drastic step for survival. In this case, it is imperative that the problem of employment and survival is dealt with.

The tables below are an analysis from the respondents' opinion on socio-economic situation, which gives a glimpse of the wider panorama of economic disparities at the grass roots level.

Table no. 5

The size of the family from respondents' own situation:[132]

Family size	6 & above	5	4	3	2
	35	32	18	10	5

As the table indicates families on the larger side with 35% followed by 32% covering the total members of five and six and above, usually each Naga family prefers a large family. There are a few others who prefer it to be small in size. However, the point here is to analyse their economical survival against the size of the family. The table on the employment status from respondents' family situation will give the picture in regards to this.

131 Source: Questionnaire. Questions, 55-58.

132 Source: Questionnaire. Questions, 1-2. Family here implies parents and children in each home.

Table no. 6

The employment status in the respondents' family:[133]

	None	Occasional	One	Two	Three	Four	Total Respondents
Government	40	-	25	15	12	8	100
Private organisation	62	-	28	6	2	2	100
Self-employment	49	7	20	10	11	3	100

Out of the total family size indicated above, the findings from the employment on government sector shows that only 25% against one member are employed in most homes. The rest are 15%, 12%, and 8% against two, three and four members respectively in each home. 40% are against 'none' who are not employed.

The findings in private sector show 62% of them are completely not employed. 28% are employed against one member in each home and the rest 6%, 2% and 2% against two, three and four members respectively in each home.

The findings from self-employed show 49% of them are not employed. The following 20%, 10%, 11% and 3% are against one, two, three and four members respectively in each home. There are other 7% who are involved occasionally.

A handful of people among those who are not employed in any of these three sectors own a business, farm or commercial building. There are people who completely depend on parents, family members, relatives and friends.

55% of the respondents express the reason for unemployment as dependence on government jobs, which are not sufficient to accommodate everybody. The second reason is due to partiality and injustice from the administration, government and officials, which practice bribery and other illegal means. Therefore poor people though qualified are kept out of opportunity. 3% expressed the concerns for population growth in regard to employment problem.

133 Source: Questionnaire. Questions, 4-12.

10% of the respondents feel that unemployment problem is because of the lack of educational qualification. 32% realize that people are ignorant about work, lazy, lack skill and interest, look out only for government jobs and therefore bypass the opportunities that come their way.

The above analysis sums up the socio-economic survival of the people. The number of poor people involved in earning for daily survival and the majority of them dependent on other members of the family. These families live a hand to mouth existence, which hardly suffices for their immediate survival.

Table no. 7

The monthly income from the respondents' own family situation:[134]

Monthly income	Below 500	500-1000	1500-2000	2500-3000	3500-4000	4500 & above	No Response
	-	7	12	20	16	35	10

The finding above indicates single or a few members employed are majority from a larger family. In a few cases there are none employed in a family. As Nagas having preferred large family system do not suffice with the little or average income they receive. Only 35% of the respondents show the income of Rupees four thousand five hundred and above and the average income of the rest is from Rupees four thousand to one thousand. With the increased need of each person, family as a whole remains unsatisfactory. All these

134 Source: Questionnaire. Question, 3. With the influence of women organizations and a few educated persons now everywhere in the village communities and in town areas, local people have started to gain confidence and enthusiasm of selling their products like clothing, arts and crafts, and eatables from gardens and farms. They usually have specific days and hours and also places assigned to sell their local products. With the increased demands of children and family people are now conscious of having money in their hands to meet their felt needs. There are new groups coming up especially among the ladies forming themselves as self help group such as; lending money to others, planting flowers, handicrafts, poultry and engaging in days work if need arise among themselves and others. These groups are seen in villages and Dimapur town areas. The next chapter will deal with this particular concern.

reveal the economic imbalance of the Naga family and community in general.

The above discussion shows a core scenario of the ground reality of economic survival among the Naga society at large. The church of God cannot remain silent spectator to the whole scene. It should be encouraged to turn its narrow understanding of mission within the traditional regularity of preaching into teaching and practically involving to the extent of solving the problem. In this, the church can become a transforming agent within its institutional boundary and beyond, networking with the other representative bodies in the state.

7. Political Aspirations

As late as 1940's, when the British rule was almost over, large parts of today's Nagaland did not even exist on their maps. Instead of showing villages the maps showed large blank white spaces with the words "Unadministered and Unsurveyed".[135] The Nagas led a primitive, uncivilized and brutish life in the villages with the traditional village polity under a chief in all aspects of power, economy and status.[136]

The word of Christ was unknown and unheard, life beyond the village boundaries was unknown and diseases went unchecked. People lived and died without even leaving their villages. They had no idea of the concept of a nation or independence or nationhood, though each village functioned as an independent unit. However, the village lost its traditional practice of governance of the villagers as a compact political unit. The villages were incorporated into the new

---

135 "Nagaland a profile and map".

136 J. H. Hutton, *The Sema Nagas* (Bombay: Oxford University Press, 1967), 36-37.
Sumi organized themselves into 5 groups - *Akukau* (the chief), *Mughemi* (the chief's dependents, followers, supporters, etc.), *Chochomi* (pre-eminent members, normally elders who advised the chief), *Kokomi* (chief's relations or nobles, but without much power), *Aluzhi* (groups composed of both sexes, that were responsible for the day to day labour in the process of cultivation and other community undertakings). The unit of the class division is the lineage, i.e., the chief's lineage of a ruling clan.

political order as a unit within a larger system. This does not mean that they lost all their indigenous political character.

The desire for wider ethnic recognition appeared with the socio-political developments in the Naga Hills. The Nationalist movement, which took to insurgency in mid 1950s, and the eventual creation of Nagaland as a State in 1963 are important developments, which made the name Naga a prestigious ethnic symbol for many hill tribes particularly in Manipur and other North-East India in general.[137]

Within the framework of this new political situation and in the light of the newly political aspirations, the Naga Club represented a small section of the Naga society, to explore the means and channels in pursuit of Naga political movement. It gradually developed into an intermediary pressure group between the British on one hand, and the traditional village power set up on the other. Since the formation of Naga Club the tribal identity has remained strong with common Naga identity.[138]

Persons awaiting this new opportunity could transcend the traditional polity and begin a new era in terms of politics. Sections of the new political activists manifested class character in terms of power. Such developments in the early stage of the Naga society explain the emergence of the class situation in the society in terms of power and class. It resulted in the emergence of middle class. It is difficult to say that without the intrusion by the British, such a development might not have taken place.[139]

The national record shows that the Naga National Council representatives and Indian leaders had a number of bilateral talks since 1946. These talks were held at the highest level possible at that time. The purpose of talks was to establish friendly relationship and mutual respect for one another as good neighbours. However, after the assassination of Mahatma Gandhi, the attempts to talk with the then Indian Prime Minister, Mr. Jawaharlal Nehru became quite

---

137 Ray, *Tribal Identity and Tension,* pp. 46-47.

138 Ibid, p. 49

139 Aier, "The Emerging Middle Class in the Naga Society," *From Darkness to Light*, 74-76.

difficult. Thereby, this led to the invasion of Nagaland by the Indian Army in 1954.[140]

The Naga territory was split between Assam and the North East Frontier Agency after Indian independence in 1947, despite a vocal movement advocating the political union of all the Naga tribes; one faction called for secession from India. In 1957, following violent incidents, the Indian government established a single Naga administrative unit under Indian rule. The Naga people responded by refusing to pay their taxes and by conducting a campaign of sabotage.

In 1960, the Indian Government agreed to make Nagaland a self-governing state within India; the state was officially inaugurated in 1963.[141] Naga separatists, however, continued to show violent opposition; they had been demanding autonomy and creation of a single administrative unit comprising all the Naga inhabited areas spanning across some of the North Eastern states. Naga rebels and the Indian government agreed on a cease-fire and peace talks are going on since 1997. Recently there has been an agreement between the Indian leaders and National Socialist Council of Nagaland- Isaac Muivah (NSCN–IM) leaders to continue talks until a "lasting settlement" is agreed upon, though there are indications that differences persist on the major issues, including the outfit's most contentious demand for unification of all the Naga areas. However, the latest agreement is to maintain a "peaceful and violence-free environment."[142]

---

140 *A Brief Account on Nagaland,* prepared by Federal Government of Nagaland (Kohima: Nagaland, June, 2000), 2.

141 Cf. "Nagaland a Profile and Map," and Hokishe Sema, Emergence. "Jawaharlal Nehru announced in Parliament on July 28, 1960, that India had accepted the Nagas' "desire" for a separate state. The inauguration of Nagaland as the sixteenth state of the Indian Union on 1st December 1963 mark the beginning of a new era in the political evolution on Nagaland. It was the long sought-after and peaceful development in times of need. It was an hour of crucial importance that brought the brave, proud and sturdy people of Nagaland irrevocably within the national mainstream. Thus it helped the process of nation-building, national integrations, modernization and political development, shoulder to shoulder with the different peoples constituting the Indian nation."

142 "India Set to Resume Talks with NSCN," *Times of India*, 16 July 2003, 9.

It is becoming increasingly clear that the preponderant majority of the Naga public would accept a position within the Indian Union. The Nagas may desire some improvements in the present status. They desire the enlargement of the present State boundaries to include all the Naga inhabited areas. They wish the formation of a Naga regiment, a separate Governor and a separate High Court. The transfer of responsibility for law and order to the State Government is another change desired by all.[143] However, the major hurdle in the progress of the peace talks is the so-called issue of the demand for 'Greater Nagaland.' The media has been misrepresenting the Naga demand for the integration or unification of Naga-inhabited areas as a demand for a Greater Nagaland.[144]

This Naga national identity has however been blurred under terrible persecution and the super imposition of the Indian national identity through the Indian state of Nagaland. In the true sense, the Naga national identity and the artificial Indian national identity co-exist today in every Naga. Iralu gives a strong emphasis that 'the solution to the Indo-Naga conflict will come only when we make a clear stand on our national identity. Half the battle for our political freedom will be won if we make this stand very clear and committed to it.'[145]

However, Iralu also elaborates about the Naga freedom movement leaders that the issue of 'Naga belongs to Nagaland' is hardly remembered rather now the issue is who is right among the Naga leaders. The people are left to carnal destruction, murder, extortion, cold-blooded death and hatred with one another. The main issue has now become secondary and now the people worship hero-leaders, which equates with cult worship that benefits self-image and self-economy.[146]

There is a possibility of coming together of the leaders if they have a firm determination and faithfulness to the cause of Nagas

---

143 Singh, *Tribal Situation in India,* 121-127.

144 R. S. Mayori, "Naga Talks Enter a New Phase," *Indian Currents*, 13 February 2005, 46.

145 Iralu, *How then*, p. 21

146 Ibid., 5-11.

nationality. The further issue involved here is of 'falsehood and truth' to self and God. The Naga leaders and public would have to get rid of double standard life because the whole social and religious ethos of Naga life and Naga spirituality is monopolize. V. K. Nuh commends that the Naga political problem is no more a political problem but rather a spiritual problem. It is a question of right relationship with God and human being. Therefore, to achieve anything worthwhile one has to seek for God's will.[147]

Finally, the question arises where is justice and freedom in Nagaland? Who is responsible to bring peace and reconciliation to the people? These are the urgent imperatives to look through for the better prospects of the future of Nagas. The Nagaland Baptist Church has involved so far in peace talk and peace process, which is a part of church mission. However, to be transforming and redeeming the situation, will again depend on how the church creatively and innovatively becomes the agent of God's mission. In this situation, the Naga Church needs an exodus liberative experience from all sorts of oppressive structures outside and within themselves.

Summary

In summing up the discussion we observe that there has been ample change taken place in the context. Some of the impact on the Naga society is in the social and community life of the people. The blessing streams of the past are replaced by the deteriorating culture and values of modern elements in all aspects of life. The economy of the people, once subsistence with credibility of their work culture, is dimly noticed anywhere due to the different opportunities at government offices and the value of easy money which leads to high expenses with low or no income (which partly is also contributed by the migrants). The political life, which was conducted mutually among the clan, village chiefs and leaders for common safety is known commonly with division and clashes at present among the political leaders.

All these problems are linked with problems such as; leadership, recognition, power, possessions, political differences,

---

147 V. K. Nuh. *My Native Country: The Land of the Nagas* (Delhi: Spectrum Publications, 2002), 79.

money, unemployment, underemployment and lack of resources and management for survival. The nature of Naga life is now ruled by the standard of manipulation, corruption, varied social evils, rich and poor divide, common people and bureaucrats divide, factional divide and continuous political warfare, and tribalism.

Thus, in this situation people aspire for social integrity, political freedom, economic progress and development; which lie far behind in reality. The church mission cannot bypass the context of the people and do God's mission because God's mission takes care of the context and liberates them. The Naga Baptist Church need to reflect theologically, bringing out the missiological models of mission and practically embrace the whole context of the Naga society, that will appropriate God's way of doing mission.

The next chapter will discuss the contribution and participation of various NGOs, other social organizations and government into different forms of awareness, education, seminars, rehabilitation, counseling, programmes for the self-help groups and welfare, writings and publications, trainings at state level. Besides the Nagaland Baptist Church Council and Sumi Church are particularly beginning to contribute in small ways, which gives a glimpse of hope of mission perspective in the near future.

Chapter 3

THE DIFFERENT ORGANISATIONS INVOLVED IN SOCIO-ECONOMIC UPLIFTMENT OF THE NAGAS IN NAGALAND (Section-A)

Introduction

At present, there is a great wave of movements taking place among the Nagas on economic, political, socio-religious and cultural fronts. Nagas are at the cross road with a fast changing world. There are changes in the field of education, western life style, clothing, eating habits, patterns of behaviour and the standard of living. Psychologically, the youth are much influenced by modern culture, which has both positive and negative impact.

As we have detailed the discussion at length in the previous chapter, we would now further look into the socio-economic upliftment of the society and its impact among the Nagas. For this, an overview of a few of the organisations and bodies involved from among the NGOs, Government, Social organizations and Churches in Nagaland has been provided.[148]

148 This will be brought out from the local perspectives in their attempts towards socio-economic upliftment/development in Nagaland (although the researcher is aware of the other recognized Northeast, National and International NGOs working in Nagaland), with a purpose to explore their roles and consciousness within their own setting.

I. The Role of the NGOs

1. Entrepreneurs Associates

The Entrepreneurs Associates (EA) is an organisation of first generation entrepreneurs committed to the following objectives: to support and help people in achieving their dreams especially participating with the youth in taking up business and setting high standards for ethics and values in business; promoting the spirit of social consciousness in advancing growth and developing and disseminating EA initiatives for wider outreach and nation building.[149]

The EA is committed to the growth and development of the society by showing the way with their achievements. It looks for a paradigm shift from the desire for easy money and easy living to a renewed culture of truthful living. Therefore, in order to make this happen it introduces special limitless opportunities of business that are available to the young people inspiring them to succeed without sacrificing ethics and values in business and their social responsibility.[150]

According to EA, there are four basic economic factors such as, Land, Labour, Capital and Entrepreneur. However, without the Entrepreneur, the other factors are but latent resources. The variance in the development of entrepreneurship determines the level of economic growth and progress. EA on the basis of this dynamic is of the view that by developing entrepreneurship, one can make the utmost use of the available resources- natural, social and human, not only for one's own growth and development, but also for the world at large.[151]

With entrepreneur skills, it encourages entrepreneurs to start at the bottom line, from the grass root level with the resources at hand. EA advocates that an entrepreneur needs to be creative and must also have the courage to be creative, to see things differently with

149 "Entrepreneurs Associates," *A Brochure,* 1.

150 Ibid., 2.

151 *Katalyst,* A bi-monthly newsletter of the Entrepreneurs Associates 1/ 4 (March-April 2003), 1. *Katalyst* is a publication of the EA containing their encounters and experiences with different individuals. It contains their success stories and contributions towards the society.

different approach, to stand alone where one has courage to choose activity over inactivity.[152]

EA facilitates loan and saving schemes. This fund goes directly into their saving account for 2 years and is returned to them with the interest of 16% and if someone is interested to renew the saving account they continue at the interest of 10%. EA borrows money from investor to uplift the programme. They also sometimes organise seminars and workshops.[153]

They provide a scheme called Entrepreneurs Associates Micro Finance (EAMF). This is an attempt to offer a common platform to both the public and business entrepreneurs for developing business & trading skills, and ideas for nation building. Roping in people's savings through micro fixed deposits, the EA corpus fund generates the micro finance.[154] It operates at three levels; first, investors who mostly make micro fixed deposits in EAMF with minimal amount of Rs 1000/- only for minimal period of 1 year at 8% rate of interest per annum; second, the group fund of EA core members who deposits in the EAMF for a minimal period of 1year at 8% rate of interest per annum; third, EA manages in giving Short –Term Loans to deserving and potential first generation entrepreneurs at 16% rate of interest per annum.[155]

Enterprise for the EA does not just relate to the ability to make money, it also means feeling good enough about oneself; having self worth and a want, to see advantages and opportunities that will make a difference in the future[156] which will result in the increase of confidence, courage, creativity and self worth; the sum being an enterprising nature.

In so doing, the EA has seen how a small grocery shop has enabled a family of five to have a dignified living; some women have risked their regular jobs to run small enterprises with more

152 *Katalyst,* A bi-monthly newsletter of the Entrepreneurs Associates 1/3 (January-February 2003), 1.

153 Interview with Arenla Imsong, Office Adminstrator, EA: Kohima, 27 April 2005.

154 "Entrepreneurs Associates Micro Finance," *A Brochure,* 1

155 Ibid., 2-3.

156 Katalyst, A bi-monthly newsletter of the Entrepreneurs Associates 1/3 , 1.

income and satisfaction; some parents have raised their children by selling vegetables and fruits, utilizing their land resources, and have also watched with admiration that how some local entrepreneurs successfully ran business houses, solving social problems and fulfilling economic needs.[157]

The research attempted to receive feedback from the survey questionnaire about EA but found the majority of respondents are unaware of this particular organisation. Out of 100% only some 4% responded. This could be because EA is confined to Kohima District whereas research sampling was done in different districts of Dimapur.

Finally, EA shows that they have a keen creative planning like giving out loans through saving accounts and micro finance operations according to the durations and interests. However, there are risks in creating another banking structural system where many illiterate people are ignorant to cope with the system. Therefore, categorizing the needs based operational systems for both illiterate and literate people will safeguard in the long run. EA should reproduce its financial stand instead of depending on others. Therefore, developing one's own resource income would be helpful in future. Focus on grassroots level may sometimes have a chance of missing the targeted young people group. Some of the reasons could be because of their differing interests and motivation apart from what is being done in EA. In regards to this, it may be better to introduce other advanced vocational openings, which will benefit by this group of people.

2. Naga People's Movement for Human Rights

The Naga People's Movement for Human Rights (NPMHR) was formed on 9th September 1978 in response to the Naga people's long-felt need for an organized movement to protect and further

157 Cf. further references *Katalyst,* A bi-monthly newsletter of the Entrepreneurs Associates 2 (November-December, 2002; *Katalyst,* A bi-monthly newsletter of the Entrepreneurs Associates 1/5, (May-June, 2003); *Katalyst,* A bi-monthly newsletter of the Entrepreneurs Associates 2/1 (January-February, 2000) and *Katalyst,* A bi-monthly newsletter of the Entrepreneurs Associates 1/4 (July-August, 2004). EA collects articles/stories from individuals for contributing in writing.

their human rights.[158] Following this in 1982, the NPMHR filed a case with the Supreme Court of India, against violating democratic values.[159]

The NPMHR attempts to give organized expression to the Naga people's fight for their rights while exposing to the people of India and to the world, the imperialist policy that ruling classes have been pursuing through the mighty military machine against the Nagas. The NPMHR is a movement of the human personality through social transformation. In the context of economic exploitation, political and military domination, social suppression with the imposition of alien culture and legal system and the distortion of Naga history; the NPMHR takes the role to ensure and safeguard the people.[160]

The recent role of the NPMHR in the peace process was to facilitate democratic space for the people to come together to express their experiences of joy and pain; insecurities and aspirations; and vision of democratising the peace process by encouraging, empowering and facilitating people's participation in decision making processes and impacting people lives and future. Further, it was creating awareness and public opinion on issues of rights, preparing people for peace and reconciliation. Some of the activities achieved in the past illustrate the NMPHR role in peace process- organizing workshops[161] and meeting with College/School going students; Consultations with Naga organizations and eminent personalities;

---

158 "Human Rights Week in Nagaland 10-15 December 1978: A Report," *Souvenir* (25 years of Naga Peoples Movement for Human Right) by NPMHR. 4. In observance of the 30th Anniversary of the Universal Declaration of Human Rights by the United Nations, the NPMHR organized a Human Rights Week in Nagaland from 10-15th December 1978. Cf. Interview with Dr. Lanu Sasu, Lecturer, Nagaland University (and Human Rights Activist), Mokokchung on 29 March 2005. There are 3 Units of NPMHR in Delhi, Nagaland and Southern Nagaland: Manipur.

159 "Nagas Towards our Rightful Place Through Healing of our Spirit," *A Brochure*, NPMHR, 3.

160 "Declaration of the Naga People's Movement for Human Rights," *A Leaflet*, NPMHR, 2.

161 NPMHR, *Journal a Quarterly Publication,* April 2004. In 2003, NPMHR organized a workshop on 'Human Rights and Peace-Building' at Tagore Hall, Faculty of Arts, University of Delhi for 2 days.

meeting the public villagers; and attending the consultations and workshops of various organisations and communities at regional, national and international levels.[162]

NPMHR has various publications such as Journal, Brochures and Booklets expressing the history of Nagas, struggles and realities undergone, and the hopes and aspirations of the Naga people. NPMHR has also worked through various forms of letter within Nagaland and nationally.[163] NPMHR claim responsibility in the present peace progress by meeting different factions; the first was with Khaplang at Burma, then Isaac Swu and T. Muivah, and Naga Federation. It partners for peace with Nagaland Baptist Church Council, Naga Mothers Association, Naga Hoho and the Naga Faction.[164]

NPMHR, recognizing the weakness of conventional non-violent strategies, has launched a new initiative through 'A Journey of Conscience', to start a process of people to people dialogue with the civil society in India. The symbolic beginning commenced when a group representing 'today' Nagas sat with compatriots in Delhi at Gandhi Samadhi, Rajghat on the 30th of January 2000, the day Gandhi's life met a brutal end. NPMHR participated in the event

---

162 "Recent Activities of Naga Peoples Movement for Human Rights, NPMHR," *Souvenir* (25 years of Naga Peoples Movement for Human Right) by NPMHR. 37-41. The process of democratizing peace process involves transcending beyond the negotiation table and initiating peoples-to-peoples dialogue. Cf. *Naga Peoples Movement for Human Rights (NPMHR): One Step Back Two Steps Forward (A Report) 1999-2000*), published by NPMHR. 9-13; "Land, Forests and Human Rights of Indigenous/Tribal Peoples" at Warangal, Andhra Pradesh on 5th –7th October 2000," *NPMHR's Occasional Publication*, Winter, 2000-2001, 5.

163 Cf. NPMHR, *Journal,* April 2004. Particularly this journal gives ample examples of participation of NMPHR and articles related to women issues and indigenous women and indigenous people of Asia and further related articles and experiences; *The Nagas: Truth and Hope for the Living* Published by Naga Peoples Movement for Human Rights, Kohima: Nagaland; *Souvenir* (25 years of Naga Peoples Movement for Human Right) by NPMHR.

164 Interview with Dr. Lanu Sasu.

remembering the legacy of friendship that the Naga elders once received.[165]

The objective of NPMHR's 'journey' is to confront the deepening crisis in Nagaland by way of facilitating a peaceful and democratic solution to the protracted Indo-Naga conflict based on a foundation of mutual understanding, respect, dignity and friendship, with firm belief that through this 'journey' NPMHR will awaken the conscience of the people to resolve to struggle together towards common search for truth, justice, freedom and peace.[166] NPMHR initiation of this journey is to help in strengthening the peace process and to help facilitate a conducive and healthy environment for the negotiation to take place.[167]

The NPMHR continues in the Naga struggle to make a positive and constructive contribution through its insights and creativity. It aspires to focus on the consequences of oppression and conflict; and consciously and effectively address the root causes of conflict and the source of oppression and justice.[168] In the past, NPMHR has also extended its help through humanitarian work among the Internally Displaced Persons (IDPs) who were scattered in the four Hill districts of Manipur, Senapati, Chandel, Uhkrul, Tamenglong including the 27 Naga villages placed under the Henglep sud-division, Churachandpur district bordering Mizoram. NPMHR not only organized its visit to relief camps but also interacted with individual and groups sharing with the people's sorrows and pains.[169]

---

165 "A Journey Continues... a Call to all Nagas," *Pamphlet*, NMPHR, 2. The NPMHR also initiates People to People Dialogue on the Indo-Naga Conflict among the Naga civil society to foster and nourish a conducive atmosphere where the rights of the Nagas can be felt and solved. Cf. "A Brief Report on the People to People Dialogue on the Indo-Naga Conflict at Vishwa Yuvak Kendra, New Delhi on 29th January 2000," *NPMHR's Occasional Publication*, February 2000, 2.

166 "A Journey Continues," *Pamphlet*, NMPHR, 2.

167 "A Strategy of Hope! (No matter how long the night the day is sure to come)," *A Paper* produced by NPMHR, 2.

168 "A Strategy of Hope!" *A Paper* produced by NPMHR,1, 3.

169 "Summary report on the conditions of the Internally Displaced Persons (IDPs) from the Imphal Valley to the Naga Hill areas of Manipur - a Repercussion

Thus, the activity of NPMHR includes organizing the people for protection against violations and maintenance of human rights. It also includes awareness building, campaign, documentation and dissemination of human rights violations taking the matter to the law court, organizing relief work for the victims of human rights abuse, fact-finding teams to the affected areas, initiating intensive debates and discussions on the various issues confronting the society.[170]

NPMHR focuses more on political affairs. It organises campaigns for solidarity to arouse people about the ongoing struggle. Despite the restricted situation in the state sometimes outsiders are brought in to eyewitness the struggle of the Naga people. The interested individuals come as tourist to attend public meetings, witness and participate among the Naga people. NPMHR lacks capacity to carry out complete programmes due to the lack of resources.[171]

NPMHR participates in the building of the Naga society through various forms and activities. However, for further improvement, the author recommends that NPMHR should be encouraged to remain committed in achieving the desired goal. There could be constant follow up in financial resources so as to sustain their programmes. In relation to this, leadership continuity will be helpful for proper supervision and quality growth in the process under NPMHR. Finally, unless thrust, commitment and resources are ensured the loophole would still remain the same.

3. Akimbo Society[172]

Akimbo Society was established in the year 1993 by a handful of women who had in themselves the urge to do something for the welfare of the underprivileged and weaker sections of the society.

---

of the Indo-Nagas Cease fire," in *The Nagas: Truth and Hope for the Living,* published by Naga Peoples Movement for Human Rights, 119, 122-123.

170 *Naga Peoples Movement for Human Rights (NPMHR),* 1. cf. 14-15. Interview with Nepuni Peku, Convenor of Nagaland, NPMHR, 12 April 2005.

171 Interview with Peku.

172 "Akimbo Society," *A Brochure*, 1. The word 'Akimbo' in Sema/Sumi dialect means "I have reached a home I was searching for". It was adopted in memory of the present Director's late adopted son Akihito (pet name Akimbo).

Initially, the society worked among the drug addicts with the objective of extending care and support to the drug users to come out of their habits but now it has expanded its support to other field of activities.

Akimbo Society is a Non-Government Organization (NGO) registered under the Society Registration Act, 1860 and registered with the Ministry of Home Affairs, New Delhi. It covers the whole area of Northeast, India with Head Office at Dimapur, Nagaland. The mission of the Society is to empower the people particularly women, children and youth through participatory approach, to revive the rich culture and traditions among the youth and children, and to bring about sustainable development of the underprivileged. On the whole it envisions the emancipation of the people and equitable social order.[173]

It targets intervention for prevention of HIV/AIDS and STD among Commercial Sex Workers and among drug users, empowering women through skill training, and provides lump sum scholarship for underprivileged students.[174] It also networks with other NGOs such as Prodigal Home and Guardian Angel in Nagaland and other states.[175]

The Akimbo Society conducted its first survey in 1995 through funding of National Foundation for India and found out that there were around one thousand sex workers (both local and non-locals) in Dimapur, Nagaland. The places were raided leading by then administration; police, factional groups and many times the houses were burnt. However, the pimps along with the sex workers were scattered and resumed their businesses in different areas of Dimapur. A decade later, a rough survey again revealed a sharp increase that around three thousand commercial sex workers were still operating in various pockets of Dimapur alone.[176]

---

173 "Akimbo Society," *A Brochure*, 1-2.

174 Ibid., 4.

175 Interview with Pheuba James, Director, Akimbo Society, Dimapur, 14 April 2005.

176 Khumpila Anar, "Increase of Local Girls in Sex Trade: A Matter of Concern," *Nagaland Post,* 17 April 2005, 8.

The Society started its work with drug users till the year 1998, but later changed its focus to HIV/AIDS. Presently, the Society is focusing on some parts of Dimapur town and Akuluto, Sub-division of Zunheboto district. In 2003 and 2004, the Society went directly and worked with sex workers. The HIV/AIDS prevalence rate was showed as 4% in both 2003 and again in 2004. On seeing the successful result the Society got encouraged. Every year, the Society conducts a survey on HIV/AIDS along with National Aid.[177]

The Society promotes condoms to the people to avoid unnecessary pregnancy and disease. They also provide needles/ syringes to drug addicts. Although their work had positive results in the past, the church remains adamant and critical of this approach, expressed the Director of the Society. The church 'believe in promoting abstinence, holy living and chastity rather than condom promotion.'[178] However, irrespective of the criticism, the Society looks forward to the future building of these victims. At present, the Society seeks to request the government for demarcation of the red light areas.[179] As a result, though the government is willing to do so, there is a tough opposition from the church. Thus, there is not enough interaction between the NGO/Social Organisations and the Church right now.[180]

The Society found out that the commercial sex workers were mainly drug users. There are three main reasons to this, they are driven out of their homes without support; some are women from poor background, villages and orphans and there are also people who are involved due to the lack of morality and pleasure. According to the Director of the Society, 50% of them are non-locals and other 50% locals (mostly drug users) who are involved.[181]

The Akimbo Society is one of the well-established societies in Dimapur Nagaland. Its purpose and social actions are excellent.

---

177 Interviewed with James.

178 Interviewed with Pongsing, Director, NDO, 14 April 2005.

179 Khumpila Anar, "Increase of Local Girls in Sex Trade: A Matter of Concern," 8.

180 Interview with James. The criticism of the church is that it is attached to the biblical religiosity without looking into the ground reality of the people.

181 Interview with James.

However, the researcher has a difficulty in understanding how it determines its future stand. The question is whether the present approaches help the situation or encourage the victims to continue with the old behaviour and commitments. The problem of the victims cannot be minimized, yet the concern is whether there are better alternatives to bring them out of the situation. The positive counts on research statistic and report shown in the recent past may not suffice in the long run. The Society has to work positively to bring out relevant approaches to the situation.

The approaches applied to the situation risk the traditional and cultural concerns particularly the providing of syringes, condoms and red light area, which might seem successful in urban areas. However, what could be another approach to fit the Naga situation in the future? Naga cultural context must be safe guarded from any element of foreignness, which is generally not acceptable. Further, the rescued young and old people are to be ensured with long-term security rather than immediate treatment.

II. The Role of the Social Organizations

1. The Naga Hoho[182]

The Naga Hoho is a federation of all Naga Tribes, which is the third traditional institution of the Nagas.[183] It was formed on 25th June 1994 with its motto as "Nagas are One", at Wokha and its constitution was adopted after official formation of the Naga Hoho during 11th–12th March 1998 session at Zunheboto.[184] The Naga

---

182 Along with the Naga Hoho the researcher brings out the work of Naga Council, Dimapur since they are an integrated body, which has similar concern towards Naga Society.

183 *White Paper on Naga Integration,* compiled by the Naga Hoho, 2002. IX. The second institution of the Nagas is institution of a group of villages of one language known as Hoho and it has been in existence since time immemorial. Every Naga tribe has its own tribe organization which functions without any external interference, not even from another Naga tribe. Therefore, Naga Hoho, which is the apex body of the Nagas, come in line with this as the third institution body.

184 Interview with, H. K. Zhimomi, Assembly Secretary, Naga Hoho, Dimapur, 6 April 2005.

Hoho is the tribe-based apex body of the Nagas under the traditional system and practice of the Naga people. Its objective is 'to uphold the solidarity of the Nagas, to rebuild the Naga family. To safeguard and protect the Naga system and tradition, to promote the social, cultural, economic and political heritage and to facilitate early settlement of the Naga issue.'[185]

The Naga Council, Dimapur came into existence in 1972.[186] It has a similar kind of role and objective towards contributing to Naga society in general though there are differences in geographical administration.[187] Both the Naga Hoho and Naga Council, Dimapur are traditional in administrative functions. Over all the concern of the Hoho is intertwined within 3 functions- Political, Socio-economic and Welfare.[188]

Politically, Naga Hoho is very involved in Naga political movement to achieve the aspiration of the Nagas, to live together as one people under a single political roof for all-round growth of the Naga people. They also look for an integration of all Naga inhabited areas, including the present Nagaland state removing all the imposed boundaries, government and systems. Thus, in relation to this issue the Naga Hoho has published the present 'White Paper', which has documented important events, agreements, memoranda, and

---

185 *White Paper*, IX-X.

186 Lhoutuo Loucu, "Back-ground of Naga Club, Naga Youth Club and Naga Council," *Naga Council Golden Jubilee, 1949-1999, Souvenir*, 48. Historically, it is said that after the Second World War ended many Nagas came to settle at Dimapur with no proper leadership to guide the community or regulate the system of living. Therefore Pehielie an Angami volunteered to contact the Nagas living in Dimapur and founded an organization called the Naga Club Dimapur, in 1948. With a view to strengthen the Naga position the Naga Youth Club was organized under the leadership of Phielie who was a good sportsman educated in Shillong. Although, Naga Club was the main body the Naga Youth Club practically played the key role in all activities including sports. Later, these two former bodies, Naga Club and Naga Youth Club merged together as Naga Council, Dimapur.

187 *Constitution of the Naga Council*, Dimapur. 8.

188 Interview with Hekhevi Achumi, Finance Secretary, Naga Hoho and Chairman Sumi Council, Dimapur, 5 April 2005.

historical records relevant to Naga integration.[189] Hoho in the past had been able to enforce the Restricted Area Permit and the Law for the safe guard of the borders. In 1998, election process was boycotted sticking to the banner of 'Nagas are one', Nagas need solution and not election, projecting to the Indian government and to the world that Nagas are free people. Therefore, to live Nagas as Nagas- 'free people.'[190]

It is evident that the Naga Council, Dimapur as premier social organisation has always played a pivotal role in guiding the society during the crucial times through fighting and voicing for justice against the army atrocities and advocating for peace and unity.[191] Zhimomi states that though the integration of the Nagas is the concern of Naga political movement it goes much beyond to a social integration of the Nagas to live together as Nagas. Therefore, it is recommendable that Nagas come under one administrative body.[192] Naga Hoho has contributed efforts in bringing peace talks between the Government and National workers but the main set back is factional differences.[193] Hoho participates in political struggles through various letters to particular political leaders and Prime Minister; and continuous effort in bringing the political dialogue between the Indians and Nagas. On 20th December 2002, the Hoho started to initiate open reconciliation - politically, socially, fictionally and in the church.[194]

Socio-economically, Naga Council invests its interest in fighting against anti-social activities like, black market, selling liquor, theft and burglary through appointing a vigilant force that goes around Dimapur. In one incident 150 immoral commercial sex workers were arrested and deported. It caught many cases of corruption directly

---

189 *White Paper*, X-XI. Cf. "Naga Hoho reaffirmed its political stand to work for integration of all the Naga areas," 7th General assembly of the Naga Hoho, May 20-22 2002. 63.

190 Interview with Achumi.

191 N. T. Longkumer, "Naga Council-Its Achievements," *Naga Council Golden Jubilee 1949-1999, Souvenir*, 38.

192 Interview with Zhimomi.

193 Interview with Zhimomi.

194 Interview with Achumi.

and indirectly. This council also reaches out for relief; an example can be cited from 1984 where a big fire broke out at Railway Bazaar and Burma Camp.[195] Economically it is not equipped to have a dominant role. Yet it approaches through appealing to work culture and setting awareness and conducting seminars highlighting the endangered economy that is foreseen in the influx of illegal immigrants and outsiders.[196] On the other hand, Naga Hoho organizes campaigns on dignity of labour and against corruption at the higher level. However, there are also a few general improvements seen at manual level such as- tea gardening, crafting and handlooms, flora culture, vegetable gardening into market economy, aromatic oil and money lending among the urban women and self-help groups.[197]

Naga Council, Dimapur attempts to have collective property of the council for the welfare of the Nagas. In 1979, the President of the Naga Council took initiative to contact officers and to mobilise Naga public to do social work on an abandoned deep pond. Later it was preserved (for) as the Naga people's common property, since then Naga Council maintains and rears fish in it.[198] Naga Council fosters harmony in all Naga society playing a supportive role and assisting to maintain law and order for the welfare of the people. It lends support to the individual when faced with crisis and denied justice. In the cases of crime or death from any tribe it organises bandh and protest rallies to project the case. For instance in 1995, the random killing of Inashe Aye and in 1998 of Theza Wor was taken up for justice.[199]

---

195 Lhoutou Loucu, "Naga Council Dimapur," Naga Council, *Naga Council Golden Jubilee, 1949-1999, Souvenir*, 55-56.

196 Interview with Savi Legiese, President, Naga Council, Dimapur, 4 April 2005.

197 Interview with Achumi. He is one of the examples contributing to flora culture in Nagaland, which he started in 1985 till date through his constant self-education and self application individual in this particular field. He also extends his teachings through seminars, church and to individuals.

198 Loucu, "Back-ground of Naga Club, Naga Youth Club and Naga Council," Naga Council, *Naga Council Golden Jubilee, 1949-1999, Souvenir*, 49.

199 Interview with Legiese.

Apart from the first hand repeated stories from the Naga Hoho and records of their activities contributing towards the Naga society we shall also turn to another side of the coin how the public look at it. Here is the analysis and findings from the respondents view during the filed survey.

42% of the respondents opined that Naga Hoho lacks tribal representatives while they talk of unification. The Hoho portrays itself as a political body than social, which hampers their set objectives. An other 35% of the respondents felt that the Hoho is engaged very strongly in uplifting socio-economic life. They expressed that the Hoho impacts the social life of the people by voicing the needs of the people to the government for implementing developmental schemes, and by checking the corruption at the high level, facilitating justice and acting as backbone to the Naga society. 5% of respondents were not sure of the situation. 12% of the respondents were balanced in their response; they were satisfied with the Naga Hoho's role in the society but also expressed the Hoho's limitations on tribal representatives and lack of implementations of their objectives. The rest 6% did not respond to the question.[200]

Finally, the majority of the respondents strongly felt that Naga Hoho is a fully politically motivated body. However, it can be balanced if they look into the possibility of holistic implementation in all spheres of life. Of all the efforts contributed by the Naga Hoho, there could be a serious self-reflection of the organisation to represent all Naga members in its Body, which will exhibit its action-oriented goal for Naga peace and security.

2. The Naga Students Federation

Naga Students' Federation (NSF) is the apex student body of the state. It was formed in 1947 with the vision and sacrifice of educated Naga youth.[201] It underwent periods when its function was threatened owing to the abnormal circumstances due to the protracted Indo-Naga political conflict. NSF took an uncompromising stand on issues, in view of their corrective perspectives and concern for Nagas

---

200 Source; Questionnaire. Question, 75.

201 *The Naga Foundation: Towards Fulfillment of a People' Unwavering Aspiration* (Kohima: Naga Students Federation, 2002), 3.

as a people. According to its president, NSF aims to protect the rights and interests of the Naga people.[202]

In support of its socio-political concerns, NSF has a resolution that 'Nagas need solution and not election' which is kept in black and white but has seen no implementation so far.[203] NSF has a vital role in the political scene. When the Nagaland Pradesh Congress Committee (Indira) published the derogatory "Bedrock of Naga Society," NSF unequivocally condemned and out rightly rejected the booklet stating that it attempted to distort and nullify the facts of Nagas, the course of immense struggles, pain and sacrifices in history. NSF went further, challenging and calling the authors to a democratic and healthy political debate on the contents of the so-called "Bedrock of Naga Society" to at least give the NPCC (I) a dignified chance to defend themselves but it remain unsuccessful with no response from them.[204]

Therefore, NSF set exemplary measures against this heinous publication on 30th November 2000. They made a bonfire out of the thousands of circulated copies of the "Bedrock of Naga Society" that were collected and submitted to NSF by Naga Public. The booklet "The Naga Foundation" was published to prevent further distortions of Naga history in 2002.[205]

The NSF with joint commitment with Naga Mothers Association (NMA) and Naga Peoples movement for Human Rights (NPMHR) affirms to stand for the values and rights of the Naga people in better relationships.[206] It seeks compensation from the British who plundered the resources and destroyed cultural and its deliberate political blunder relegating the fate of the Nagas; emphasises mutual respect will happen only when India and Burma surrender

---

202 Interview with Pushika Awomi, President, NSF, 16th May 2005.

203 Interview with Zeito, Former President, Sumi Kiphimi Kuqhakulu, SKK and Advisor, All Nagaland Students Union, ANSU, 8 April 2005.

204 *The Naga Foundation,* 3. All other Naga social organizations and concerned individuals condemned the booklet as "demeaning" and "dehumanizing" to the Naga people.

205 *The Naga Foundation,* 4.

206 "Nagas are What Nagas were," *A Brochure*, by NMA/ NPMHR/ NSF on 14th August 2003. 6.

the Naga occupied territories; argues that by expediting Sovereign powers to Nagas by Neo-liberal and Neo-colonialist Indian and Burmese regimes will then strengthen cooperation between nations; continues the struggles for freedom; and affirm that unification of all Naga areas is a must for any political settlement.[207]

NSF participates actively in the peace process through Seminar, Workshops, Meetings, Concerts, Bandhs, and Rallies. It organizes programmes according to the demands of the situation and involves both with political bodies and other social organizations, within the State and outside.[208] An example can be cited from the pursuance of the decision made by the Presidential Council held on 17th July 2001, when the NSF organized a mass rally on 25th July 2001 throughout the Naga inhabited area through its federating units and sub-ordinate bodies in support to the declaration of ceasefire between the Government of India (GOI) and NSCN (IM) opposing the central government's decision to review the cease fire area coverage. It further observed a bandh on 3rd August 2001 extending to all Naga inhabited areas to express its strong resentment.[209]

NSF contributes towards relief and social awareness of the people. In year 2001, upheavals consequent to the cease-fire, thousands of Nagas were compelled to leave their homes and take refuge in other Naga areas. In consecutive year 2002 again thousands of Nagas were made homeless in eastern Nagaland of Burma (Myanmar) during the so-called punitive strikes against the Naga Freedom Fighters. On both occasions NSF took initiatives for relief work to the affected brothers and sisters.[210] There was an other such

---

207 "Nagas are What Nagas were," 6. cf. "The Stand of the Naga Civil Society on Naga Integration," in *White Paper*, 62. It is cited that on January 8 1995 the NSF launched a booklet entitled "For a Unified Naga Lim," which clearly outlines the aspiration of the Naga people to live together under one political roof in spite of the diversities of Naga tribes."

208 "Tenure 2001-2003 at a Glance: Brief Report of the General Secretary of the NSF," *Vanguard*, Vol. 1 (May-July 2003), 13-19.

209 Ibid., 13.

210 "Presidential Address Delivered on the 20th General Conference of the Naga Students' Federation by Eno. Vipopal Kinsto at Niuland on 23rd April 2003," *Vanguard* Vol. 1 (May-July, 2003), 10.

case in Senapati District in Manipur, here NSF made an attempt to pay a visit along with 17 members on 21st August 2001 and delivered materials worth about 2 Lakhs to the people displaced due to the anti cease fire protest in Manipur Valley.[211]

The NSF in its social awareness programmes highlights on the issue of immigrants in relation to the problem of limited job avenues in the state government. It has also urged that the non-locals cannot hunt for job opportunities that belong to the Nagas and also it is against the marriage between immigrants and Naga women.[212] NSF maintains economic balance through social awareness; the business people including non-locals are advised to maintain uniform marketing prices to ensure equality to every consumer. It creates awareness among business people to co-operate towards the development of the State. It also advocates that the selling of intoxicants and alcoholic products will not be tolerated.[213] The NSF for the betterment of Naga economy maintains peace and security by creating awareness.

In the past NSF has organized seminars like "Impact of Transmigration on the Nagas" and certain issues have been taken into consideration, for example to check on Inner Line Permit (ILP) and the Bengal Eastern Frontier Regulation Act, 1873 and its relevancy to present context; and increase growth in alarming numbers resulting in cultural assimilation of the Naga race by non-Nagas.[214]

NSF genuinely felt the need of the people to determine their destiny by way of making laws suitable for native use (which unless early solution of Indo-Naga problem is settled the problem still will continue); need for thorough and unbiased electoral revision (since in the past inclusion of non-Nagas in the electoral roll by some vested politicians has given them powers and claim for indigenousness; need

---

211 "Tenure 2001-2003 at a Glance: Brief Report of the General Secretary of the NSF," *Vanguard*, Vol. 1 (May-July 2003), 14.

212 "NSF Pulls Up Non-Local Community," *Eastern Mirror*, Dimapur, 19 August 2003, 1.

213 Ibid.

214 "Seminar on The Impact of Transmigration on the Nagas organized by the Naga Students Federation at Dimapur, 4th-5th April 2002," *Vanguard*, Vol. 1 (May-July, 2003), 25.

to revive the glorious Naga work culture in an attempt to reduce the influx of illegal immigrants; and the need for transparency and accountability at all levels of functioning. Nagas might preserve the right place of work according to one's capabilities and interests, therefore, avoiding corruption, exploitations and manipulation at all levels of governance whereby equal opportunities in all fields are provided to the deserving Nagas).[215]

Further, NSF resolved in its first federal meeting to deal with the issue of immigrants vigorously through various seminars, workshops and some effective measures to check and prevent further influx and infiltrations of immigrants; since this issue has become threatening to the very fabric and identity of the Naga society.[216] In relation to this, NSF is also aware of Border disputes with Assam, in the past Assam government acquired rich Naga resources and under British policy of expansion began planting refugees and migrants in the Naga area with protection of their Police and Para Military forces. Thus, NSF is continuously working towards solving the issue through dialogue and mutual understanding with All Assam Students' Union, AASU.[217]

The Naga Students' Federation are taking HIV/AIDS into serious consideration taking necessary steps to reach to all Naga areas for effective prevention and management of the disease. NSF calls all Nagas especially the students' community, young adults, and the affected population to actively participate in creating sensitive, conscious and motivated society in this issue in a constructive nature.[218]

NSF is concerned for educational reform and they look forward to work out the modalities and pursue the one that they deem fit

---

215 "Seminar on The Impact of Transmigration on the Nagas," 26-27. Cf. " The Achievements and Failures of NSF," *Souvenir* (Naga Students Federation Golden Jubilee, 1947-1997), 36.

216 "Minutes and Resolutions of the First Federal Assembly, Camp at Tamenglong on 27 June 2003," *Vanguard* , Vol. 1 (May-July 2003), 33.

217 Achumbemo Kikon, "NSF on Border Dispute," *Nagaland Post,* Dimapur, 9 April 2005. 4.

218 "Awareness Programme for HIV/AIDS," *Vanguard,* Vol. 1 (May-July, 2003), 35.

for the future.[219] In regards to unemployment the Federation has scrutinised some Government departments on prevailing irregularity and manipulative practices and situation. Therefore, NSF urges the Government to take prompt action on the following - the particular cases of contract, ad-hoc, deputation against any vacant post under department's purview and regular posts for recruitment and promotion through political pressure and manipulation attempting to regularize such appointment and making it clear that the said appointment should not be entertained but terminated.[220] NSF enforced the Government to conduct competitive examination for any post. However, they failed to get it implemented. Zeito comments that NSF needs cooperation and ample proof from the office and officers to succeed such implementation.[221]

Presently, on employment issue NSF continuously appeals to the senior officials to vacate their chairs if they reach superannuation age so as to 'let young minds get a chance to serve the people.' The federation pursues that the justice and equality are ensured for the upcoming Naga generation.[222] Federation make an appeal to execute measures on the rampant prevalence of the anomalies in state department, for instance on the cases of extension of service and on

---

219 "Minutes and Resolutions of the First Federal Assembly," 33. cf. Interview with Zeito, similar concern for education is acted upon by various other student unions. The Sumi Kiphimi Kuqhakulu (Sumi Students Union) discovered that there were many proxy teachers and teaching happened in the local government schools. Therefore, a tour over 200 villages was organized and met with Villagers and Chiefs to implement proper teacher and teaching in their own villages and areas. There were about 70 teachers found under proxy teaching in 2000. The SKK forwarded the case to the Government and action was taken at one point.

220 "To The Hon'ble Chief Minsiter, Nagaland by Nezokhotuo Belho, General Secretary and Achumbemo Kikon, President, NSF," *Vanguard,* Vol. 1 (May-July, 2003), 49.

221 Interview with Zeito.

222 "NSF Reiterates Stand on Superannuation," *Nagaland Post*, Dimapur, 6 March 2005, 2.

job reservation.[223] NSF has dealt with the problem extensively yet it persists.

Finally the study is done in bits but it is amply clear that NSF performs a complementary role for the attainment of the Naga aspirations and the welfare of the Naga Students. On the other side, the findings reveal the following on the NSF's role -

35% of the respondents were of the opinion that the NSF is a strong students body, which participates in the political struggles and peace process by all possible means. 20% expressed the NSF role more as contribution to social awareness and welfare of the people such as, influx of the immigrants, HIV/AIDS, unemployment and the concern for job opportunities, equality, justice and sharing of the opportunity and resources, dignity of labour to revive the work culture and schools and educational relevancy of the people. Another 40% of them felt negative at NSF, a few among them expressed that NSF in some ways is becoming the mouthpiece of political party. It has become a complacent and self-interested group and rash organization, with little or no contribution towards socio-economic achievement especially in students/youth welfare. Some commented on improvement and to be practical for the cause. The rest 5% gave no response to the question.[224]

Although the purpose and aim achieved by NSF are varied the findings show that the majority 40% of the respondents are not satisfied with what NSF is presently doing pointing towards their weaknesses. 35% of the respondents opined siding that NSF sides towards political issues, which does not particularly qualify the students concern and welfare. NSF needs to concentrate and act practically to their cause as 20% of the respondents expressed.

The NSF's contribution is noticeable from the discussion. However, the earlier focus towards student concerns could be lifted higher. NSF lacks representatives from all tribal Nagas, which could be checked as it stands for all Naga Student.

---

223 V. Phushika Aomi and W. H. Maring, "Extension of Service Flayed," *Nagaland Post*, Dimapur, 2 May 2005, 3.

224 Source: Questionnaire; Question, 66.

3. The Naga Mothers Association and Related Local Association[225]

Naga Mothers' Association (NMA) was formed on 14 February 1984 as a state level voluntary organisation with the clear objective of combating social evils. The women's issue is one of the interest issues that mothers addressed and uphold the dignity of motherhood.[226] Recognising the social problems and challenges NMA took up the responsibility towards women and youth, and the need for sustainability. NMA with its motto "Human Integrity," has been consistently working with the objective to uphold womanhood, human values and rights. It serves as a channel of communication particularly for Naga women's mutual interests and welfare, and the Naga people in general.[227] Therefore, a society under its organization called "NMA Youth and Women Welfare Organization" got registered under the Societies Act Vide No. R.S. 1072 on 28th October 1986.[228]

In the past, the Naga mothers whose children were immediate victims of drug abuse started to gather determination to fight the dreaded diseases of drug addiction. Thus, the first task for NMA was to start checking drug trafficking, which was rampant, by going after drug peddlers in various localities and also assisting the state enforcing agencies such as, Police and Excise personnel. This approach generated a high level of awareness but could not sufficiently control the problem. They also set up Mount Gilead; Drug De-addiction-cum-Rehabilitation Center for addicts on 12 February 1989.[229]

Since then NMA has started awareness campaigns on prevention of drug abuse all over Nagaland with the help of counsellors and recovering addicts. The NMA organised a series of seminars and workshops, the first workshop on "Drug Trafficking and Abuse"

225 Under this section we will study the umbrella wing of Mother's Association and parallel contributions particularly from Western Sumi Totimi Hoho, WSTH (Western Sumi Mother's Association).

226 "NMA 'Human Intergrity' ," *A Brochure*, Naga Mothers' Association. 1.

227 Gins Shangkham, "Naga Women and Peace Process," *NPMHR's Occasional Publication*, 2000-2001. 8. cf. Interview with Khesheli Chishi, President, NMM, 16 May 2005.

228 "NMA 'Human Intergrity' ," *A Brochure*, Naga Mothers' Association. 1.

229 "NMA 'Human Intergrity' ," *A Brochure*, Naga Mothers' Association. 1.

on 20-22 February 1990, at the State Academy Hall, Kohima.[230] The next seminar was organised for 2 days on "Causes, Effects and Treatment of Drug and Alcohol Abuse"[231] and in the following year 1991, Youth Reformation Crusade for Drug Addicts was held at State Academy Hall, Kohima.[232]

NMA also pioneered the responsibility of social health by dealing with HIV/AIDS. The first hand experience of these mothers is tremendous since their knowledge was limited to treat this disease. However, they prepared the drug patients with pre-counselling on HIV/AIDS tests, after which the first batch were tested in the month of June 1990 in the presence of the counsellors and some NMA members. Thus in the month of October the results were positive indicating that the disease had come to stay in Nagaland. These people were further given extra care and post counselling, and other supports to help them retain the same sense of belongingness. NMA had no option but to acquire more knowledge on this subject; they started taking active part in all seminars and workshops organised on HIV/AIDS by any agencies in regional and National level.[233] NMA

---

230 "NMA 'Human Intergrity' ," *A Brochure*, Naga Mothers' Association. 2. This was organized along with Narcotics Control Bureau and Collectorate of Customs and Central Excise, Shillong. It was the first North East Regional Workshop held.

231 "NMA 'Human Intergrity' ," *A Brochure*, Naga Mothers' Association. 2. NMA and Kripa Foundation, Bombay jointly organized the seminar at the premises of Holy Cros School, Dimapur on August 1990.

232 "NMA 'Human Intergrity' ," *A Brochure*, Naga Mothers' Association. 2. NMA in collaboration with Operation Dawn International, Hong Kong organized the crusade.

233 "NMA 'Human Intergrity' ," *A Brochure*, Naga Mothers' Association. 3. They also extend health care and support to the victims outside the state. An excellent example can be cited from their visit to Imphal Jail where the inmates isolated themselves to stay inside the cell and accordingly food was served to them through the windows of their cells. Seeing this pathetic experience made NMA members ask permission from the authority to allow the inmates to interact with them. Later, they were brought out and shook hands openly and converse with them. This impacted the authority of the jail and this news was published in 'Times of India' (28 June 1994) citing their excellent example. Thus, this report also boosted the morale of NMA and encouraged the members to make deeper commitments.

on this particular issue continues to bear witness, help and support in envisioning society's health.

Socio-economically, Naga Mother Association encourages women at different fields; they give recognition to selected persons for their outstanding contribution towards Naga society.[234] NMA does this in order to uplift the status of women in various fields. NMA along with various governmental agencies envisions education for a girl child and takes steps to network with relevant agencies.[235] Side by side, Western Sumi Totimi Hoho, WSTH is also involved locally voicing for women's upliftment in every field – for equal opportunities, equality and women's empowerment at all levels.[236] WSTH further engages in economic upliftment by introducing self help groups and through seminar and workshops teaching them particularly, home economic, encouraging children to work and for equal education for female child and to become self made women in economic scenario. WSTH rescue girls from prostitution, counsels them, invests money in them and send them back to their respective villages and communities.[237]

The NMA and Naga Women's Union Manipur, NWUM have been corporately working on human rights issues, afforestation and conservation, empowerment of women, against construction of the multi-purpose Tipaimukh high dam and on alcoholism and drug addiction.[238] The NMA and NWUM has been participating in

234 "Social Issue to Top NMA Meet," *Nagaland Post, Dimapur,* 27 April 2005, 4.

235 "NMA General Session Adopts Resolution," *Nagaland Post*, Dimapur, 5 May 2005, 3.

236 Interview with Hukhali Chishi, President, WSTH, Dimapur, 8 April 2005.

237 Interview with Chishi.

238 "Women for Peace in Nagalim," *NPMHR's Occasional Publication*, 2000-2001, 3. They have worked with other leading Naga organizations such as the Naga Hoho Summit (Federation of Traditional Tribal Councils), the United Naga Council, the Naga Student Federation, the All Naga Student Union, Manipur, the Council of Churches and Naga People' Movement t meet all the groups and factions even before cease fire was allowed to Naga civil society to come out in the open and actively participate in the discussions on Naga Political issues and engage in dialogue with groups from the national movement. The NMA president has received the Padma Shri Award, a very prestigious award for outstanding social work, from the Indian Government in recognition of

training to improve their capacity which is part of empowerment process, to ensure women's views and position are taken into account in the discussions on the future of Naga society.[239]

NMA has recent concern particularly for their economy and culture, therefore plans an indigenous Naga food festival in future as part of resource mobilization and to promote Naga indigenous food culture.[240] Along this same line of thought, R. S. Pandey Chief Secretary of Nagaland speaking on the theme "creation of health" exhorted the womenfolk to move forward towards income generating sectors so as to strengthen the state economy and also to initiate to advance their agricultural production. The chief secretary emphasized on the need to have basic infrastructures, marketing avenues and transportation in the modern society, and that the government would assist the same.[241]

It looks into the cultural promotion and preservation of the rich Nagas cultural heritage, which has unique feature and identity.[242] NMA is taking interest to bring about electoral reforms in Nagaland through awareness campaigns in various district head quarters. [243] At present, this is a crucial issue related with the influx and economic

her work. Cf. " Nagas are What Nagas were," *A Brochure*, by NMA/NPMHR/NSF.

239 "Women for Peace in Nagalim," *NPMHR's Occasional Publication*, 2000-2001, 4.

240 "NMA General Session Adopts Resolution," 3.

241 Cited, "Pandey Exhorts Womenfolk," *Eastern Mirror*, Dimapur, August 21st, 2003, 1. During the inauguration of the two-day exhibition sale cum workshop at Kohima Local ground under the Angami Women Organization, the Chief Secretary expressed that the indigenous designs and traditions of the Nagas occupy an important place in the world map and so hoped that the Nagas would give due importance to such areas. For instance, the women folk belonging to Angami Naga tribe were high lighted in 'Eastern Mirror' in relation to their hard work. There is new 'self help' women's group coming up, they organize exhibitions on flowers and variety of delicious eatables; they also have their common collected amount through selling and earning in groups in small ways, which help them to manage their families and homes.

242 "NMA General Session Adopts Resolution," *Nagaland Post*, Dimapur, 5 May 2005, 3.

243 Ibid.

exploitation that is taking place. The influx of refugees to the state is a parasite to Naga socio-economic life comments Chishi.[244]

Politically looking at the past the Naga women have been tortured, raped, and left widows and orphans in many instances. In this tale of the Naga saga, the prime victims who faced and are facing the brunt of the Indian repression are the women. The Naga women, a vital component of the Naga society cannot remain silent spectators and are actively involved in confronting the situation along with Naga men folk.[245] NMA stands in support with Naga Peace process and looks for creating better understanding among the National workers and at all levels of Naga society to facilitate finding a settlement acceptable to all.[246]

NMA along with Naga Women's Union Manipur (NWUM) and Manipur State joined in the efforts to consolidate peace in Nagalim at the National level.[247] Since the beginning of the peace talks, the two women's organisations have become deeply involved in the peace process focusing on three areas: peace and reconciliation; participation in capacity building; and the "peoples to peoples dialogue" with Indian civil society. Thus, Naga women are playing this role effectively.[248] There are such others, like WSTH, which is totally committed to peace talks within Nagaland. The characteristic approach is mainly through personal meeting with factional leaders and upholding peace among the Naga political leaders in Nagaland.[249]

The findings from the survey analysis shows that 70% of the respondents are pleased and satisfied with the activities of NMA giving

244 Interview with Chishi.

245 Gins Shangkham, "Naga Women and Peace Process," 1.

246 "NMA General Session Adopts Resolution," *Nagaland Post*, Dimapur, 5 May 2005, 3.

247 "Women for Peace in Nagalim," *NPMHR's Occasional Publication*, 2000-2001, 3. Cf. This is an extracted article by Shimreichon Luithui from "Indigenous Women," in *Indigenous Affairs*, No. 3, July-September 2000, 24-27.

248 "Women for Peace in Nagalim," *NPMHR's Occasional Publication*, 2000-2001, 3-4. The NMA and the MNWUM have been actively participating in several workshops and training programmes on peace and capacity building so that they can positively impact the on-going Indo-Naga peace talks.

249 Interview with Chishi.

them credit as the best and strongest body, which provides better service in the social arena. The examples expressed are particularly its active contribution towards controlling social evils such as: drugs and alcohol; prostitution and rehabilitations; handling rape and unlawful divorce cases. However, they also opined that NMA should not divert the focus from women issues- on equality and justice for women's rights particularly in raising women's social status in all fields. In taking peace initiatives and for women's cause, NMA sometimes become politicizing body. 26% expressed that NMA is doing very little in confronting social evils, economic upliftment and in peace process.

Further the comment expressed was 'they are no better than any other organizations or NGOs.' The activities are often in the media but have less practicality, and often they have their own organizational constraints. In spite of their busy activities- meetings, seminars, training and workshops it shows limited impact. The rest 4% did not respond to the question.[250]

Along with the respondents' positive response on NMA, the researcher is of the opinion that they can expect economic upliftment of the society in future.

4. Sisterhood Network, Morung and Mother's Hope

a. Sisterhood Network

The Sisterhood Network (SN) is in the process of formally launching out as a registered society. The realities of the plight of the women challenged Alongla Aier and two women alumni of Oriental Theological College, Dimapur to start SN. The first survey was done among the married women at Lingrijan colony and it came out with the concept of 'self help group' (SHG).[251] It has worked for 3 years under the theme 'Helping One Another', SN works with the disadvantaged, neglected, low income, and illiterate women in and around Dimapur. The main objective for SN is to empower women to grow towards social, economical and spiritual well being;

250 Source: Questionnnaire, Questions, 69-76.

251 Interview with Alongla Aier, Consultant/Director, and Sisterhood Network: Dimapur, 14 April 2005.

facilitating them through various activities; letting them learn to take initiatives by living a full balanced life; and making difference in their individual, family and social lives.[252]

SN advocates the holistic approach as it seeks to help women towards empowerment. The first group formation began in May 2001.[253] At present, there are six active groups involved with three full time staff members that are fully responsible for the activities and projects and two other volunteers who regularly assist the various activities and programs.

The group has started saving banks with regular collection each month, which is self-generated money. They have income generation activities such as conducting 'sales day'; reselling wholesale products at retail price among themselves; growing plants and flowers, working on craft items and collecting popular ethnic food items from rural area which are sold. SN encourages in utilizing their talents for generating the money. Weaving is one of the talents and some of them have successfully completed loom trainings. SN has helped some SHGs by giving them loans of Rs 5000 to Rs 10,000 to acquire looms for self-employment projects. Out of this newfound trade three of them are generating income.[254]

Other activities include 'learning seminars' where food making, savings, health issues, family matters, building leadership and spiritual programs are organized. The groups also attend seminars arranged by other organizations on 'women empowerment' and small-scale industries. Finally, SN looks forward to help some selected groups to begin a major project by networking them with the right financial agencies that would be willing to support them financially and will also provide skill trainings towards attaining their project goals.

In its survey for locating women to begin SHGs. SN has found a large number of girls in teens and early 20s who are schools dropouts and some educated unemployed.[255] In the beginning SN collected

---

252 "Sisterhood Network (SN): A Profile," *A Paper* produced by Alongla Aier, Consultant /Director, SN, 1.

253 Ibid.

254 Ibid.

255 "Sisterhood Network (SN): A Profile," *A Paper* produced by Alongla Aier, Consultant /Director, SN, 2.

these girls from colonies through word of mouth. However, recently they started coming by themselves seeking to join the SN.[256] On seeing the need of such girls SN welcomed them willingly. SN gives them orientation to life process, counseling and spiritual emphases, and session on inspiration and motivation. They are taught crafts, embroidery and skills such as card making, sewing and handicrafts to help them grow independent and responsible adults and citizens, keeping them busy for three months periods at least. If they succeed they are further sent for relevant programmes. With the help of Khadi Industry, SN has sent three batches to Trichur, Kerala. Due to the want of space there are only 20 girls enrolled in a program at a time.[257]

All these initiatives has helped SN women members in many ways. Their self confidence and enthusiasm, feeling of being significant and useful has drastically increased. Many of these groups are experiencing the empowering support of being in a group there are also setting up small shops in the neighborhood, making and selling handloom products, growing and selling flowers, greens, saplings, poultry, pigs and vegetables in the weekly market.

b. Morung

Morung was founded in 2003 in Dimapur. The term Morung is understood as a 'place of learning' or in other words a 'community of learning.' This was brought out with the hope of bringing together all like-minded people to 'contribute towards process of contribution' on issues such as peace, reconciliation, culture, human capacity, art and indigenous people.[258]

For generations, Morung has been a place of co-learning, sharing experiences, story telling, and healing; encouraging the creative growth and unique gifts each individual contributes to the society. The idea and practice of the 'morung' have assumed a historical place and practical role in Naga society. Encouraged by the

256 Interview with Aier.

257 Ibid.

258 Interview with Akum Longkumar, one of the founding members, Morung, Dimapur, 12 April 2005.

morung's profound contribution and vibrant spirit in Naga society, the Foundation has consciously decided to name itself after the morung so that it can emulate the positive and constructive role. Morung then was a non-profit foundation, which seeks to bring critical minds to a meeting place. The Morung intends to contribute in the process of collectively generating a culture of critical consciousness and critical solidarity. It envisions of building a compassionate and dignified society freely determining its economic, social, cultural and political development.[259]

"The Morung is a non-partisan foundation having no affiliation to any political organization."[260] It functions independently on the basis of the principles laid down in its working guidelines. It aims to extend support and encouragement to non-political organizations founded on similar values striving for common aims and objectives and nurture partnerships that are issue-based.

Morung is instituted to enable cross-sections of people to share, exchange and create ideas towards a shared common vision founded on the realization of human dignity. It is committed to working with the grassroots, the marginalized and the unrepresented people based on their wisdom and experiences to find the most relevant and effective ways for structural transformation and healing of the society.

At present, Morung focuses on news and publications, and workshops for leadership, peace building, human development, critical responsibility, empowering people in decision making and envisioning, designing, HIV/AIDS and exploring indigenous ways of life. Morung has started networking with Artisan and Organisations, and is researching into the past cultural documentations.[261]

These are some of the activities outlined by Morung for future involvements such as Study and Research, Publications and Media, Humanitarian Service, Art and Creative Works, and Training & Workshops.[262]

---

259 "Morung: for indigenous affairs and just peace," *A Brochure,* 1.

260 Ibid.

261 Interview with Bandi Angami, one of the founding members, Morung, Dimapur, 14 April 2005.

262 "Morung: for indigenous affairs and just peace," *A Brochure,* 3. It may be a small contribution yet the researcher brings it out to show a sense of awareness

c. Mother's Hope

The Mother's Hope (MH) started in June, 2001 with a reason to provide home for crisis pregnancy, specifically targeting unwed mothers. There are many young girls between the age 12-19 and early 20s who face unwanted pregnancy where they feel their only option is to have an abortion. Hence, the Hope Center comes to their rescue, to show them that God is love, helping them to realize the sanctity of life and its preciousness. There are medically trained nurses to look after the pregnant mothers and the process of delivery.[263]

It has so far taken up 120 cases and sent 77 babies for adoption. There are about 2-3% non-locals involved but most of them are local Nagas.[264] The process is under taken in such a way that the mother of the baby is given the choice either to have the baby or relinquish it for adoption. Couples are screened properly by the center before adoption takes place. The couple should have been married for minimum 7-10 years and should not exceed 45 years of age. Both the couple and family members should agree on adoption, and the couple must be economically sound. The baby is then sent for adoption with no charge except Rs 1000/- against release form. Presently there are five pregnant girls and twelve nursing babies in the Center. MH networks with other NGOs on Pre-marital sex awareness in order to educate people about the risk of involving in it. The Center is looking forward to these babies growing in families of a married couple with two to three children, so that they may grow in a family environment.[265]

Sisterhood Network, Morung and Mother's Hope are small openings of transformational avenues, which have just begun to discover the reality and to work in small ways. One has to wait and see their contribution towards the upliftment of the socio-economic situation of the Nagas.

---

towards social movement that is present among the Nagas today.

263 Interview with Moamenla Ao, Founder of Hope Center, Dimapur, 14 April 2005. Both Moamenla and her brother found this Center. Moamenla trained in HongKong and has experience in Mission Field, HongKong Social Service.

264 Interview with Moamenla Ao.

265 Ibid.

The over all findings from the questionnaire show that 72% of the respondents are aware of the existence of NGOs and Social Organizations working in Nagaland for the upliftment of the society, in terms of: creating awareness of HIV/AIDS, drug and alcohol, health care and prostitution through seminars, rehabilitations and counseling; development programmes through publications, newspapers, media, SHGs: cutting and tailoring and self-employment; free education; and contributing towards reconciliation and Naga peace process. Some of the bodies mentioned were Naga Hoho, NMA, World Vision, NEICORD, NSF, NPMHR, CASA, Rotary Club, Lion's Club, Prodigal Son, Eleuterous Society and Akimbo Society. Another 20% of the respondents were partially aware of these existing organizations. 8% of them did not respond to this particular question.[266]

55% of the respondents felt that the prevailing works and contributions are not done upto the level of satisfaction. Although the programmes run are helpful; the limitation is that they often do not touch the grassroots level and hence cannot have much impact on the people. 35% of the respondents felt that these organizational works are not at all helpful because of limitations of area coverage; limitations of methodologies used in creating awareness and seminars, that actually do not touch the grassroots level. It can be observed that the comments given by the respondents and the workers in the NGOs and social organizations, diverge themselves on their views from the above discussion. However, the works done in attempt for the socio-economic upliftment of the society should be appreciated. It is recommendable to improve for effectiveness of their role in future.

7% did not respond to the question and 3% of the respondents were unsure of the situation. However, 86% of the respondents felt that the organizations should maintain transparency at whatever resources received are distributed faithfully to people. Finally, they also opined that the organizations need to promote self-supportive

266 Source: Questionnaire. Questions, 65 and 66. Cf. Source: Questionnaire. Question, 79. The researcher found out that majority of the respondents did not respond to the question- the reason could be because they are unaware of the NEICORD working in Nagaland. Only 3% opined that their activities through seminars, relief and HIV/AIDS awareness.

resources then depending on special funds or others. 14% of the respondents did not suggest anything.[267]

III. The Role of the Government

Under this section, we shall particularly study the role of the State Institute of Rural Development (SIRD) of Nagaland, Kohima and few other general concerns.

SIRD is a State-level training institute established during 1990 with the assistance of the European Economic Community and the Government of India. The department has a total strength of 40 regular posts. The SIRD has a three-tier institutional set-up for training of Rural Development functionaries with the National Institute of Rural Development (NIRD), Hyderabad and NIRD, Regional Center for Northeast at Guwahati, the State Institute of Rural Development (SIRD) at State Level and the Extension Training Centers (ETCs) at the district level (Phek and Tuensang). There is one more ETC under consideration by Ministry of Rural Development (MORD), Government of India.[268] Administratively SIRD in under State Government but the advice and guidelines come directly from Government of India.[269]

SIRD aims to provide training facilities to various levels of people from all walks of life by organizing training programs, seminars, conferences, and workshops according to the categories of developmental functionaries/agencies from state level to the grass-root level. It undertakes research studies, evaluation, monitoring on various subjects relating to rural development (RD) in the state; disseminating information on RD programs, rural technology to the rural people; providing orientation training to village level functionaries, i.e., Village Council, Village Development Boards, Voluntary Organizations in the field of rural development; bringing better co-ordination amongst the Government departments by way of organizing seminars and workshops on common specific issues to the people of the State; and providing basic computer training to all

---

267 Source: Questionnaire. Questions, 67-68, 80.

268 *Annual Administrative Report of SIRD 2004-2005,* by Government of India.1

269 Interview with Velu-o-swuro, Deputy Director, SIRD, Kohima.

allied agencies/organizations.[270] The SIRD operates for up-lifting the rural poor, which constitute the major population of the State.

Some of their work includes socio-economic empowerment of socially and economically disadvantaged groups such as women. This is said to be most effective and sustainable if done through Self-Help Groups (SHGs). With financial support from the Ministry of Rural Development it endeavors to create broad-based public awareness especially amongst rural women by conducting training on "Empowerment of Women Through Self Help Groups." SIRD has evolved an innovative farming system known as 'Self Sustainable Integrated Farming (SSIF) that is based on friendly, eco-friendly, and pro-small & marginal farmers.[271]

Health care and nutrition for women and children in rural areas is a continuous need and there is priority to create awareness and educate the rural masses. SIRD intends to organize programs in all districts of Nagaland covering health workers, social workers and women groups to upgrade their skills and knowledge. To fully utilize the District Informatics Centers, the SIRD has ventured into conducting computer training to all middle level officers of the RD department including Village Development Boards / Village Councils and NGOs.[272]

One of the major training programmes introduced during 1999-2000 was the 'Rural Development Foundation Course'. This is a compulsory training course for 6 weeks for all the officers of the department of Rural Development, starting from the level of a Assistant Project Officer (APO) or Block Development Officer (BDO) up to the level of Assistant Director or Deputy Project Officers (DPO).[273] The SIRD has undertaken orientation trainings and seminars on various rural developments related subjects in

270 *Annual Administrative Report of SIRD*, 2, 9.

271 *Annual Administrative Report of SIRD*, 6.

272 *Annual Administrative Report of SIRD*, 6.

273 "Past and Present Status of Training Conducted by SIRD, Nagaland," in *Action Plan of Panchayati Raj Training for The State of Nagaland for Chairman, DRDAs/Ex-Officio Chairman, VDBs and Village Council Members/VDB Members/ G.Bs.*, prepared by State Institute of Rural Development, 2003. 6.

the district and sub-division levels, where members of the Villages Council and VDBs including women, attended the programmes.

It has trained more than 2400 VC and VDB Members with fund from the Ministry and in ten years of its establishment it has conducted 138 training programmes at the state level besides seminars and workshops, benefiting 7822 participants. In 2002-2003, the Institution completed 18 training courses, enriching the knowledge and skills of more than 600 officers and others.[274]

Mostly they focus on health of women and children; empowerment of women; management of youth: NGOs; Village Council and Development Board; computer training to village development members; employment and HIV/AIDS cooperatively with the medical department. In case of trainings related with women, health and empowerment, the focus is laid on the church since it is the best to connect to the rural areas. For instance, in the the past, programmes were held at Mon, Tuensang, Wokha and Dimapur through linking with church women's departments.[275]

The SIRD has published 10 research works successfully with vital issues relating to the rural development in Nagaland in 2003, and there are another three in the process.[276] SIRD has established and registered a Society under the aegis of Society for Training and Research on Rural Development (STRORD) in order to facilitate training and research in the field of rural development, for viewing in near future to collaborate with other agencies for financical assistance and logistic support. This Institute has prepared and brought out

274 "Past and Present Status," 6.

275 Interview with Swuro.

276 *Annual Administrative Report of SIRD*, 8. Some of the research works are- Kiyasetuo Vizo, *Self Sustainable Integrated Farming: An Alternative for Sustainable Agricultural Development in Nagaland* (State Institute of Rural Development, Nagaland: Kohima, 2003); Yongdang, *Impact of Topography on the Activities of Rural Life in Nagaland* (State Institute of Rural Development, Nagaland: Kohima, 2003); Kiyasetuo Vizo, *A Case Study of Cattle Rearing in Kohima Village Kohima R.D. Block Nagaland: A Socio-economic Perspective* (State Institute of Rural Development, Nagaland: Kohima, 2003); and Phola Konyak, W., *Sample Survey on Consumption of Imported Meat, Fish and Eggs in Kohima Town 2003* (State Institute of Rural Development, Nagaland: Kohima, 2003).

reading materials in different dialects for the elected members of the Village Councils and VDBs.[277] It is also engaged in comparative studies with other states in administration and development.[278]

The State Government provides full budget provision for SIRD like any other sector for recurring expenditure. MORD, Government of India reimburses 50% of the recurring expenditure to SIRD on submission of the prescribed form. MORD also reimburses 100% to meet the salary expenditure of staff. Finally, MORD also sanctions grant depending on the genuine requirements and justification of the proposals on the basis of 100% central assistance for the infrastructural development of the institute. [279]

The following findings are not limited to SIRD:

64% of the respondents were not satisfied with the present role of the Government in the socio-economic upliftment of the people. They felt disillusioned by the reality that exists in the form of corruption, self-gain, and misusing of power and richness, and self-centeredness. 20% of them were unaware of the prevailing role of the Government. While 10% felt satisfaction, expressing that despite facilities and opportunities from the Government, the corruption at top level does not permit it to implement practically which means only the able, powerful political leaders in the society are benefited. The rest 6% did not respond to the question.[280]

70% of the respondents pointed out that there are ample opportunities provided by the Government if people implement it appropriately. The opportunities are mainly loan facilities like PMRY, CM Corpus Fund; Subsidies; various Central schemes and developmental fund; Loan relief; scheme such as SHGs, Angawadi; Below Poverty Line (BPL) loan; Agri department helps in plantations, seedlings and equipments; vocational training opportunities; and

277 "Past and Present Status," 6. Cf. Training of the Members of Village Councils and Village Development Boards (VDBs) *Reading Materials* prepared by SIRD, Kohima: Nagaland, 1999.

278 Interview with Swuro. Cf. "Comparative study on Panchayati Raj (West Bengal) and VDs/VCs (Nagaland)"- this book is in process. *Annual Administrative Report,* 8.

279 *Annual Administrative Report of SIRD*, 13.

280 Source: Questionnaire. Questions, 82-84.

schools and colleges. 13% did not respond to the question while 7% were not sure of the situation. 10% felt that the situation is neglected and unimproved.[281]

65% of the respondents felt that the government has failed to act fairly towards the common people. 28% of them were neutral in expressing that the government does a fair job in granting opportunities but the bureaucrats' misuse it for their own purposes- utilizing for family, relatives and clan. They are manipulated accordingly with the politics of favoritism, nepotism and tribalism. The 7% of the respondent failed to respond.[282]

61% of the respondents said they are never benefited from the opportunities given by the government. There were also 10% of the respondents who said that they are partly benefited through public roads facilities, water irrigation projects and employment facilities. 8% said they never tried and 7% as government servants benefited through receiving salary. 15% of them did not respond to the question. In relation to these responses, below are the findings of who benefits from the opportunities and programmes given by the government.

Table no. 8

Opinion as indicated by the respondents during the field survey on Government beneficiaries:[283]

<table>
<tr><td>The Party Workers</td><td>78%</td><td rowspan="3">No Response 4</td><td rowspan="3">Total 100%</td></tr>
<tr><td>The Rich</td><td>16%</td></tr>
<tr><td>No Partiality</td><td>2%</td></tr>
</table>

52% of the respondents felt the lack of implementation of the government's upliftment programmes and facilities are due to late information or one's ignorance, negligence in determining the needs of the people and development in the state, corruption and influence of politics and political movement, inconsistency in nature of power exercise, and particularly self-centeredness of the powerful. 22% of

---

281 Source: Questionnaire. Question, 86.

282 Source: Questionnaire. Question, 87.

283 Source: Questionnaire. Question, 89.

the respondents expressed a balanced opinion that the government release schemes and opportunities are misused by the people at top. However, the government also executes its programmes through the NGOs strengthening their function for the common people and therefore it depends on the functions of the departmental level which cannot be generalized. 18% did not respond to the question whereas the other 7% felt pleased, expressing that in most of the cases the government is strict in implementing the community projects and developmental schemes.[284]

The following finding shows particularly on the government's role towards social evil. 78% of the respondents were not pleased with the situation. The opinion expressed by them were- the bureaucrats, politicians and people at any higher authority lack honesty and sincerity in their respective jobs. The best example drawn was on liquor ban in Nagaland, which continues to overflow in all corners of the state. The people responsible for this job have turned it into illegal business for themselves and getting a lot of money out of it. The criminal cases and bankruptcy at the top level is another corruption the people face today. 14% of the respondents opined that the government has taken certain steps enforcing the law system in the state through local police authority and security, the existence of jail and also the declaration of Nagaland as a dry State. 16% did not respond as they were either ignorant or hesitant while 2% were unsure of the situation.[285]

88% respondents aspire that the responsible persons at high authority should take their responsibility seriously giving way for common sharing, justice and honest implementation, scrutinizing the needs and development of the people. For instance, promoting resource management, creating job avenues, opportunities at grassroots level and sustainable economy. They also expressed that each department should ensure that no individual hampers the socio-economic development. The 22% of them did not respond

284 Source: Questionnaire. Question, 90.

285 Source: Questionnaire. Question, 91.

to the query. They were either hesitant or not serious about the situation.[286]

Of all the contributions made by the government the researcher is of the view that the government has to build up better thrust and commitment in executing policies responsibly ensuring stability in its governance. Transparency and systematic function for the public welfare may be identified fairly and strictly for the benefit of common people and development of the state.

The general opinion on the contributions of government towards socio-economic development is not implemented as it sounds. Implementation of opportunities and privileges especially for the poor, youth and common people are hardly executed sincerely by the administrator and people in power and authority. The government should look into the issue of whether the participants involved in trainings do their responsible job after completion and receiving the advance money. How is the need being identified in the process of programming the development projects? Are the projects fulfilling the purpose of development? Are these programmes also meeting the needs of the people?

Summary

This section touches the core perspective of the social-economic move incorporating the traditional and cultural values, and the modern elements. The sense of community and commonness; sharing and caring that emerges particularly from the discussion of Naga Hoho and Naga council, NMA, NSF, Sisterhood Network, Morung and Mother's Hope give a tremendous social impact on the Naga people with reviving spirits and renaissance in the form of health care, socio-political struggles, care for women and underprivileged people, moral and community building and economic awareness through developing creatively the human power and potentiality, all these challenge the Nagas to relate to the experiences and realities of life.

However, there is failure on the part of Nagas to unite for peace, essence of community life and the nature of hard labour, fidelity. Degradation of moral values, economic bankruptcy and dependency

---

286 Source: Questionnaire. Question, 92.

has uprooted the social ethos of Naga life. The need for the Naga church at the moment is to identify its spirituality on the basis of life realities. There is a serious breakdown of Naga spirituality and commitment to God somewhere along the way. Thus, the present church could reconsider its mission to work towards reconciliation and peace.

To study each of the different departmental activities of the Government on socio-economic upliftment would be difficult and vast. Therefore, SIRD is studied since it is one of the main bodies that work towards socio-economic development of the State.

Discussing on the SIRD we could find two major contributions (i) educating people of all stages and professions through trainings, workshops and seminars towards economic upliftment and self-reliance, (ii) and undertaking major research work on social-economic issues at grassroots level considering the peoples' relevant need for survival. However, the over all impact has to be put into consideration: How has it been helpful and responsible? The criticism often faced by the government should be evaluated carefully for the growth of the socio-economic situation of the people.

In the following chapter we shall continue to discuss the contributions of the Nagaland Baptist Church Council (NBCC): Nagaland Development Outreach (NDO), which functions independently under NBCC and Council of Naga Baptist Churches (CNBC) in the socio-economic upliftment of the society. These organisations have religious flavour and interpretations in their approach, which is a part of mission commitment to build the Naga society, especially contributing to the political peace process, social integrity and economic development.

Chapter 4

THE DIFFERENT ORGANISATIONS INVOLVED IN SOCIO-ECNOMIC UPLIFTMENT OF THE NAGAS IN NAGALAND (Section-B)

Introduction

The present chapter is the continuation of the previous chapter (Section – A), it deals with the role of the Nagaland Baptist Church Council (NBCC) and also the Council of Naga Baptist Churches (CNBC). We shall attempt to overview churches' ministry in the context.

I. The Role of the Naga Baptist Churches

1. Nagaland Baptist Church Council

The Nagaland Baptist Church Council (NBCC) is the central organization of the Baptist Churches in Nagaland. It was first established in 1935 as "the Naga Hills Baptist Church Advisory Board," and later renamed as "the Naga Hills Baptist Church Council" at the bungalow of Rev. I. Tanquist on April 5, 1937. It was reorganized in 1953 and functioned provisionally until 1960. At the final stage, it was formulated again and given the name

"The Nagaland Baptist Church Council," after the inauguration of Nagaland as a separate state.[287]

The latter part of 1970s and the early part of 1980s saw a great spiritual awakening in Nagaland Churches. It resulted in strong ministerial leadership and strengthened the ministry itself. At present, the Nagaland Baptist Church Council is a constituent member of the Council of Baptist churches in Northeast India (CBCNEI), with its headquarters at Guwahati, Assam (India). The NBCC also maintains its historical relationship with Baptist International Ministries, USA through CBCNEI and is a member body of the Asian Baptist Federation and the Baptist World Alliance since 1992 and 1993 respectively.[288] The 125 years period of Christianity in Nagaland have taken the initiative in political and educational field, and in protesting social evils under the slogan "Nagaland for Christ."

The NBCC has empowered Nagaland Missionary Movement (NMM) for its ministry since 1962 and its secretary was appointed in 1969. The inaugural function was observed on 5th January 1970 in Dimapur.[289] The NMM promotes evangelism and church development in Nagaland. It supports evangelists and fledgling associations in the nine fields initially targeted by the Home Mission Board in 1967. By 1973, NMM ministry was extended beyond India's borders. With the financial aid of Rs 15,000/- through Council of Baptist Churches North East India (CBCNEI) missionary work was done in the Fiji Islands.[290]

'Nagaland Congress on World Evangelism' was conducted by NMM on March 1st–9th, 1975 in Dimapur. A major outcome was the adoption of Nagaland Congress Covenant, which propelled the churches into revival and a greater thrust in evangelism. They began

287 "The Formation of Nagaland Baptist Church Council," in *From Darkness to Light,* edited by P. Alongla, Aier (Kohima: NBCC, 1997), 104.

288 Ibid., 106-107. NBCC celebrated 125 years of Christianity in the land in 1997. Some of the tribes such as the 'Aos' celebrated its 125th years of Christianity in the same year 1997 followed by the 'Sumis' in December 2003.

289 Ibid., 117. The Late Rev. Longri Ao initiated formation of Home Mission Board to complete the unfinished task of evangelism at the annual meeting at Mokokchung in 1960.

290 Ibid., 120. cf. NMM Board Meeting Correspondence, 16 January 1973.

to minister among the Adhi tribe of Arunachal Pradesh.[291] The NBCC provides the broad guideline for carrying out the mission task to Naga Tribal Baptist Associations. The NBCC resolved during its 41st annual council in October 13-16, 1977 to enlist ten thousand Naga volunteers for mission outreach from all Baptist Associations. Nagaland Baptist women's union and youth movement urged all the churches to involve themselves seriously in enlisting the volunteers within six months from the 15th of October 1977, when this campaign was officially inaugurated.[292]

Today, NMM continues to reach out through sending missionaries to India, Andaman and Nicobar Islands, Andhra Pradesh, Assam, Bhutan, Manipur, Meghalaya, Orissa, Sikkim, West Bengal, and in foreign countries like Burundi, Cambodia, Myanmar, Nepal, Thailand, and South Africa. NMM extends students chaplains to Delhi, Bangalore, Kolkata, Shillong, Pune, Guwahati, and hospital ministry in C.M.C. Vellore, Civil Hospital Dimapur and Mokokchung. There are six evangelists working with the non-locals in Nagaland.[293] NMM keeps up the prayer day during its mission week May 1-7 every year.

A fresh impetus arose among the leaders of NBCC and other prominent Church leaders who were very concerned about the new trends of socio-political life of Nagaland. They were convinced that the Church was the only competent body who would speak for peace. Immediately, the third Nagaland Baptist Convention held at Wokha January 1-February 2, 1964 passed a resolution to form a "Peace Mission" for the restoration of peace in the state.

This peace initiation was side by side welcomed by the Government of Nagaland and later approved by the Government of India. Thus, the "Peace Mission" held its first meeting at Kohima in May 1964 and they continued their work with sincerity and dedication in consultation with the leaders of Naga Federal

291 O. M. Rao, ed., *Longri Ao; A Biography* (Calcutta: Swapna Printing Work, 1986), 62.

292 Hevukhu Achumi, "Revival Movement in Nagaland and its Impact on the Nagas" (M.Th Thesis, New Zealand, 2000), 87.

293 Anjo Keikung, "Nagaland Missionary Movement Mission Week May 1-7, 2005," *NBCC NewsLetter* 5/2 (Janaury-March, 2005), 4.

Government, the leaders of the State Government and the Church leaders as well.[294] However, the original objective of the Nagas for self-determination and the quest for peace and communal harmony continued to maintain.[295] The NBCC leaders perceiving another period of difficulty and nightmares enforced the peace team and top leaders of national workers to maintain peace immediately.

Later, in support of peace, the NBCC Women department conducted a statewide peace procession on 29th February 1996. About 5,000 women joined the procession in Kohima alone. Likewise several people participated in all the district headquarters followed by seminar "Peace work" held on March 13th, 1996 at NBCC office for all the executive secretaries under it. Later a special day of repentance was organized on 2nd December 1997, in which all the churches in Nagaland were involved. The Government granted mass casual leave to government servants to attend the prayer and fasting program in their respective churches.

The year 1997 was declared as Jubilee Year and therefore the peace team appealed to all the sections of people in Nagaland to maintain peace. The statewide peace rallies were launched on 7th - 22nd March 1997. Rallies were held in all the districts and sub-divisional headquarters. The peace rally team called upon every citizen and all sections of people to desist from violence.[296]

The team continues to work to foster peace and unity among people in the Naga inhabited areas of northeast. The two apex bodies NBCC and Council of Naga Baptist Churches (CNBC) organizations of Nagaland called for reconciliation among the Naga underground groups. The meeting was termed as 'peace conference.' These organizations called the Nagas to hoist white flags on each Naga house on August 14th and 15th 2001 to symbolize peace and non-violence. Thus, they also appealed not to boycott the August 15th independence day functions.[297] These organizations expressed

---

294 "The Formation of Nagaland Baptist Church Council," in *From Darkness to Light,* edited by P. Alongla, Aier (Kohima: NBCC, 1997), 113-114.

295 Ibid., 115.

296 Ibid., 116.

297 "Two Apex Naga Church Groups Call for Reconciliation," (10 August 2001), 1 http://www.rediff.com/news/2001/aug/10naga.htm (2 March 2003).

the 'serious concern' over the 'plight' of Nagas, who had fled the Imphal valley in the wake of anti-ceasefire stir in the valley. They extended their solidarity with the Nagas in Manipur.[298] This joint venture shows the churches' commitment to people at the crucial juncture, which defines a moment in the history of the people.

They also expressed their concern over the reported threats and intimidations on February 21st, 2003 by political parties and underground groups in the run-up to the February 26th Assembly elections in the state. The people were urged to leave the decision to the electorate's best judgment.[299] Moreover, the NBCC in a separate statement enforced the idea of free and fair elections for strengthening the spirit of democracy in the Naga society. Hence, the years of participation have shown the aims and objectives of the NBCC for the proper exercise and stewardship of political resources in a spirit of peace, understanding, and co-operation. It also continues to call for peace in this highly divided Naga society today.

NBCC also works towards peace among the factions inspite of the criticism received from different NGOs, Naga Peoples Movement for Human Rights, NPMR and others, setting allegation against the church as they approach each factional group. The Secretary of NBCC states that NBCC is not or against any political agenda rather the concern is, if sovereignty is demanded certainly it should be agreed upon in negotiation between the Indian government and coming together of all different factions.[300]

NBCC took an initiative to fight against liquor and make Nagaland a "Dry State." This is one of the best examples of social activities seen. Liquor was identified as a major root cause of social evils that hit the society, churches, and the government as well. The

---

298 "Two Apex Naga Church Groups Call for Reconciliation", 1.

299 "Church, Naga Unhappy with poll process," (20 February 2003), 1 http://newsarchives.indianfo.com/spotlight/election2003/21nagapoll.html (2 March 2003).

300 Interview with Zhabu Terhuja, Executive Secretary, NBCC, 28 April 2005. cf. "Peace Conference," organized by CBCNEI/NCCI/MBC/CASA, October 12-14, 2001 at MBC Center Church- *A Report*. 19-20. There are other recognized bodies that work actively towards 'peace' mission – the CBCNEI, NCCI and CASA.

resolution was passed to bring liquor prohibition as early as mid forties. This stance was once again revived and a meeting was held on February 5th, 1962 at Mokokchung. It requested the Governor of Nagaland to abolish immediately the sale and use of liquor in Nagaland and divert the funds to other welfare projects. NBCC observed 27th and 28th September 1972 as demand days for total prohibition in all the towns of Nagaland.[301]

Despite several memoranda submitted to the Government for total prohibition, liquor shops have increased. [302] Having seen the situation, another resolution was passed on October 25th- 27th, 1988. Thus, a big protest was launched on November 15th, 1988 and about 10,000 people participated in Kohima. The Church leaders submitted a memorandum to the Governor of Nagaland signed by over 5,000 people in demand of 'Total Prohibition.'

The Roman Catholic Church and other organizations such as the Tribal Unions, Naga Students' Federation, Naga Mothers' Association and the Naga Scholar Society were in support of the prohibition movement. Having gone into various protests, hunger strikes, indefinite fasts, the Government of Nagaland took heed of the demand by passing an act on 'Total Prohibition' of liquor in the State of Nagaland on March 29, 1990. Therefore, churches in Nagaland observed a thanksgiving day on June 3, 1990 and this day is observed as NBCC Day of Prayer every year.[303] Presently, Zhabu agrees that NBCC lacks constant coverage and voicing in this aspect. However, he says a lot is done at the local level in some Associations -the Konyaks, Chakesang and Abum.[304]

---

301 "The Formation of Nagaland Baptist Church Council," in *From Darkness to Light,* edited by P. Alongla, Aier (Kohima: NBCC, 1997), 111.

302 The flow of liquor brought about moral destruction to both young and old and created disciplinary problems in the family, schools, and colleges and even in Government offices. It left many homes bankrupt economically and ruined potential public leaders, and prospective youth leaders etc.

303 "The Formation of Nagaland Baptist Church Council," in *From Darkness to Light,* edited by P. Alongla, Aier (Kohima: NBCC, 1997), 111-112. The role of the Naga Students Federation and Naga Mother's Association is specially discussed in the previous section.

304 Interview with Terhuja.

Particularly NBCC Women Department is involved in socio-economic development in its own way apart from the political and social involvement in history. Short-term training is given to mothers on health and leaders to discover local medicine available instead relying on Western medicine. Important training on psychological health and the rudiments of Western medicine are given.[305] Further in regard to 'health care training' the methods of healing were taught in 2004 with the resource persons coming from Chennai. They also look forward to three more times training on the same to complete course.[306] Seminar for young girls, family and very rarely singles are organized touching topics like careers, sex education, HIV/AIDS and self-awareness. [307]

They actively encourage women to generate income through their handloom productions, piggery, baking bread, farming, gardening and any local products. They further encourage the setting up of Self Help Groups. For this, Naro comments that the Chakesang tribe and tribes of Tuensang District are the best and most successful example at present.[308] Overall they teach cleanliness and maintenance of proper sanitary system in local areas and preservation of foods.

The counseling department, 'New Life Ministry'[309] in its annual report gives the character of its work among the various groups of people. Especially its ministry focuses toward drug addicts, HIV/AIDS and other general ministry as well. It has two main projects at Jalukie and Grace Home Rehabilitation Center, Tuli. The services offered are counseling, training and referral. They also concentrate on various seminars like youth management, drug addiction, HIV/AIDS, career guidance and premarital counseling. The important

---

305 Interview with Naro, Women Secretary, NBCC, 26 April 2005.

306 *A Brief Report of the NBCC Women's Department Secretary from October 2003 to September 2004 at T. Chekri, Pfutsero During its 22nd Annual Meeting*, October 8-9, 2004. 2. Presented by K. Kapfo, Women Secretary, NBCC. A resolution made to this point was to continue the training in South India for 15 days and twice for 10 days at a slot in the consecutive year.

307 Interview with Naro.

308 Interview with Naro.

309 Structurally 'New Life Ministry' is under NBCC but it has its own independent function.

groups and meetings are addressed to especially youths, parents of children affected by drug abuse and HIV/AIDS, female addicts both married and singles who sometimes become commercial sex workers in order to support their addiction habits. It further has a special Detoxification and Rehabilitation Programmme.[310]

NBCC has an Educational Programmme. According to Terhuja one of the main projects of the NBCC is schools and colleges so as to educate people and allowing them to save their money which otherwise they would have spend in going to a distant place for education.[311] Christian English School, which was established in 1967 and are under private management, is one of the best school in Nagaland. The school conducts regular activities like Morning Chapel, Vacation Bible School and Youth Evangelistic Camps.

The Oriental Theological Seminary (OTS), a special project of the NBCC was established in June 1993. It aims at preparing the students to be thoroughly oriented in contextual ministry and dialogue with the society and its people. Clark Theological College at Mokokchung is jointly sponsored with Ao Baptist Arogo Mundang (ABAM) since 1974. This college was established in 1972 in memory of the first American missionary to Nagaland. The NBCC is also involved with Union Biblical Seminary (UBS), Pune, Maharastra as a lifetime sponsoring body. The main purpose of having a theological seminary is to educate men and women for a worldwide Christian ministry. NBCC is a joint sponsoring body with Manipur Baptist Convention for Patkai Christian College since 1974. The college has three departments namely, Arts, Science and Music.[312]

---

310 *Annual Report of the New Life Ministry, NBCC,* October 2001. 1-3. There are other recognized bodies like CBCNEI and NEIDAC-Shillong (North East India Drugs and AIDS Care), who work within the North East States. NEIDAC came into existence 5years ago for action in the area of drugs and HIV/AIDS in NEI. Dr. D. Ratno is the Director with their office at Laitumkrah, Shillong. Cf. "Church Consultation on Drugs Abuse, HIV/AIDS," *Baptist News* 53/1 (January-March, 2002), 35-40.

311 Interview with Terhuja.

312 "The Formation of Nagaland Baptist Church Council," in *From Darkness to Light,* edited by P. Alongla, Aier (Kohima: NBCC, 1997), 109-110. Historically the need of a Christian college for higher education was brought out in the meeting of NBCC Executive and Church elders at Kohima during

Apart from this formal set of education, NBCC education department of Nagaland provides Alternative and Innovative Schooling. This is a programme for children who never had a formal education called "Never enroll Children" under the leadership of Arenla Education and Communication Secretary, NBCC. This programme was organized for few months, it started on 17th August and ended on 30th of November 2004. NMM also has 65 centers for non-residential children. According to Weyeite Lohe this program helped the underprivileged children to receive free tuition classes in all centers. These children's performance and learning capacity was more than volunteer teacher's expectation.[313]

Along with this, NBCC encourages the associations and pastors to give importance to Sunday school ministry, making affordable sufficient material and training. In 2004 CBCNEI donated Rs. 20,000 for the Vacation Bible School ministry in five affiliated schools under NBCC. The Baptist World Alliance also sponsored towards Sunday school ministry. Through BWA training 11 associations were benefited strengthening 317 ministries and 341 teachers under them.[314] NBCC conducts a state level Sunday School Teachers' Training designed to lead the trainees from a teacher-centered approach to leaner-centered approach. A lecture was given in creative play method for involving children in the learning process which was attended by 106 teachers.[315]

NBCC has related ministries in the area of development in collaboration with the Church's Auxiliary for Social Action (CASA), particularly on relief and development; Comprehensive Rural

---

June 27th-29th, 1967. In the meantime the proposal also came from Tuisem Shishak for the possibility of establishing the college in that region. Thus, NBCC became a major sponsoring body.

313 *NBCC NewsLetter* 5/1 (October-December, 2000), 3-4. He is the former coordinator of Alternative and Innovative Schooling.

314 Arenla Longchar, "Education and Communication," *NBCC Newsletter* 4/4 (July-September, 2004), 9.

315 *The Nagaland Baptist Church Council in 2004: A Brief Report Presented at the Annual General Meeting of the Council of Baptist churches in North East India Held at Sivasgar,* April 21-24, 2005, 5; presented by Zhabu Teruja, General Secretary, NBCC.

Development Services (CRDS) operates in co-operation with NBCC against poverty, injustice and responses to emergency relief work and needs; Bible Society of India (BSI) which has branches in various parts of Nagaland; and World Vision of India (WVI) that sponsors educational institutions and developmental projects. NBCC has close ties with Evangelical Fellowship of India, North East India Committee on Relief and Development, and National Council of Churches.[316]

NBCC have a continued relationship with these particular ministries, but they are now in the hands of the Nagaland Development Outreach, NDO (a development wing of NBCC). We shall look into some major activities involved by NDO in the following section.

2. Nagaland Development Outreach (NDO)

The Nagaland Development Outreach is a developmental wing created by Nagaland Baptist Church Council in 1999. It is the first indigenous development organization commissioned by the Nagaland Baptist Church Council to initiate socio-economic development program for fostering a wholesome change in Naga society. This is a registered body of development organization under the Societies Registration Act of 1860.[317] It is also registered under Foreign Contribution Regulation Act, Ministry of Home Affairs, Government of India and granted Income Tax Exemption registration. Thus, in this way NDO fulfils all the statutory requirements to function as a development organization.[318]

---

316 Sashinungla Ao, "A Study of the Role of the Nagaland Baptist Church Council in the Socio-Political Life of the Nagas in Nagaland from 1947-1997" (M.Th. Thesis, Senate of Serampore College, 2000). 56. Cf. A report of NBCC Submitted to the CBCNEI 39th Annual Council at Jorhat February 15-19, 1998; NBCC Annual report of 2004.

317 "Nagaland Development Outreach," *A Brochure*, by NDO. NDO defines "development as discovery and the responsible utilization of human potentiality to the extent of fostering other resources giving a wholesome growth in all spheres of life, which involves people's participation towards a sustainable existence."

318 "Nagaland Development Outreach," *A Brochure* by NDO.

The NBCC organized a major consultation on development at Kohima in 1995 involving development agencies like Churches Auxiliary for Social Action (CASA), Comprehensive Rural Development Service (CRDS), North East India Committee on Relief and Development (NEICORD),[319] World Vision of India and Indo-German Social Service Society (IGSSS). The consultation of these bodies help to recognise the need for creating a development agency to dialogue and communicate with government, national and international agencies. As this need was recommended to the NBCC Executive committee accordingly they resolved for creation of a Development wing of the church. The Quasiqui Century participants held the same resolution during the celebration at Kohima in 1997. Therefore, they aim for effectively proclaiming the message of Love and Salvation in Jesus, participating in holistic human development and social transformation in Christ.[320]

The NDO networks in partnership with Development of Human Potential (Imphal); Action Aid India; British High Commission, New Delhi through Action Aid; Board of International Ministry, USA; Churches Auxiliary for Social Action; Medical Ministry International; Forest Department, Horticulture Department; and the Nagaland State Government. Along with these NDO is involved hand in hand with twenty Baptist Associations and over 13000 churches covering the entire Nagaland.[321] Financially, NDO raises its own resources from individual well wishers, funding agencies and grants from the government.

In the past years, the Baptist churches gave a prior focus on spiritual dimension of ministry, as it was a necessity then. The

---

319 Cf. "Introducing NEICORD," *A Brochure; In Touch,* A Quarterly Publication 2 (October 2004).` NEICORD has been involving in relief and development in the NE States for India for 23 years and now plan to move forward with a greater focus on Micro Enterprise Development, MED, Health and HIV/AIDS response and on sustainability. It operates from its head office situated in Shillong in the state of Meghalaya and programmes are implemented through partnering with Churches and like-minded NGOs at the grassroots level.

320 Profile of Nagaland Development Outreach, *A Paper* produced by NDO office. 1.

321 Ibid., 2. Western Sumi Baptist Church comes under this.

entire resources were used for spiritual development, evangelism and mission outreach programmes. Apart from these, churches did not pay adequate attention to socio-economic development of the state. The church continued to raise its voice against the failures of the government from a distance thinking that it was the sole responsibility of the government. At present, the church has realized that the ministry of the church should be holistic. Now NDO is on the move and perhaps the best development agency in Nagaland as far as organization is concerned.[322] Thus, NDOs priority and emphasis is given on development as a process in which human beings become central, along with their environment.[323]

NDO runs a holistic programme on environment, community empowerment and delegates the power in the hands of the community people. It also works through the help of the association touching the grassroots levels. Inspite of short sightedness and instability on the part of government and the initial taboo of the church to talk on development NDO could succeed. Gradually, there are changes taking place in almost 20 Church Associations with developmental wings being established. Now even the government has accepted NDO as the biggest indigenous developmental agency in Nagaland.[324]

NDO involves in mission empowerment to the underprivileged and marginalized through awareness program, capacity building, and assimilation of information, advocacy, lobbying and networking. It promotes activities towards self-sufficiency and welfare of the total person and nature. Finally, it also strives for unity and peaceful co-existence through conflict resolution and peace building. There are different departments, which carry out these programmes, namely, Human Resource Development Center, Peace Promotion Program, Self Help Group, Community Based Health Care, Public Relation

---

322 Pongsing, "Nagaland Development Outreach," *Nagaland Post*, 14 December 1999, 5.

323 Ibid., 6.

324 Interview with Pongsing, Director of Nagaland Development Outreach, Dimapur, 14 April 2005.

and Resource Mobilization Department, and Finance Department.[325] We shall in brief look into the activities done by these departments.

a. Human Resource Development Center

NDO Human Resource Development Center situated at Nikhekhu Village, Nuiland Division, Dimapur District acquired its name on 4th September 2003 at Kohima.[326] The Power Department of the State Government helped the NDO to complete it and get the transformer installed along with the Cafeteria and a Cottage.[327] The other activities involved are- Middle Education School, tree plantation, horticulture farm, construction of dams and football ground with donations of cash and machinery. Besides, NDO has other construction work of Christian Higher Secondary School Dormitory, which can accommodate 100 children; and a tribal school at Dimapur and Tizit to implement in the future.[328]

b. Peace Promotion Programs:[329]

Peace Promotion Programs have been organized for the churches and community leaders whereby they can begin to take peace promotion activities at the local level. NDO has developed trainers or facilitators to help as resource persons, with the purpose that when conflicts resolution arise these people will be able to solve it at the earliest, not expecting others to solve the problem but to manage within the

---

325 *Annual Report of 2004 Nagaland Development Outreach,* Towards Fuller Life. Presented by Pongsing, Director, NDO. 1-6.

326 Profile of Nagaland Development, 2. This 30 acres land was donated by Mr. Isawoto Zhimomi of Nikhekhu village

327 *Annual Report of 2004,* 1-2.

328 *Annual Report of Nagaland Development Outreach* Submitted at 16th Triennial Convention Nagaland Baptist Church Council on January 30-February 1, 2004 by Pongsing, Director, NDO. 4-5. cf. Profile of Nagaland Development, 3. Mr. Asungba Sangtem, Mr. and Mrs. Neibu Nagi, Mr. and Mrs. Chuba Chang, Mr. Apok Jamir, MP (Rajya Sabha) and the Director of Horticulture have made donation.

329 *Annual Report of Nagaland Development Outreach,* 5. NDO decided to work for peace promotion and Action Aid India and British High Commission, New Delhi support the project.

community itself.[330] Thus, this program endeavours to channelize the energy engaged in destructive conflict into constructive work by addressing pressing issues, problems and needs of the regional people.[331]

These programs are mostly discharged in the form of seminars and workshops such as, conflict resolution, peace promotion, peace & development, and youth leadership & development. People are trained and mobilized with skills and capacity building to perform right leadership in their community.[332]

c. Self Help Group

NDO organizes this self-help group for the credit needs of the poor to meet small amounts. A formal banking system is unable to address their needs adequately. Therefore the need for SHGs arises to provide a source of credit for the poor, which can be return with a minimum interest after a specific period. In the process of time people may achieve certain self-sufficiency.[333] For this reason, NDO has launched a program called 'Micro Finance for Self Help Group' (SHG). NDO gave a revolving fund to 13 SHGs after evaluating them. There are another 116 SHGs who have registered under this program. They desire to link them to urban banks moving themselves from non-formal to formal sector for larger benefits preserving old values of self-help and dignity. NDO so far has 74 SHGs and many of them have been linked for credit facilities while others could not do because of non-availability of the banks. NDO is looking for ways and means to either link them up with banks or assist them directly.[334]

NDO targets women because of their discipline and capability in managing the household economy and further to build in them self-confidence and a positive self-image. This program expects women to participate in community building that will lessen their burden once they reach a certain stage of self-sufficiency. The other

330 Interview with Pongsing.

331 *Annual Report of 2004,* 2.

332 Interview with Pongsing. Human Resource Development Program partly comes under it.

333 *Annual Report of 2004,* 2.

334 *Annual Report of Nagaland Development Outreach,* 7.

objective is to empower women to become entrepreneurs and raise their status which will enable them to live life to its fullest.[335] Finally, it raises the image of women making them earning members in a family and society therefore enabling to acknowledge their role as a mother, wife and mother maker.[336]

d. Community Based Health Care

The NDO realized the need for health care, which is one of the neglected dimensions in Nagaland. Medical Ministry International (based in USA) agreed to develop partnership with NDO in order to extend service for health care programs in Nagaland.[337] NDO is attempting to provide health for all which means people's health in people's hand.[338] Thus, in relationship with the church, government, NGOs and international organisations; it conducts Community Health Programs like curative and preventative activities, annual medical camps for the poor who cannot go to hospitals, free medicine and check up, and health education to the church community leaders through seminars and trainings (training the trainers).[339]

NDO along with Catholic Relief Services (CRS) is heading the program on HIV/AIDS project. From November 2004 two trainings under this were held with Yimchunger at Shamator, and WSBAK at Kaziranga, Assam. The project is part of the Community Based Health Care program of NDO and its objectives are as follows- to increase church leaders involvement in the HIV/AIDS prevention initiative thereby reducing ignorance, denial, fear, sigma and discrimination. It is also to develop a resource pool from among the

---

335 Interview with Pongsing.

336 *Annual Report of 2004,* 3.

337 Profile of Nagaland Development, 4. cf. *Annual Report of 2004,* 3-4. MMI came for the first time to Nagaland in 2003 to conduct medical camp at Tuensang, Impur, Mokokchung, Wokha, Kohima and Dimapur. In 2004 they were at Mon District and by August 2005 they will be at Longleng District.

338 *Annual Report of 2004,* 3.

339 Interview with Pongsing. Mainly this program is to train NBCC women's department, which represents 20 Women's Association Secretaries and Evangelists in order that these trainers would train their own Associations and local churches.

church leaders for the prevention initiatives and management of the HIV/AIDS pandemic. Finally, it advocates and facilitate a network working in HIV/AIDS.[340] Thus, NDO undertake this program from Christian perceptive. On one hand, NGOs are promoting condoms, on the other hand NDO promotes principles of abstinence, holy living and chastity.[341]

e. Human Resource Development

Human Resource Development is another major program done by NDO. People are trained to enhance and acquire the skills and knowledge to be effective in service. In the same way, some students are sent to colleges and universities abroad in countries like USA, Germany and South Korea. Staff are also sent for exposure and training programs, such as, Conflict Resolution, Peace Building, Advanced Leadership Training, Gender and Women Empowerment Training, Globalisation,[342] SHG Training, Developing Training Manual, Initiative for change, peace and reconciliation, and Advance Level Training on Conflict resolution and Peace Building Skills. NDO over all do have their staff exposures and evaluation program for themselves.[343]

f. Public Relations and Resource Mobilization Department

NDO received help both from secular and church organisation in meeting the needs of different projects. Inspite of the contribution and resources received NDO has to look for resources from outside to meet the felt need. Therefore, NDO created a small department with an aim to build relationship with the Baptist Churches and Associations in order to share the needs and ministry of NDO. This department came into being in the year 2004 and has different projects and funding agencies.[344]

---

340 NDO, "HIV/AIDs: A Development Issue," *NBCC Newsletter* 5/1 (October-December, 2004), 10. cf. *Annual Report of 2004,* 4.

341 Interview with Pongsing.

342 *Annual Report of Nagaland Development Outreach,* 10-11.

343 *Annual Report of 2004,* 4-5. 12 full time staff spent time at Kaziranga, Assam on exposure trip and evaluation program from 12th -13th November 2004.

344 *Annual Report of 2004,* 5.

The survey analysis shows the following findings – About 40% of the respondents were aware of the NDO's work in Nagaland. They say that NDO is doing much in the area of awareness programmes on HIV/AIDS, creating competitive spirits in various schools and colleges, and organising seminars. However, it needs to generate transparency in State and Church developmental projects. The other 47% percent of the respondents did not respond to the specific question; it could be either out of their ignorance or insufficient work done by NDO. The rest 13% of the respondent opined that there is no proper implementation of development work seen rather NDO focuses only on spiritual side.[345]

II. The Council of Naga Baptist Churches

CNBC covers the churches of the whole inhabited Naga areas. According to the statistical report, the total population is 6,41,994 with 2,536 churches (NBCC, Assam Nagas, Naga Baptist Convention: Manipur, Naga Baptist Convention: Myanmar, and Arunachal Nagas).[346] Its main focus is on Myanmar areas. In 1813 Burma received the gospel message through the first American Baptist Missionary Adoniram Judson. It has the most number of Baptist memberships in Asia. In 1936, when Htay Pung belonging to Somra tribe went to study at Ukhrul he was then introduced to the Gospel.[347] It was only in 1993 the Nagas came to realize their existence and they came together under Naga Baptist Convention, Myanmar. CNBC in administration with Nagas cooperates with NBCC.[348]

345 Source: Questionnaire. Question 76.

346 Statistical Report 2005 Produced by V. K. Nuh, General Secretary, CNBC, 4. NBCC has total 4,06,794 baptized members and 1,327 churches; Assam Nagas 8,500 and 62 churches; Naga Baptist Convention (Manipur) 23,099 and 1070; Naga Baptist Convention (Myanmar) 80,240 and 242; and Arunachal Nagas 18,000 and 154 respectively. 1-4.

347 The 19th Annual Assembly Council of Naga Baptist Churches March 18th-20th 2005, Zeme Baptist Churches Dimapur, presented by V. K. Nuh, General Secretary, CNBC. 3.

348 Interview with V. K. Nuk, General Secretary, CNBC, 26 April 2005.

CNBC is actively involved in mission. CNBC is sponsoring two missionaries through different churches and 30 others who are studying at different theological colleges. There are 21 evangelists, 32 pastors and each year Rs. 30.000/- is sent to the Mission Center.

CNBC is much involved in peace work. It confronts various conflict situations without compromising its prophetic voice. CNBC so far has responded to any challenge of peace work. Along with the General Secretary, the President is deeply involved at different levels for peace and reconciliation. On this account both the leaders attempt to meet NSCN-IM collective leaders in exchanging views. For CNBC failure or success in not in question but contribution towards the struggle.[349] V. K. Nuh comments that Nagas are heavily suffering from theological imbalances; theologically trained people and church leaders are not ready to confront the political situation practically. Therefore, it should be protested from spiritual bankruptcy that the Naga face today.[350]

CBNC has a research wing, which publishes CNBC bulletins and provides many materials to research scholars. Presently, it possesses more than one thousand documents on 58 years of Naga political affairs, theological study and church history. CNBC aspires to have an archive for research work and establishment of academic research students in Christian study, conflict resolution and peace study in the near future.[351]

Summary

The church role (NBCC; NDO and CBNC) as discussed above is not to be taken as the complete account of their activities. The church mission commitment and its main involvement are for political peace and reconciliation, seminars and trainings, health concerns especially on HIV/AIDS and protection against social evils in the form of liquor. An educational concern is another aspect that includes the importance of Sunday schools.

349 The 19th Annual Assembly Council, 4.

350 Interview with Nuk.

351 The 19th Annual Assembly Council, 4.

The author observes that NBCC participated in socio-political struggles particularly in the peace process since the 1960s, but its impact has not been effective for the Naga people and among the factional leaders till date because of taking a neutral position. Perhaps NBCC has to be more prophetic in its approach. The church needs to be self-reliant in terms of resources inspite of regular collections and donations from the people.

The impact of the NDO is seemingly not known to most of the Churches although a few of the local churches/Associations/villages may have started with some similar programmes by way of conducting seminars, workshops, SHGs and others. The NBCC continued role on anti social evils should be lifted once again. What has been discussed is mainly of the act done in the past, especially towards drugs and liquor in Nagaland. NBCC could step forward from regular systematic programming to the needs of the time.

NDO should be encouraged to look into building up an individual and the community rather than concentrating on the physical construction within the campus. NDO need to concentrate to reach out to all the churches and villages for growth in socio-economic spheres since it represents the NBCC in Nagaland. CNBC on the other hand, has wider concerns and coverage of all the Naga inhabited areas and political concerns it has to continue to strive for peace among the Nagas.

Thus, the book gives a bird's eye view covering their major involvement in socio-economic aspects, in order to highlight the glimpses of their ministry and acknowledge their roles in further development of the socio-economic concerns. In the following chapter we shall continue study the contributions of the Sumi Baptist Church in the present context.

Chapter 5

THE ROLE OF THE SUMI BAPTIST CHURCH MISSION IN THE SOCIO-ECONOMIC CONTEXT OF NAGALAND

Introduction

Traditionally, the census of India labeled the Sumi religion as animism[352] although the idea of Creator '*Alhou*/ *Timilhou*' was present among them.[353] He was believed to be benevolent god who lived in a remote higher place. G.K. Ghosh argues that they cannot be strictly labeled as animist but rather can be said as polytheists.[354] However in the researchers view, animism does not necessarily mean 'spirit worship', rather a quest for the Supreme God and security. Therefore,

352 J. H. Hutton, *The Sema Nagas* (London: Oxford University Press, 1968), 192-193.

353 Ibid., 191-193.

354 G. K. Ghosh, *Tribals and Their Culture in Manipur and Nagaland*, Vol. 3 (New Delhi: Ashish Publishing House, 1999), 33. cf. A. Wati Longchar, *The Tribal Religion in Northeast India: An Introduction* (Jorhat: Eastern Theological College, 2000), 8. According to Wati Longchar, tribal religion cannot be termed as animism or primitive which would be a misleading label that needs to be completely relegated by all. He argues that in tribal religion one discovers certain traditional religious ideas such as the concept of the Supreme Being, the Spirit, spirits, relationship of humans and supernatural beings and animals to the world around them and therefore one sees ethical values well developed.

various spirits were appeased to keep them away from disturbing their daily life and activities.

History reveals two major factors that influenced Sumi Nagas to Christianity. First, the contributions of American Baptist Missionaries,[355] although it was for a short period of time during the year 1948-50 (B. I. Anderson) and 1950-55 (Rev. R. F. Delano);[356] and second, by way of 'Power Encounters.'[357] Soon a "mass movement" swept among the Sumis everywhere. The local evangelists from neighbouring areas evangelized Sumis before the American Baptist missionaries reached them out. For instance, Christianity among the Sumis can be dated back to the first converts in 1904 and 1906. While by 1929, a tremendous increase in Christian membership that grew to three thousand members was seen. The mass movement, which started in 1927 continued throughout the 1930's having great impact upon the Sumis.[358]

By 1955 after a short period of foreign missionary work the Sumis were left to continue the task of establishing the church. At the beginning, although the situation was difficult, the local leadership began to form and organize. Mission centers were established in different locations due to the geographical difficulty of coming together. The first mission center was established in 1937 (Sumi Baptist Akukuhou Kuqhakulu) while the American missionaries were still there.[359] The later two came into existence in 1962 (Western Sumi

---

355 *Sumi Baptist Diamond Jubilee Vesulho Eno Xughili, 1904-1978* (A Souvenir and History of the Sumi Baptist Association), 53.

356 Lhotohe Ayemi, "Nagami Yeghilo Eno Sumi Gholo Ayehkulu Ighikeu," *Souvenir* (Sumi Christian Centenary-WSBAK 1904-2003), 39-40.

357 P. T. Philip, *The Growth of Baptist Churches in Nagaland* (Assam: CLC, 1976), 109.

358 Ibid., 111-112.

359 Inaho G. Swu, "A Study of the Growth of the Baptist Churches Among the Sumis with Special reference to Southern Baptist Churches" (Clark Theological College: Unpublished BD Thesis, 1996), 58. However, the first mission center is now divided into two: the old remain in the same location (named as Original Baptists) and the separated new center shifted to Nito Mount: Zuheboto (named as Baptist Revivalists). This split can be traced back to 1968-1976 when the Sumis encountered the Charismatic movement in the Southern Baptist Church.

Baptist Association, at Akuvuto, Dimapur),[360] and in 1977 (Sumi Aphuye Baptist Akukuhou Kuqhakulu, at Phughoboto, Kohima district).[361] These Associations cover around 400 local churches of which 150 local churches are covered by WSBAK alone.[362] These Associations are affiliated under Naga Baptist Church Council (NBCC). In 2003, the Sumi Baptist Churches celebrated 100 years of Christianity among the Sumis at their respective places under each Association.

Besides these, there is an independent organization called Unite Revival Fellowship (URF), which had mission outreach from 1985. Initially this worked partly under SBAK though it functioned independently. It should be recognized as representative organization that works cordially with them.[363] It especially works among the Adi tribe of Arunachal Pradesh in North East India. Some of its achievements are Bible translation in Adi dialect (New Testament was completed in 1987 and the Old Testament in 2000), free education, construction of church buildings and establishment of Bible Institute.[364]

---

360 Hetoni Swu, "A Study of The Holistic Concept of Mission Found in Luke's Gospel in Relation to the Concept of Mission of the Sumi Naga Churches" (BD Thesis, Bishop's College, 1997), 32. WSBAK was permitted to function as a branch Association under the supervision of SBAK., it was only in 1979 the permission was granted to WSBAK for its separate independent body from the parent body (SBAK). Cf. "Western Sumi Baptist Akukuhou Kuqhakulu Shiluve Keu (Establishment of WSBAK Center), *Souvenir* (Sumi Christian Centenary-WSBAK 1904-2003), 46-47. WSBAK underwent four stages of process in geographical location, first at Qhehoi in 19471956; second, Zhuikhu in 1958; third, Pherima (Sakipheto) in 1959-1971 and fourth at Thahekhu the present location which was dedicated in 1972 though the process of work was already started as mentioned above.

361 Sumi Aphuyemi Baptist Akukuhou Kuqhakulu (Association) Diamond Jubilee Xulhe 1912-1987. *Souvenir*, 17.

362 Sumi Christian Centenary (WSBAK) Cum 45-U Western Sumi Baptist Akukuhou Kuqhakulu 2003 Yepithi (Report), 4th–7th Dec 2003, 17.

363 Interview with Rev. Inaho on 27th Sept 2004 at Dimapur Town Church.

364 A Short Report of URF Outreach Mission to Adiland, Arunachal Pradesh, From 1985-2000, presented by Rev. I. Khala, Director, URF, 4.

This chapter will focus particularly on the Western Sumi Baptist Akukuhou Kuqhakulu (WSBAK)[365] concentrating side-by-side on the Sumi Baptist Town Church, Dimapur. The chapter aims to explore the mission of the Sumi Baptist Church in the present context.

I. Brief History of WSBAK Mission

WSBAK mission has its place of struggles and strivings in the process of growth. WSBAK began under a few people's leadership in 1960s and 1970s in different contexts and environments. At the beginning it is told that people were less receptive, ignorant and less supportive financially, although some were wealthy, and the church leaders lived without proper roof above them in mud houses. There was no in depth teaching and preaching of the Word among the people. They lacked motivation for mission work.[366]

WSBAK shifted in leadership from early 1970s with the coming of Rev. Toniho who became the pioneer of Akuvuto Bible School in 1973. Rev. Luhoyi became the first Secretary to WSBAK (1970-79) followed by Rev. Hevukhu Achumi from 1980 till 1995 as Field Supervisor and Executive Secretary, during 1979-80's a great wave of spiritual revival touched the Western Sumi people. The visible impact was seen through the gifts of Holy Spirit, people materially flourished turning their hearts towards God, which expressed in self-giving for the mission.[367] In 1980, there were only 91 local churches and by the year 1995 they increased to 137. From 1980s onwards

365 The term 'Western Sumi Baptist Akukuhou Kuqhakulu' and 'Western Sumi Baptist Church Association' are both of the same. Therefore, the researcher would use them interchangeably in this book/chapter.

366 Interview with Tovishe Awomi, Evangelist, Akuvuto, Thahekhu, 7 September 2004. He is the senior residing Evangelist. He has been appointed at various posts in WSBAK Center.

367 Interview with Awomi. Beside the people mentioned there were a few others like Mr. Ghonito, Rev. Shiwoto and Rev. Yeluvi, who shouldered the responsibility.

there was great mission consciousness among the Sumis particularly in WSBAK.[368]

The scriptural basis for mission of WSBAK is specially quoted from Genesis 12:2; Psalms 2:8; Isaiah 52:7a;[369] Romans 15:21; Mathew 25:36[370] and frequently from Mathew 28:18b-20a.[371]

WSBAK for the first time in history sent a missionary to Arunachal Pradesh in August 1984 among the Nyishi tribes of Arunachal Pradesh in joint partnership with Dimapur Baptist Town Church.[372] It resulted in establisment of 246 churches and over 23000 Baptized members between the years 1984-2000 AD. The missionary pioneers were Rev. Luhoyi Jakha (who was a graduate of Bible School, Jorhat) and Rev. Nihozu Kiho (Layman; he is still working under Dimapur Baptist Town Church as full time missionary) who represents WSBAK for Cross Culture Mission.[373]

At present, there are 7 missionaries and missionary teachers in various mission fields and other locals working in various staff posts such as pastors, executive secretaries, women secretaries, field secretaries, and evangelists.[374]

WSBAK from 1984 to 2005 has been mainly involved in five places namely- (1) Dimapur Area-Nepali Baptist Fellowship started

---

368 Interview with Vitoshe Swu, Mission and Evangelism Director, Akuvuto, Thahekhu, 7 September 2004 (he is presently Executive Secretary elect of WSBAK). As mentioned earlier at present there are 150 local churches under WSBAK.

369 "WSBAK Mission Kumla Eno Jukucho Nhetsu," *A Paper* by Mission Department, Akuvuto,Thahekhu.1.

370 *WSBAK Mission Sutsa/News,* Mission Department, Akuvuto, Thahekhu, June 2004, 1.

371 Vitoshe Swu, "WSBAK Mission Ghili" (WSBAK Mission History), *Souvenir* (Sumi Christian Centenary-WSBAK 1904-2003), 49.

372 Ibid., Cf. Although, according to the interview with Awomi- in 1960s while WSBAK was still functioning under SBAK, Aizuto (The first Sumi Church Association) they sent a missionary to Arunachal Pradesh. This happened only after WSBAK began to function independently.

373 Vitoshe Swu, "WSBAK Mission Ghili" , 50.

374 Vitoshe Swu, "WSBAK Mission Kumla Yepithi 2004," *A Report,* (46th Western Sumi Baptist Akukuhou Kuqhakulu 2004 Yepithi at Nikhekhu Baptist Akukuhou on 3rd-5th, December 2004), 17-18.

from 1989; it has 1480 baptized members at present. (2) Hewa Naga Mission, Namphainong, Arunachal Pradesh started in 1993; it has 625 Baptized members. (3) Dimasa Mission, Kothalguri, Karbi Anlong started in 2002; it has one church with 14 baptized members and 20 believers. (4) West Kameng Mission, Bomdila, Arunachal Pradesh started in 1999; it has 417 baptized members. (5) Kurung Kumey Mission Sangram, Arunachal Pradesh started in 2002; it has 52 established churches out of 392 villages.[375]

WSBAK has made an attempt to reach out to the people making disciples in order to carry out the same responsibility. WSBAK has fulfilled thus for obedience to Jesus' commandment. Its foremost concern from the beginning was on cross-cultural mission, which continues till today.

The research survey shows that 63% of the respondents were of the opinion that mission is to 'send.' Again when the question was asked why missions? 58% respondents said because it is the commandment of Jesus. Finally, 81% of the respondents felt that mission is a part of the church structure.[376]

The present majority of the people understand mission as to 'send.' In this case one might observe that WSBAK is mission conscious and active in reaching out to the people outside Nagaland. WSBAK sees mission as an important part of the Church structure, in obedience to the commandment of Jesus. From this discussion one could observe the urgency of spreading God's word and saving souls as mission priority of WSBAK towards God's mission.

II. Recent Missions Activities and Functions under WSBAK

Western Sumi Baptist Akukuhou (Church) Association is an apex body, which covers about 150 churches in the Western part of Nagaland. It is a centralised body which regulates all power and authority, having representatives from each area and sometimes even

375 Sumi Christian Centenary (WSBAK), 18 f. cf. Interview with Rev. Nihozu Kiho (Missionary to Kurung Kumey among the Nyishi tribe of Arunachal Pradesh) on 9th September 2004 at Dimapur.

376 Hetoni Swu, "A Missiological Study on the Mission Application of the Western Sumi Baptist Church Association" *A Seminar Paper Submitted to Consortium for Indian Missiological Education in October 2004,* 53-54.

from local churches. There are a few able local churches in town areas, which in certain instances function independently within limits and in contact with the Association,[377] for instance, in sending missionaries to the mission field or having a separate mission field. Appointing a person for any post in a local church can be worked out between the candidate and the particular church. It is then further processed to WSBAK for their consent on the matter, also WSBAK sends its representative for official installation.[378]

The overall finance matter is taken care of by the Association. In the case of the salary of a missionary, collection of membership fee per head is taken on yearly basis and allotments from each village. It is possible to decentralise resources and finances to the local churches. For example, owning income resources like commercial buildings and common farming, and the collection of tithes and offerings are used for the maintenance of the particular local church which includes the pastor's and staff salaries, specific projects and developments within the church. The apex body WSBAK has all rights to set rules and regulations for the churches affiliated under it, but it is flexible in functioning depending on the circumstances.

In this section, we will discuss the various bodies, their activities and functions in executing different responsibilities to promote mission development and concerns under the Association.[379]

1. Executive Board

The Board members are usually representatives from the local area and churches under WSBAK. It also includes other departmental staff occasionally, according to the situational demands. All the represented members of this body have tenure limitations.

This body functions and decides as the head of all the departments, and works for the welfare and growth of WSBAK. It

377 Interview with Heniho Swu on 26 September 2004 at Dimapur. He is the ex-chairman of the Sumi Baptist Town Church and also a representative (member at large) to WSBAK in the recent past.

378 Interview with Rev. Phughoto Aye, Executive Secretary, WSBAK on 6 September 2004 at Akuvuto Mission Center (WSBAK).

379 This section comes from the knowledge and experience of the writer while working with WSBAK in May 1997 - May 1999.

takes up the appointment and replacement of the staff according to the need. This body sanctions the policies and nature of functions, and reviews them occasionally for implementation. There are other developments and projects within WSBAK like creation of departments and posts which are decided when the need for such arises.

2. Departmental Bodies

WSBAK has five main Departments - General Department, Mission and Evangelism, Women Department, Youth Department and Christian Education Department. In addition, the association developmental works are carried out through the General Department. We will discuss them in brief in the following paragraphs.

a. General Department

The Executive Secretary looks after this department. It administrates the rest of the departments mentioned, coordinates with other departments and plans out the programmes for a year, including all general activities and developments to be unfolded. It is generally concerned with WSBAK Centre developments and projects, such as schools and financial matters. For any constructions and physical developments within the Mission Center a person is assigned as an incharge officer over the works. It networks with local churches, Sumi Baptist Church Council (SBCC)[380] and Naga Baptist Church Council. It also organizes conferences, revival meetings, camps and various trainings at the Center.

b. Mission and Evangelism

The Director of Mission and Evangelism coordinates with the Executive Secretary and plans out the yearly work within WSBAK,[381] for instance, scheduling the days for evangelism, specifying the areas and local churches to each evangelist. This also includes all

380 This is the Council of the three Associations, SBAK, SABAK and WSBAK.

381 Interview with Rev. Vitoshe Swu, Director, Mission and Evangelism, WSBAK on 7 September 2004, at Akuvuto Mission Center (WSBAK). He was previously Principle of Akuvuto Bible Institute (ABI) and he is the present Executive Secretary elect of WSBAK 2005.

the departmental secretaries for church visitation and evangelism. It has its coordinating Mission Board. It is significantly engaged with outreach mission[382] other than mission activities within the WSBAK.

c. Women Department

WSBAK women department work with all the structural and administrative departments particularly WSBAK Executive Board and Executive Secretary. The Women Secretary runs the department, intimating its works to the Executive Secretary. The department has women standing committee - representatives from various areas and local churches. They are very actively involved in various projects and missionary activities. They have their resources and income from different means.

d. Youth Department

The Youth Secretary of WSBAK looks into the needs of all the youths of different local churches. The Secretary coordinates with the Executive Secretary by getting his consent in pursuing the plans and activities. The most significant activity is to organise conferences and youth camps on the requests of particular local churches and WSBAK youth camp once a year. The other programmes are youth rallies and handicraft competitions that encourage the young people to develop their skills and creativity. It has its own resources and income through various donations and membership collections.

e. Christian Education Department

WSBAK Christian Education Department is run by the Secretary who is entitled to carry out the work in corporation with the Executive Secretary. It imparts education mainly to children below 10th standard. A few exceptional local churches, for example, Sumi Baptist Town Church, concentrate a little above this level, teaching them according to their learning capacities. This department is now taking initiatives in translating materials into local settings. It has its income projects and resources accordingly.

---

382 Outreach mission will be discussed at later stage.

3. Home Mission

The activities of WSBAK (Home Mission) are flourishing tremendously in all the mentioned departments. We will discuss them under the following headings.

a. Education

At present, there are two regular educational schools (Kuhuboto Baptist School and Rev. Inache Memorial Mission School). Each has a motto "Rise and build"[383] and "Saving a Child is saving the Nation" respectively.[384] The teachers are from different communities and the children come from the surrounding places. The Headmasters of the schools with the consent of the Executive Secretary look after the educational administration. These schools not only impart secular education but also give Christian moral and ethical teaching as well, for which chaplains are appointed.[385]

WSBAK has a vital role in theological education for which it has a joint project with SBCC.[386] In the year 1993, Trinity Theological College (which was proposed on 4th June, 1992) came into existence (the college was in the WSBAK campus for few years).[387] But later it shifted to the present campus. It aims at educating people so that they manifest the Almighty God, the Son and the Holy Spirit. The graduates of this institute are expected to give preferences for ministerial appointment in Sumi Baptist Churches.[388]

---

383 School Policy/ Guideline, Baptist School: Kuhuboto, Nagaland. 1.

384 Prospectus 1998 Rev. Inache Memorial Mission School, WSBAK Centre Akuvuto, Nagaland.

385 Prospectus 1998. 1.

386 Constitution of Sumi Baptist Convention (now changed into Sumi Baptist Church Council, SBCC) 2nd edition, 1995. SBCC is also engaged in literature promotion works for the Sumi people, such as, translation and revision of the Holy Bible, Sunday school material, Pastor hand book, Hymnal and others. Besides, it has a coordinating Board of Ordination to which each association can recommend people. Further, it aims at extending an outreach mission.

387 Trinity Theological College 1st Annual report, 1993-94 presented by Principal, Trinity Theological College on 24th April 1994. 1.

388 Constitution of Sumi Baptist Convention, 9.

WSBAK attempts to provide wholesome education in all spheres of life. It is significant to take into consideration the contributions of the Sunday schools. The Sumi Baptist Church Dimapur (local church) is one of the best examples under WSBAK. The materials for the Sunday schools are in the process of translation. The Director of Christian Education Department is responsible for imparting and promoting Christian education in all the local churches under WSBAK. The activities conducted are camps, songs, dramas, skits, reciting scriptures and various other programmes for which they have competition programmes every year. They also organize joint picnics at the end of the year.

b. Evangelism and Camps

These programmes are conducted in all the departments. As the previous discussion indicates the Mission and Evangelism Director with the consent of the Executive Secretary plans out the schedule for evangelism and church visitation yearly. In this, the evangelists usually look into the church matters, attend services and present themselves available for the church members, elders and leaders to discuss the progress and development or any crisis faced within the church. The evangelists also take opportunity to visit a few homes on their visits looking into the spiritual life and other needs of the people. The activities performed in evangelism are mainly prayer, Bible studies and meetings on church concerns.

The general department has started recently Father's camp. It impacts many young and old lives through the camp experiences. These can be seen from the change in their lives and testimonies that many has confessed. Many villages and local churches wish to organise youth camps at least once a year and WSBAK (Youth Department) officially calls for youth camps and picnics. These bring tremendous change among the young people resulting in many bearing witness and becoming leaders in the society. Activities like recreation, singspiration, competition, prayers, counselling, devotion, teaching relationship between husband and wife (to the Fathers) and to the young people the relationship of man and woman above all in relationship with God, and other physical fitness concerns let them to develop healthy and to have wholesome lives. These programmes are led by the evangelists with the consent of both the Youth and Executive Secretary at the request of the local churches whenever need arises.

c. Conference, Revival Meetings and Crusades

The various local churches under WSBAK come together for youth, women and annual conferences every year to strengthen the spiritual growth and unity among the churches. Each church rounds up to minimum 30-40 and maximum 50-70 members (especially in youth conferences). The core activities that take place in these programmes are particularly yearly reports, handicrafts competitions, worship and preaching.

The revival meetings are conducted at least twice a year at different places and churches. Each church prepares its counselors, prayer warriors and people for other help before arriving at the place. Many come and experience the power of God through healings from physical and spiritual sickness such as casting out of demons and evil spirits, and healing of broken relationships with God. Apart from these programmes crusades are held depending on the churches' need. This also happens every year at the local level for about 1-3 months depending on the size of the church. Prayer is one of the most important and powerful element performed where many experience God's power in their individual and family lives.

d. Pastors' Refresher Course and Training

Pastors' Refresher course is especially for the people who are already involved in the field and churches. This programme focuses on practical teaching on church related matters (in administration, finance and management of the church and congregation and others) and meeting physical needs (work ethic and values of work), for instance, effective farming and raising resources for survival. Besides these, other physical fitness and health programmes are introduced. They are in return expected to go back and mobilize people, teaching and promoting health in all spheres of life. Women, youth and Sunday School departments also organise their departmental training every year.

Occasionally, WSBAK invites Government officers from different fields, to help and encourage them to manage their responsibilities in their own settings. The village chiefs to wives are also invited at different timings to the WSBAK Mission center and discuss the importance of their role in the improvement of the society.

e. Social Involvement

WSBAK participates in other social activities although they are almost fully engrossed in church activities and evangelism. The main involvements are their participation in peace march and rallies organised by NBCC or any other social organisation. The recent Sumi mass participation in the rally which was organised against the 'torture and murder' of one of the outfits by another of the same, is worth noting. [389] WSBAK also participated in peace march at recent incident of the twin blasts in Dimapur; Nagaland giving a tremendous move to the people to come together, to express their solidarity.[390]

Women department started the Samaritan Home project in 2002, which seeks to empower women through counselling and vocational training; it aims to share the burden with the victims of the society, the poor, the orphans, the widows and the helpless. It seeks to rescue the commercial sex workers, the less able, women substance abusers, and to give spiritual nurturing.[391] The second graduation took place on 25 May 2004 and presently there are 12 girls in the Samaritan Home. The women department also attend any training or meetings on women's empowerment or related issues, for instance, conference on "Women in Holistic Ministry", in March 2004 at Guwuhati; and "Naga Women in Search of Holistic Ministry" in 2005 at Life's Spring Corner, Dimapur. There are other programmes

389 The term 'outfit' here refers to Naga Political activists.

390 The researcher personally witnessed on 5th and 6th of October 2004.

391 Interview with Kanili Aye, Women Secretary, WSBAK on 6 October 2004. cf. WSBAK Women Department Brochure on *Samaritan Home Project* (Networking with Priscilla Center Guwahati), which aims at empowering women.

like- SHGs; 9 groups have a Federation Bank account and money was collected from them, which amounted to Rs 98,000/- in 2001.[392]

f. Financial, Material Supports and Sponsorship

Finance is one of the strongest backbones that sustain the mission work of WSBAK. The individuals, families and churches contribute generously for the expansion of God's kingdom.[393] Apart from the contributions received, WSBAK has attempted to generate its own resources through various means, e.g., rental income, fisheries and school.

Recently WSBAK contributed Rs 10,00,000, for the development of Trinity Theological College (TTC) building (with the Executive Secretary's own interest during his tenure in WSBAK), Rs 15,00,000 for the cost of library books and 2 sets of computers installed in the college. WSBAK also distributed New International Version Bibles and 12 series of books to all in the churches. It also distributed quilt to the poor and old people at some parts of villages under WSBAK through the help of CASA. WSBAK has Rs 4,00,000/- for its library development. All these large amounts of money have been directly received from foreign funds.[394]

g. Development Works

Development work initially was confined to looking after the construction work, properties, fisheries and schools. Recently new developments have taken place in education and socio-economic aspects with various projects like, weaving trainings, self employment through weaving and looming, alternative schooling programme.[395]

392 "2004 Mpe, WSBAK Women Department Kumla Yepithi," *A Report,* (46th Western Sumi Baptist Akukuhou Kuqhakulu 2004 Yepithi at Nikhekhu Baptist Akukuhou on 3rd-5th, December 2004), 25-26. Cf.

393 Sumi Christian Centenary (WSBAK), 24-25. The annual report of WSBAK presents the list of the contributors every year.

394 Phoghoto Ayemi, "Executive Kumla Yepithi/ Report 1995-2004," *A Report,* (46th Western Sumi Baptist Akukuhou Kuqhakulu 2004 Yepithi at Nikhekhu Baptist Akukuhou on 3rd-5th, December 2004), 8-9.

395 Hetovi Ayemi, Development Officer, WSBAK , Letter to the author, 4 January 2005.

There is also a Micro-Financing Scheme loan distributed to Self Help Groups and churches to uplift the society, creating employment avenues for about 3 years of duration.

There are now 5 buildings raised from various departments-general, women, and youth for WSBAK self-reliance project and schools at Akuvuto and Kuhuboto. In the future the development department is also planning to set up a fruit and food-processing unit worth Rs 1.13 crores. They look forward to the Government of India to finance the project.[396] WSBAK built residential buildings for the staff workers in mission center apart from generating income resources, building school and hostel, roads in the mission center and others.[397]

4. Outreach Mission Activities

With the sending of the first missionary to Arunachal Pradesh, WSBAK continued to work passionately among the tribes of Arunachal Pradesh and others.[398]

First of all, mission field is established on the basis of an agreement with the local people for certain period of time according to the need of the people.[399] These mission fields have permanent local evangelists, pastors and mission secretaries, working among them besides missionaries sent by WSBAK.

WSBAK invests widely for church constructions and schools. They help in all church developments, managements and programmes.[400] For instance, the report on Nepali Baptist Fellowship shows tremendous dependency on WSBAK for any church programmes and salaries for evangelists, teachers and pastors. Likewise, the other mission fields have developed structurally with financial and material support from WSBAK, which comes from individual, family and church donors under WSBAK.[401]

396 Hetovi Ayemi, Development Officer, WSBAK , Letter to the author, 4 January 2005.

397 Phoghoto Ayemi, "Executive Kumla Yepithi/ Report 1995-2004," 6-7.

398 Interview with Phughoto Ayemi.

399 Interview with Hekuto Ayemi on 2nd September 2004 at Dimapur.

400 WSBAK Mission Sutsa/News, July-August 2004. 3-5.

401 Sumi Christian Centenary (WSBAK), 24 f.

Some of the important activities are conferences, rallies, revival meetings and evangelistic camps and sometimes medical camps. They experience power encounters and healing miracles through prayers. They also occasionally involve in social ministry such as relief and charity works whenever the situation arises.[402] The educational ministry (e.g., New Era School at Namphainong) is used as an opening to proclaim the gospel. Many young people are trained and a few sponsored for theological education for future local leadership.[403]

Construction and development are seen as important aspects, constructing especially houses for missionaries and roads for easier communication. Any major construction works is entrusted to the local people and the materials are supplied to them by WSBAK. In a few cases the WSBAK staff physically help them in construction.[404] The major works are evangelism and church planting (if above 50 members) or establishing fellowship (if below 50 members). Along with evangelism the teaching happens especially in domestic affairs (cooking, washing, cleaning, dressing, gardening and family planning). They are taught English songs and local people interpret the message preached to them. The most common languages used for communication are broken Assamese, Hindi and English. Despite the language and cultural barriers the missionaries face, one can observe the progress of WSBAK mission work through their untiring commitment towards God.[405]

The general opinion received from the questionnaire analysis on 'church role' is detailed in the following-

First, with regards to the church's activities in the socio-economic context, 33% of the respondents felt that the church is busy into development projects and improvements within the church jurisdiction; conducts seminars; raises awareness on health;

402 Interview with Phughoto Ayemi.

403 Sumi Christian Centenary (WSBAK), 20, 25.

404 Interview with Phughoto Ayemi.

405 Interview with Kiho. cf. Interview with Ahoto Chophy (he was a missionary to West Kameng, Arunachal Pradesh for few years in the past. At present he is the Asst. Pastor for Sumi Baptist Town Church, Dimapur) on 27 September 2004 at Dimapur.

drugs and other social evils; reaches out to the poor and bereaved in the community; gives importance to children's religious education through Sunday schools; has occasional programmes for youth, rallies, crusades and seminar. Particularly women are practically involved in self-reliance projects, seminar and workshops at local churches. Further comments that these programmes and activities impact people's social life and spiritual growth transforming individual and society bringing peace and unity; to reduce social evils; to become more sensible, forgiving and submissive to God; and to be religiously and morally obliged to one another.

Another 50% of the respondents expressed that church does not get practically involved in the socio-economic upliftment of the people. They rather are involved in the financial improvement of the church and Associations and therefore take away the material resources in terms of cash through donations and collections from the people; in doing so, indirectly it encourages the rich and government officers to involve in corruption due to the demand laid on them in many instances. Church is much involved in teaching and preaching, and outreach mission but corrupted within. Therefore, Church hardly has any direct concern for the socio-economic upliftment programmes in the society.

The rest 17% of them expressed the grievance that church presence in the society does not produce sufficient impact on the people. Many people worship their own work and money, and with increased social evils and corruption the church is recommended to seriously think about relating their preaching and teaching to grassroots problems of the society. [406]

Second, the following opinions were received on asking whether the church involvement in socio-economic and political situation would be appropriate.

75% of the respondents felt that it is appropriate for the church to involve in the socio-economic and political context of Nagaland because the church is part of the society. Many of them commented that church is the appropriate Christian body to give positive directives to the society through preaching and teaching,

406 Source: Questionnaire; Question, 93-94.

involving in social problems, setting awareness programmes, and alleviating social evils. There were also a few who commented that church should refrain from its direct involvement in politics (apart from giving voting right) but through its teaching and guidance, the church can became a powerful influential body.

The other 15% of the people felt that church is a purely religious body therefore it should confine its ministry only to spiritual growth of the people. However, it could bring out concern on honesty, fairness and other moral values in the society.[407]

Table no. 9

The following findings are the respondents view on the over all expectation of the church role in the society during field survey. [408]

	Very Important	Less Important	Not Important	No Response
To set social awareness	45	0	48	6
To be creative agent in all social spheres of life	34	13	66	7
To involve in nation building	33	18	43	6
To work for social action	22	28	43	7
To preach	55	1	49	5
To transform	56	5	34	5
To promote Christian education for all people	34	17	43	6
To teach	44	4	46	6
To train and provide skills for survival	30	26	38	6
To evangelize	53	5	37	5

407 Source: Questionnaire; Question, 97.

408 Source: Questionnaire; Question, 98-111.

	Very Important	Less Important	Not Important	No Response
To provide tools and facility for survival	24	29	41	6
To promote opportunities for survival	23	25	50	7
To work for human right and dignity of all	33	22	38	7
To promote relevant education	63	7	23	7

The above discussion and table shows what the people perceive towards spiritual and social change. In this context the researcher is of the opinion that the church has done too little or has not raised any serious concern on the present socio-economic context of the people. It needs a serious theological and action oriented involvement in transforming the society.

The following responses were received when the respondents were asked to express their view on present mission work. Thus this will give the clear indication on the evaluation of the above table.

The majority 59% of the respondents expressed satisfaction at the ongoing mission and evangelism work taking into consideration outreach mission; spiritual awakening; increased church memberships; baptism and conversion and number of activities in relation to this purpose. 21% expressed dissatisfaction. They also commented that the church terribly neglects the social aspects of mission and there is also ample need of personal evangelism. An other 11% of the respondents were not sure of the situation. The rest 9% of the respondents did not respond to the question.[409]

Summary

The 100 years of Sumi Christianity have given a fresh impetus and enthusiastic passion for mission and church growth. Sumis have given their maximum spiritual and moral effort under various mission

409 Source: Questionnaire; Question, 95-96.

centers -SBAK, SABAK WSBAK, SBCC (the apex body of first three Associations) and existing Para church organization (URF).

Of these Associations, the focus here has been mainly on WSBAK, which is the apex body for Sumi Baptist churches within the Western part of Nagaland, Dimapur District. WSBAK with its flexibility in functions carries out the structural role and policies for the rest of the affiliated local churches. WSBAK is widely involved in mission and evangelism, outreach mission, church planting, educational ministry and partly in social ministry.

However, the author is of the opinion that WSBAK mission needs to broaden its mission horizon in all spheres of life. WSBAK has fallen short of understanding what it means to be a mission. The short sightedness of mission understanding has also hindered the Sumi Baptist Church from reflecting theologically on their mission perspectives. For this reason, the Sumi Church could formulate a strong biblical and theological approach to mission. Moreover, the missionaries and evangelists sent for mission work need to be thoroughly mission-oriented persons both by qualification and spiritually because the lack of appropriate mission approach to the context affects a great amount of work in mission progress. It is imperative for the Sumi Church to relook into the mission progress of 100 years of Christianity and redefine the mission outlook in the socio-economic context. Apart from the development work within the WSBAK and partly social concern now raised by women department, on the whole the WSBAK has not touched the socio-economic or any other social concerns in their mission involvement. Therefore, Sumi Church has severely failed to accommodate the right spirituality in mission perspective, which is depicted clearly in the division of the church, community (socially, politically and economically) and among them.

WSBAK with all its enthusiasm for mission 'outreach' has to revive according to the present changing context, which would then accomplish a wider impact of its mission consciousness. This could be the present mission approach fulfilling and reaching out within WSBAK. WSBAK needs to strengthen the concept of mission by moving away from the traditional approach of mission to the contextual issues involving practically the socio-economic context of Nagaland. As V. K. Nuh stated, the Church has an obligation to speak to the contemporary realities and the theology of truth to liberate the people from every kind of oppression participating in the story of God's act of liberation in history.[410] Hence, WSBAK by way of educating and practically involving in the relevant mission approach would help the mission to grow in future.

The following chapter will throw light on the biblical and theological relevance for furthering the mission of the Sumi Baptist Church in the socio-economic context of Nagaland. The discussion in this chapter will cover the understanding of God and His creation; and how human beings are responsible and related to God as created in His image; and the issue of justice/righteousness and prophetic role, community concerns from Old Testament and New Testament perspective; on poor, widow and rich; wealth, and human rights.

410 V. K. Nuh, "Liberty in Socio-Political Transformation," *A Paper*, presented at Sumi Baptist Centenary on 4-7 December 2003, Zunheboto.

Chapter 6

A BIBLICAL-THEOLOGICAL BASIS FOR CHURCH MISSION IN THE SOCIO-ECONOMIC CONTEXT OF NAGALAND

Introduction

Any study of a Christian view on development and participation in God's economy need to be influenced by Christian principles found in the Bible. Economic realities are not purely profane. They come from God and must be directed to God. This is because, for Christians, the Bible correctly interprets and enables a person to discover the Word of God for a particular time and context in a unique way. This discovery in turn would enable one to discern and obey the Will of God in a particular situation.

The author believes the same for the Sumi Baptist Church, that unless the basis of its mission is completely on the biblical teaching there is always a danger that church would misinterpret the relevance of God's message to the people in a context. Sumi Church has been seriously contributing to the growth of the church mission and evangelism, laying down finance, resources and time. However, the author is of the opinion that the present mission involvement shows only some part of it. Mission understanding and role could be enhanced from continuing the same old pattern in future.

Sumi Church has not discovered the biblical relevance to its context. It needs a fresh reflection and thorough biblical knowledge at present. Doing so would allow itself to rectify its mission understanding from flaws and lop sidedness. For this reason, the book presents biblical and theological insights for the Sumi Baptist Church to direct its mission perspective and to gird them to involve in the socio-economic context of Nagaland. The Naga context calls the church for transformational development of the society.

Therefore, this chapter will deal with the biblical and theological basis for mission understanding and its implications in the socio-economic context bringing out a few themes relevant.

First of all, to understand the word economy one has to look into the Greek word *oikos* which means "household." The concept of the household involves not only husband, wife and children but also an "extended family", including servants and slaves. Originally, the managing of the household was, in a typical, small household, in the hands of the wife; in a large unit, it was left in the hands of a skilled slave or freeman known as an *oikonomos,* "steward" or "household manager."[411] The ultimate extension of *oikonomia* terminology was to the largest "household" imaginable, that of the world or universe. According to Meeks, 'steward' signifies one who cared for the livelihood and survival of the household.[412]

Thus the world, its various parts, and its people were understood to have a certain order, an arrangement or regulation by God or nature. God was viewed as "administrator" managing the affairs of human beings and the whole universe in such a way so as to fit the divine design and will.[413] The understanding of God's economy takes us back to the events in the Old Testament, for example, Jonah 4:6 where God in His economy appointed a plant to provide shade to Jonah at Nineveh. Similarly, in New Testament Saul of Tarsus was called to preach Christ. All these show the arrangement and divine economy of God to save the world, as He is a divine steward who

411 John Reumann, *Stewardship & the Economy of God* (Grand Rapids: William B. Eerdmans Publishing Company, 1992), 11.

412 M. Douglas Meeks, *God the Economist: The Doctrine of God and Political Economy* (Minneapolis: Fortress Press, 1989), 76.

413 Reumann, Stewardship & the Economy of God, 13, 15.

plans and manages the salvation for creation.[414] God is the source of everything and in His divine management He cares for His household, creating, liberating and sustaining every creature to make them enjoy the fullness of life in Him.

For this we see Trinity as the model where God's greater involvement is demonstrated in, with and for the world.[415] As Martin Buber puts it, "In the beginning is relationship,"[416] from the beginning God is relational for He created all beings and things. A relationship of friendship existed between God and human: "God walked with Adam in the cool of the evening."[417] His relationship with fellow human beings is concretised in the close relationship between Adam and Eve. One is not a solitary individual, neither is God. In the ecological, economic worldview and in Christian faith, beings are individuals-in-community. The trinity, then, is central to Christian faith. It expresses the entire God-world dynamic. More basically, the trinity is about God's love for the world and the world's response.[418]

In this regard, study of the Old Testament and New Testament will enlighten one in discovering God's economy of creation throughout the ages. This will also help one to understand and relate to the rest of creation participating in God's economy of creation. The following is an attempt to uncover the biblical truths and their relevance for Naga context today.

---

414 Reumann, *Stewardship,* 28, 31-32.

415 Sallie McFague, *Life Abundant: Rethinking Theology and Economy for a Planet in Peril* (Minneapolis: Fortress Press, 2000), 143. Each of the three Persons in the Godhead has his own part to perform in governing, sustaining, and directing the entire universe toward its appointed end. To the Father the creeds ascribe the work of creation; to the Son the work of human beings' redemption; and to the Holy Spirit the work of sanctification.

416 Cited in Fague, *Life Abundant,* 143. cf. Carl S. Meyer and Herbert T. Meyer, eds., *The Caring God: Perspectives on Providence* (London: Concordia, 1973), 21.

417 Desmond A. D' Abreo, *Turning the Tide of Injustice* (Mangalore: Margaret D'Abreo, 1991), 5.

418 Ibid.

I. God in/and Creation

In creation, God made His purpose known to human beings. God created nature and human beings and worked through history to bring His creation to fulfilment. Part of His providence is the gift of freedom and creativity.[419] The things of nature are, in themselves, not complete, but await human's work to give them their full significance in the pattern of the universe in submission to the plan of God. Thus, their task is to develop all aspects of human life and activities in such a way that the whole of the human race becomes a hymn to the Creator, and human themselves grow in the process. Human beings created in His image, received the mandate to govern the world with justice and holiness and acknowledge the Creator, the Lord of all.[420]

1. God the Creator

God the 'Creator' protects His creation. It signifies God's loving relationship with His creation. The creation is about God's total graciousness and the gift of life in total commitment to the life.[421] The Scriptures clearly depict that the created world is His handiwork and He controls it determining its beginning and end as the apostle Paul puts it "From Him, through Him and to Him are all things" (Rom. 11:36). All created things flow from the will of Him who commands the morning and causes the dawn to know its place (Job 38:12).[422]

Thus, God is neither an absentee Landlord nor a watchmaker God, but is involved in an ongoing creation. Within the all-encompassing horizon of creation as household, the economy of God, most briefly put, is the distribution of God's righteousness.[423] This doctrine of God as the sovereign Creator and Sustainer of all existence is one of the foundation stones of the theology of Stewardship,

419 Angelo Fernandes, *Towards Peace with Justice: The Role of Religion Today* (New Delhi: Indian Social Institute, 1991), 82.

420 Ibid., 82.

421 Fague, *Life Abundant,* 145.

422 Carl S. Meyer and Herbert T. Meyer, eds., *The Caring God: Perspectives on Providence* (London: Concordia, 1973), 21.

423 Gerhard Von Rad, *Old Testament Theology,* Vol. 1. (New York: Harper & Row, 1962), 370.

which is inseparably connected with Creator's sovereignty and ownership.[424]

In creation the aspect of work has an important part in God's economy. As it is a divinely instituted element, work becomes an integral part of human existence. [425] The work of God as a Developmentalist is to be reflected in the work of the human being as developmentalist for God and the creation. To be a human means to be sent as God's developmentalist to live and work for God's will for the creation.[426] The Genesis creation account's twin injunction 'to work' (change and develop) on creation and 'to take care of it' seem to capture entirely the central meaning of the term 'sustainable development' when used with reference to the natural environment.[427] Work is also viewed positively as the ordained means by which people, under God, are to develop the created order and provide for their basic needs (2 Thess 3:8,10).

Emil Brunner summed it up concisely when he described work as "science of human conduct as it is determined by divine conduct,"[428] and when it is applied in the sphere of environmental care it means that in the same way as God is just, loving and merciful,

---

424 T. A. Kantonen, *A Theology for Christian Stewardship* (Philadelphia: Fortress Press, 1956), 31.

425 Richard S. Gnanakan, *Work in God's World: Insights into a Theology of Work* (Bangalore: Theological Book Trust, 2003), 41 cf. Gerhard Von Rad, *Old Testament Theology*, Vol. 1. (New York: Harper & Row, 1962), 370; Kantonen, 31, 41. "It is noticeable as well in the changing definition of "work" itself. Over most of the past, work has been the universal prerequisite of social continuity, which crowded out much else of life. Even in the most advanced nations today, work continues to be an inescapable requirement for the majority, although its demands have been incomparably lightened over years. This importune and exhausting predominance of work is certain to be markedly diminished in the not too distant future. The discussion would continue towards the end of the writing."

426 Meeks, *God the Economist*, 89.

427 Deryke Belshaw, "Socio-economic Theology and Ethical Choices in Contemporary Development Policy: an outline of Biblical Approaches to Social Justice and Poverty Alleviation," *Transformation* 14/1 (January-March, 1997), 6.

428 Cited in John Drane, "Defining A Biblical Theology of Creation," *Transformation* 10/2 (April-July, 1993), 8.

these same qualities should characterize human relationships to the creation.

The key Bible teaching on this subject is that work is a positive gift, and a God-given context for relationships. As a promise of blessing and fruitfulness human being are to work the outcome of good management or be stewards over animate and in-animate nature. These truths are distorted by mere materialism. It is true that human beings work in order to eat. The difficulty arises when one takes work as a path to conspicuous consumption. No doubt, today people have taken this for granted in the consumerist and exploitative sense. This gives a concrete base for Sumi Church to rethink its creator's relationship to Naga community. It also calls for divine management of Naga socio-economy and to view critically its essentials of work aspect in response to God's created image in us.

2. God the Sustainer

The best place to start is the Old Testament view, Sustainer is with the creation account itself. God himself set a pattern of work in the six days of creative activity. There is an understanding of work in its loftiest sense, and that is creative activity. God has a similar role for humans as well.[429]

Most of the texts emphasize that God with or without human's help provides sustenance. The labourers in the Old Testament had the right to demand every day a wage for their work (Lev. 19:13; Deut. 24:14f; Mal. 3:5; cf. 2kgs 12:14ff; Jer 22:13ff; Ezek. 29:18ff). In Deut 20:5-7, the thought that one is to live on one's work is specifically prominent. Here work does bring results, but the worker himself is not allowed to enjoy them, as is normally his right. It is obvious that work yields bread or other reward (2Sam 9:10; 1Kgs 11:28; Isa 5:1ff; Amos 4:6ff; 5:11; Job 4:5; Prov 12:11; 14:23; 24:27; 28:19; Eccles 10:18).[430]

The specific principle is presented often in proverbs: "He who works his land will have abundant food..."(12:11; 28:19). It is also

429 Gnanakan, *Work in God's World*, 41.

430 Goran Agrell, *Work, Toil and Sustenance* (Sweden: Verbum Hakam Ohlssons, 1976), 25-26.

presented by the writer of Ecclesiastes: "so I say that there is nothing better for a man than to enjoy his work, because that is his lot..." (3:22). This has been planned since the creation of the universe and is God's plan for us today.[431]

God the sustainer is a further elaboration of how the Creator and liberator God operates to insure planetary well-being. This God cares about just and sustainable planetary management, so that all creatures may flourish.[432] The combination of the inherently life-sustaining capacities of God's created world was to be vastly enhanced when allied to humankind's God-given creative abilities. Hence, the creation story envisages the 'filling' or peopling of the earth without damaging it (Gen. 1:28; 2:15).[433]

The provision of God generally does not come by magic or miracles, but rather through productive economic activity. Abraham often stated that "God will provide", and this is seen in animal husbandry and farming. When God called him to Canaan, or even when in trouble with the Egyptians, he said, "God will provide." The provision of God for His people in the Old Testament is generally through agricultural production that requires work.

Certain Old Testament texts speak of sustenance without work.[434] Then sustenance is a gift from the Lord to the people, or to a certain group within the people Ex.16 is a typical example, telling of the feeding of Israel in the wilderness. The people grumbled and wished they were still sitting down to pots of meat in Egypt, i.e., they preferred bondage, if they only had food. But the Lord provides the people with meat and bread (16:11f). They gather from it, as much as they need (16:15). But none is to gather for tomorrow (16:19).

---

431 David Befus, "Discovering a Role in God's Provision: Sustainable Economic Development for the Church and Poor People," in *The Local Church in a Global Era: Reflections for a New Century*, edited by Max L. Stockhouse, et al., (Michigan: William E.Eerdman Publishing Company, 2000), 50.

432 Fague, *Life Abundant*, 146.

433 Deryke Belshaw, "Socio-economic Theology and Ethical Choices in Contemporary Development Policy: an outline of Biblical Approaches to Social Justice and Poverty Alleviation," *Transformation* 14/1 (January-March, 1997), 6.

434 Agrell, *Work, Toil and Sustenance*, 24.

The Lord miraculously without the work of the people here provides sustenance, meat and bread.

According to other texts, God gives sustenance without work especially to certain groups, the poor and those at the bottom of the social scale. The motivation behind is the sabbatical year in Ex. 23:10f for example, is that a break of one year from sowing and harvesting allows the poor to gather their living from that which they did not sow.

It can perhaps be interpreted to mean that the earth itself brings forth something for them to eat (Lev. 19:9f. and Deut. 14:28). According to Lev. 25:5-7, all in Israel are to live on that which the land's sabbatical yields. God through His land provides sustenance for men, the master, slaves, day labourers, and even beasts; and He does it without their working.[435]

In the providence of God, Israel was called to a new future that was set forth in terms of the suffering Servant. His progress is not marked by conquest and glory, but by quiet labour, infinite patience, and suffering. His suffering was both exemplary and vicarious. Glory lay beyond that ignominy and agony, which was to be part of His mission.[436]

The researcher understands the basic blessings of God in creation as God's sustenance on humanity and the rest of the creation. God's care is demonstrated in sustaining His creations with every basic need. The insights from the discussion show no boundary in His dealing with His creation. God's providence is assured through human labour or work to sustain them and also God's gracious providence sanctioned to the poor who do not engaged in work or possessed the resources. This draws the theological meaning and practicality of the human needs materially in all stages of life. It insists on human input to labour and to produce and be a life source to other creation. This challenge comes to Sumi Church to become a co-creator and sustainer to Naga community in developing the ethics of socio-economic life in the context. In this case church should

435 Agrell, *Work, Toil and Sustenance*, 24.

436 Meyer and Meyer, ed., *The Caring God*, 32.

become a facilitator, and motivate the whole Naga community to have better commitment to life.

3. God the Liberator

God the Liberator underscores that God is there for us no matter what. God as saviour or liberator continues the work of God as creator who preserves human beings with His love from any evil acts that separate them from Him.[437] In the Old Testament God reveals Himself to us as the liberator of the oppressed and the defender of the poor from an oppressive social structure, demanding from human beings faith in Him and justice towards man's neighbour. This liberation is simultaneously political, economic, religious and spiritual.

The liberating intervention of God in the Exodus is the fundamental experience that was repeated and deepened in the conquest of Canaan, in the ups and downs of national life and even in the deliverance from exile in Babylon. God the Liberator demonstrated as always Emmanuel, 'God with us', in their exodus from Egypt. The significant fact is that Israel never sees itself as autonomous or dependent on any other nation. Its existence as people and its calling is to recognize that it belongs and is accountable to Yahweh, the one who is present there, accompanying it on its pilgrim way.[438]

It has often been stressed in the past that the God of the Bible is revealed principally in the events and in the unfolding of the people's history. Again and again it has been a story of struggle for liberation from oppression, exploitation, and injustice. The Old Testament God is recognized as one who has taken sides in that struggle- the side of the poor and the exploited. God first spoke and was manifested in the lives and history of these people as the one who stood by them in their suffering and who acted on their behalf in delivering them

---

437 Fague, *Life Abundant,* 146.

438 Philip Potter, "The Global Economic system in Biblical Perspéctive," *The Ecumenical Movement Tomorrow,* edited by Mac Reuver, et al., (Geneva: WCC, 1993), 21.

from the slavery of Egypt.[439] The God of Israel continues to put His liberating action into effect through the Judges (Judg. 2:16-18; 4:12-16) and Kings (1 Sam. 8:7-22; 10: 17-24).[440]

Naim Ateek sees liberation and hope for the Palestinian Christians in Psalms 42 and 43, which can be used as the real cry of a refugee. Further Ateek describes how the psalmist apparently has been forced out of his homeland. Living as a refugee in Jordan or Lebanon remembering happier times, friends and neighbours, the worshipping congregations- especially the great feasts, when people celebrated together with excitement, with songs and praises to God. He also talks about how the Psalmist reminisces about his own participation in these joyous festivities and found trusting God as the only better future, hope in God, the only medicine and cure for a depressed spirit.[441]

In Psalm 43, the Psalmist is praying for God's vindication of his rights, recognizing that injustices have been done, that he is dealing with ungodly, deceitful, and unjust people. He asks God to remove his troubles and restore him to his country. His joy and hope will remain in God. Thus, for Palestinian Christians these Psalms carry special significance because God hears the cry of the oppressed. In the midst of a refugee life and in the heart of a life of exile, God is there with them.[442]

The author brings out the similar situation of the migrants in Nagaland in comparison with the life of exile as also discussed in the previous chapter. The Nagas have taken these people for granted, they are used basically for manual labours and domestic work. Generally, many of them are economically exploited and manipulated for individual benefits. The church has not touch the life's of these people least along with masses they are deprived and less cared. The church

---

439 Anthony R. Ceresko, *The Old Testament: A Liberative Perspective* (Mumbhai: St. Pauls, 2001), 405.

440 Thomas Punnapadam, *Justice as Spirituality: The Challenge Posed by the Synodal Document Justice in the World* (Bangalore: Kristu Jyoti Publications, 1991), 152-153.

441 Naim Stifan Ateek, *Justice, and Only Justice: A Palestinian Theology of Liberation* (Marynoll: Orbis Books, 2001), 90.

442 Ateek, *Justice, and Only Justice: A Palestinian Theology of Liberation*, 90-91.

in some ways is reaching out to the neighbouring people through evangelism. Instead majority of the respondents' response during survey reveals their negative attitude to migrants and outsiders living in Nagaland. Thus, the issue is raised in regard to their interference in Naga economy and social life. The researcher believes that the Sumi Church should work towards rescuing of these people socio-economically and spiritually through playing a liberative role model and mobilising the Nagas to integration of life.

In other words, God identified himself with humanity to give liberation to the poor (from poverty), to the oppressed, the handicapped (like the blind). The reason lies in the fact that God is on the side of the marginalized (Lk 4:18-19). There are lots of passages in the OT (Ex. 22:25; Lev. 25:35-37; Deut. 23:19; 15:1) where Jews were commanded not to take interest on the loans taken by the poor and to cancel the debts of the poor every seventh year. In the year of restoration (50th year) all property that the poor had sold shall be restored to the original owner or his descendants and anyone who has been sold as a slave shall be returned to his family (Lev. 25:6-17).[443]

God's judgment is in favour of the oppressed giving them rights (Ps. 103:6; 140:112; 146:9); God's concern is in doing right where the commandment was set not to cheat the poor and the needy (Deut. 22;24:14); not to deny justice to the poor when they appear in the court (ex. 23:6); not to mistreat the Gentiles and foreigners (Ex. 22:21; 23:9; Lev. 19:33,34); not to mistreat widows and orphans etc., (Ex. 22:21; 22:22-24; 23:9; Ps. 22:21; Lev. 19:33,34; Ps. 82: 2-4; Jer. 22:3).[444]

God's continued presence as liberator is seen best in Israel history of Exodus. God's continues to defend poor from oppressive structures in spite of their sin against His graciousness towards them. Israel was a select group for God's continued liberative work. The special jubilee and sabbatical provision granted them, the right to

443 Gustavo Gutirrez, *A Theology of Liberation* (New York: Orbis Books, 1973), 360.

444 Robinson, "A New Economic Order: The Challenge of the Biblical Jubilee," in *A Vision for Man,* edited by S. Amirtham (Madras: CLS, 1978), 366.

life. Thus, God's liberative act unfolds His relationship to humanity, restoration of life and commitment, protection and security, and His immanent presence with His people in all life circumstances. This leads the Sumi Church to realize the presence of God in the midst of similar situation of the Naga community such as, the Naga political struggles, injustices, social evils, division and all sorts of threat to human rights in bringing restoration and protection in all spheres of life- politically, socially, economically and spiritually.

This whole section of discussion challenges the Sumi Baptist Church to take up God's trusted stewardship as a co-creator in His creation. In the Naga context where relationship and commitment is devalued, social and ethical values dismissed, economic and political situation corrupted, religiously and spiritually bankrupt, and freedom is misused at all levels here the Sumi Baptist Church finds a relevant message to help redeem the Nagas from all these situations. The importance of divine economy covers the spiritual realms in saving people, liberating in accordance to His divine management seeking human response to Him. God's continuing gift of freedom and creativity to human beings in total commitment to life is what God required. In other words, God demands the commitment to life and growth to enjoy the fullness of life. God's self revelation throughout history shows His love implying faith and justice, and continued liberation and redemption. Thus, God's constant revelation in human history declares His relationship to humanity so that human beings might reflect the same to the world.

II. God as Justice/Righteousness

Justice/Righteousness is a very significant basic Old Testament concept. It is a standard of human's relation to God; relationship to fellow being; and also relationship to the animals and environment.

G. Von Rad writes: "There is absolutely no concept in the OT with so central a significance for all relationships of human life as that of *sedaqah* (justice/righteousness)."[445] The centrality as well as the richness of the biblical statements on justice is the very reason

445 Cited in John R. Donahue, "Biblical Perspectives on Justice," in *The Faith that Does Justice*, edited by John C. Haughey (New York: Paulist Press, 1977), 68.

why it is difficult to give a "biblical definition" of justice. God may be defined as the God of justice because from every point of view, justice is the central theme of the OT. At the same time it is impossible to give a biblical definition of justice, as it is a "protean and multifaceted term."[446]

1. Definition of Justice/Righteousness

The Hebrew word *sedeqah* would be righteousness, which "represents an extraordinarily rich and varied group of concepts." Very clearly Righteousness has far wider connotations than moral innocence. It is totally incomprehensible outside the context of a relationship. Other terms like *hesed* (steadfast love, loyalty), *rahamin* (mercy) and *emeth* (fidelity) are all almost identfiable. In Deutero-Isaiah and the Psalms, justice and salvation appear quite frequently together. The justice of God also includes the wrath of God, which is by no means vindictive, but an integral part of restoration and aimed at the conversion of the sinner.[447]

According to O. J. Baab, "The Hebrew word *sadaq* and the related word *sedaqa* carry the idea of rightness, deliverance, or victory, depending upon the circumstances in each case." Neither the English word "justice", nor the German word "*Gerechtigkeit*" is adequate to bring out the full meaning of these words.[448]

The *hiphil* form the Hebrew root *sdq* [449] (Gk *dikaioun* means, "to be righteous" or "to be just" signifies "to justify someone" or "to declare somebody righteous)." The masculine noun *sedeq* and the feminine noun *sedaqah* (both translated *dikaiosune* in Greek), with no significant difference in meaning, are rendered "righteousness", "justice", "right" in English. The adjective *saddiq* (Gk *dikaios*) means

446 Punnapadam, *Justice as Spirituality*, 154.

447 Ibid.

448 Cited in Robinson, Gnana "Justice in the Old Testament," in *Where is Justice?* edited by Frenz, Albercht, (Madurai: Tamilnadu Theologically seminary, 1976), 1. (This article is a part of papers presented at the Dialogue- Seminar "The Understanding of Justice" held at Tamil Nadu Theological Seminary, Arasaradi, Madurai on 14th and 15th August, 1976).

449 J. Scara K., "Social Justice in the Old Testament," *Biblebhashyam* 1/3 (September, 1978), 163.

"righteous" or "just." The Septuagint almost invariably renders the Hebrew *sdq* and its derivatives by *dikaioun* and its cognates.

The Hebrew *sdq* is so rich that LXX coins other Greek terms to convey the appropriate meaning according to the context. For example *sdq* is rendered *amemptos* (blameless, faultless) at Job 22,3; *katharos* (pure) at Job 4, 17; *alethes* (true) at Is. 41, 26; *pistos* (faithful) at Job 17, 9; *eusebes* (pious, reverent) at Prov, 12, 12.

It is instructive to note the various terms RSV has employed to translate the Hebrew *sdq*: vindication: (Ps 103, 6; Jer 51, 10), deliverance (9Is 46, 12; Mic 7,9), saving deeds (I Sam 12, 70), saving help (Ps 40, 10), righteous help (Ps 71, 24), salvation (Job 33, 26), equity (2 Sam 8, 15), right (Is 5, 23), uprightness (Jer 4,2), truth (Ps 52,3), triumph (Judge 5, 11), victory (Ps 48, 10; Is 41, 2), prosperity (Prov 8, 18) etc.

The RSV has used various terms, with considerable difference in meaning, to translate the Hebrew *sdq*. This shows the depth and richness of 'righteousness' for a Hebrew. Scholars are of the opinion that *sdq* acquired this depth in denotation in the course of the Israelites' history. In the final stage of this historical development, righteousness is identified with salvation.[450]

In Arabic, the cognate word of *tsedek* is *sidq*, "truthfulness." From the same Arabic root, *sadiq* means friend, that is, "one who speaks the truth to you;" *siddiq* is a pious person, a person who lives in truthfulness before God; and *sadaq* is almsgiving, which is considered rewarding for the giver, (Deu. 24:12-13).[451]

Thus, the root *sdq* is derived from Arabic and it means, "to be straight" or "firm. The word *sadaq* could have come very easily to be used as a figure for that which is, or ought to be, firmly established, successful and enduring in human affairs. According to *Ringgren,* "*saqaq* and *sedaqa* refer to the divine order that regulates the world and the universe."[452]

450 J. Scara K., "Social Justice in the Old Testament," *Biblebhashyam* 1/3 (September, 1978), 164.

451 Ateek, *Justice and Only Justice,* 142.

452 Cited in Robinson, "Justice in the Old Testament," in *Where is Justice?* 2.

2. Justice/Righteousness as Covenant

The righteousness of God lies primarily in His covenantal rule in fellowship with His people. Righteousness as the very essence of God is completely alien to legal and juridical systems with which a modern reader automatically links the word justice. The ideas of juridical righteousness can be understood only in the context of the covenant relationship that exists between Yahweh and Israel.[453]

"Righteousness" in the Old Testament means the fulfilment of the demands of a relationship, whether that relationship is with human beings or with God. Each person is set within a multitude of relationships: king with people, judge with complainants, priests with worshipers, common man with family, tribesman with community and all with God. In New Testament (Lk. 1:6) the term righteous is explained as walking in all commandments and ordinances of the Lord, blameless. So also, the way of justice means life lived according to the commandments of God (Mt 21:32; 2Pet 2:21). In this sense the just human is one who fulfils the commandments of God.[454]

Biblical justice relates to power (Ps. 71:18-19) and love (Ezek 34:16, 23-24; Ps. 146: 7). Justice aptly focuses on impartiality, desert, and conformity with fixed and definable standards. God's intention is for people to live, not in isolation, but in society affirming the dignity of God's creatures and God's justice for them, which requires life, freedom, and sustenance.[455] Martin Luther King states that power without love is reckless and abusive; and love without power is sentimental and anaemic.[456] And so power at its best is love implementing the demands of justice. For instance, in the story of Exodus and Judges God acted in history as the one who uses His power to see that justice is done.

---

453 Punnapadam, *Justice as Spirituality,* 155.

454 "The Righteousness required of the Followers of Christ (Mt ch. VII)," *Bible Bhashyam an Indian Biblical Quarterly* 10/2 (June, 1984), 132.

455 C. Calvin Beisner, "Justice and Poverty: Two Views Contrasted," *Transformation* 10/1 (January-April, 1993), 16.

456 Cited in Stephen Mott and Ronald J. Sider, "Economic Justice: A Biblical Paradigm," *Transformation* 17/2 (April, 2000), 53.

Since God is a God of justice, the beings created in His image must treat each other with justice. Injustice to human being is desecration of God. "Whosoever mocked the poor blasphemed His Maker" (Pr 17:5). On the other hand, "He that is gracious unto the poor lend unto the Lord" (Pr 9:17). For instance, Jewish tradition went so far as to state "the poor man does more for the rich man than the rich man for the poor man."[457] Throughout the Bible, injustice is constantly identified as failure to relieve the plight of the poor (Dt. 27: 19). The concern for the defenceless in society is not a command designed simply to promote social harmony, but is rooted in the nature of Yahweh himself who is defender of the oppressed. There are a series of texts, again from different traditions, which portray Yahweh in this role (Ex. 22:21-22; Dt. 14: 29, cf Dt. 15:7; 10:18; Ps. 82:3-4; 103:6 cf. Ps. 140:12; 146:7). [458] Thus, Israel's fundamental experience is of the righteous God who sets His people free, not because they are mighty or worthy, but because He loves them and chooses them as His own.[459]

The exodus event is one among the many experience of the Israelites with a matchless significance. It was the exodus experience that gave birth to Israel as a nation (Dt. 6: 20-24; 26: 5-6; Jos. 24: 2-213). The Old Testament, Ex. 3, 7-9; 6,6-7, maintains that God's act of freeing His people from oppression in exodus played a primordial role in the entire revelation of the Old Testament. Yahweh's revelation of himself as the one true God proceeds through his manifestation of himself as sole Saviour and liberator.[460] Many of the psalms dwell on the praise of the power of Yahweh that was revealed in the historic act of liberation (78, 106, 135). Even after centuries the event, the liturgy in the temple of Solomon continued to center on the exodus event, culminating in the great solemnity

457 Richard G. Hirsch, "Judaism in Pursuit of Economic Justice," in *Contemporary Religion and Social Responsibility,* edited by Norbert and Brockman S. M. (New York: ALBA. House, 1973), 289.

458 John R. Donahue, "Biblical Perspectives on Justice," in The Faith that Does Justice, edited by John C. Haughey (New York: Paulist Press, 1977), 73-74.

459 Brian A. Wren, *Education for Justice* (Marynoll: Orbis, 1977), 45.

460 Philip Land, Justice in the World: An Overview (Pontifical Commission Justice & Peace: Vatican City, 1972), 15-16.

of the Passover.[461] Thus although the ultimate meaning of Yahweh's covenant with Israel is the liberation fulfilled in Christ, the exodus event also has its own meaning.

When Israel forgets the covenant it is the prophets, most explicitly Amos, Isaiah and Jeremiah, who proclaim to Israel that their fidelity to the covenant Lord must be manifested in concern for the poor and the oppressed. When Israel settles in Canaan, the prophets shock her leaders by declaring that Yahweh loves justice more than he loves Israel. When the rich oppress the poor, when merchants give short change or follow market economics by putting up prices in time of scarcity, when judges take bribes from the rich and refuse to hear the poor man's case, and when the kings make unjust laws and publish burdensome decrees, they condemn such injustices as a breach of the Covenant.[462]

Amos, one of the earliest and strongest prophets, calls Israel to return to justice (Am. 2:7; 5:11). Amos culminates his judgment against the rich and exploiters of his day by proclaiming that their injustice negates their worship of Yahweh (Am. 5:21; 4).

Isaiah 58 begins with a cry to declare to the people their transgression. The people assemble for worship and ask of Yahweh righteous judgments (Is. 58:2). They come in fasting and prayer, but hear no answer (Is.58: 3). The answer of Yahweh appears in verses 4-7. The cultic fast, which the people choose, is a charade because "in the day of your fast you seek your own pleasure and oppress your workers". In verse 8 the request of the people for "righteous judgments" is then answered.[463]

The researcher sees the prophetic strong stance against the context. The church in Nagaland should be encouraged to have the same attitude to oppose anything that is oppressive and unrighteous. The religiosity of the people does not conform to wholesome spirituality unless the heart of the problem is identified. There is a serious covenantal relationship break ups among the Nagas and with God which the church may need to elevate its calling to commitment

---

461 Punnapadam, *Justice as Spirituality*, 152.

462 Wren, Education for Justice, 47.

463 Donahue, "Biblical Perspectives on Justice", 75-76.

for covenantal restoration. The Sumi Church has to move out from the pulpit communication to intimate relationship with the Naga social world. In doing so the church will be effective in future.

Thus, the above discussion makes concrete that justice is 'fidelity' to the demands of a relationship. The people cannot be just before the covenant God, they cannot know or worship Him, when they do not heed His call to take the cause and defend the rights of the poor and oppressed in the community. This obligation is to be genuinely and effectively concerned for those on the fringes of society. It is so sublime and sacred that it unconditionally supersedes every other religious and cultic demand (Is. 58: 1-9; Ezek. 33: 14-19).

Further the righteousness of God in the Old Testament cannot be understood in a purely ethical or legal sense. God's righteousness is not known on the basis of set norms or codes of conduct. In Him, righteousness becomes all embracing world-order. Taking its root-meaning seriously, we may say, preserves a given situation or world order firm and established. It does not speak of a conduct, which is of universal application and of permanent value. All ethical norms are subject to the time and the context in which one lives. However, the righteousness of God is that which preserves given order on the basis of the norms to which it is subjected.

3. Justice/Righteousness an overview from the Bible

Justice is not equality or distribution of resources, but is rather the restoration of right relationships.[464] The preaching and life of Jesus confers a new and definitive depth on the Old Testament requirement and the centrality of the obligation to observe Justice in inter-personal relationships. Jesus brings the new righteousness, the greater justice. For Jesus the first commandment is the love of God. The second is love of one's neighbour as oneself. Thus, Jesus condenses the precepts of Justice in the Old Testament into a new and radical formula: "So, whatever you wish that men would do to you, do so to them; for this is the Law and the Prophets" (Mt. 7:12).[465]

464 D' Abreo, *Turning the Tide of Injust*, 6.

465 Punnapadam, *Justice as Spirituality*, 162-163.

God works for justice, i.e., restoration to community. As seen in the Jubilee year (Lev. 25:35-36), the poor are described as being on the verge of falling out of the community because of their economic distress.[466] Therefore, the conditions provided by justice are only a beginning. The receiving individuals have responsibility according to their ability to transform the condition into the reality of good life.

In this sense, righteousness goes beyond justice. It carries the meaning of kindness, compassion, and mercy. Therefore, to talk about the God's righteousness means His compassion and mercy. Injustice is condemned biblically not because the law has been broken, because a merciful God is flouted and people are hurt. This aspect of God's compassion is best illustrated in the story of Cain and Abel. Cain was condemned after he killed his brother Abel, not because he broke a law, but because his brother's blood was crying out of the ground. According to the demands of strict justice, Cain could have killed. Instead, he is spared by the compassion of God and even protested.[467]

In Matthew Jesus is a teacher of the new Righteousness. Matthew qualifies new righteousness with mercy, which reaches out to the marginal ones in the world. The parable of the unmerciful servant (Mt. 18:23-34) shows justice qualified by mercy "Should you not have had mercy on your fellow servants, as I had mercy on you?" (v. 33). Though on one level the parable seems to be an exhortation to forgiveness, on another level it is a parable of justice qualified by mercy. In the context of Matthew's theology the new law of the Christian community is that the just are those who meet the demands of fellow men because they live in a covenant relationship with a lord who has given them mercy.[468]

In the Hebrew Bible war is a dominant theme. Conflict and bloodshed receive twice the attention given to peace. The need for peace and the hope of peace were always there, "awaiting the right voice to bring them to awareness." Thus, the spiritual greatness

---

466 Stephen Charles Mott, "The Partiality of Biblical Justice," *Transformation* 10/1 (January, 1993), 25.

467 Ateek, *Justice and Only Justice*, 142.

468 Donahue, "Biblical Perspectives on Justice", 103-104.

and genius of the Hebrew Bible is found (in) its awareness of the relationship among peace, righteousness, justice, salvation and God.[469]

Peace has been used again and again to indicate shalom which obviously is part of humanness in all stages, forms and manifestations of life; it has remained unchanged like 'life', 'thirst' or 'joy.'"[470] Shalom always means the intactness or wholeness or integrity of a community. In shalom, each person enjoys justice, enjoys his or her rights and dwell at peace in all his or her relationships with God (Isa.2: 2-3), with self, with fellows (Isa.32: 16-17) and other creatures and with nature (Isa. 11:6-8).[471] Thus, peace (*shalom /eirene*) is the opposite of chaos like war and famine; and of internal chaos like lust, greed, fear, despair, anger and confusion. The peace perspectives of the bible are summed up in the prayer Jesus taught us. Invoking the God of peace, Creator of the world, as our Father amounts to embracing humankind as a family to be cherished and served.[472]

John Donahue summarizes Luke's special presentation of Jesus in the form of an OT prophet who takes the side of the widow (7:11-17; 18:1-8), the stranger in the land (10:29-37; 17:16), and those on the margin of society (14:12-13, 21)."[473] Thus, peace is actually to live the way of God's kingdom, brought near in Jesus. The fact that peace brought about by Jesus is to be understood eschatologically is made clear in John. On the other hand, this *eirene* is granted at Jesus' resurrection (20:19, 1, 26), the eschatological divine act par

---

469 Samuel Rayan, "Peace: Biblical Perspectives," *Jnanadeepa Pune Journal of Religious Studies* 4/2 (2002), 109.

470 Ulrich Duchrow & Gerhard Liedke, *Shalom: Biblical Perspective on Creation, Justice and Peace.* (Geneva: WCC Publications, 1989), 113.

471 Nicholas Wolterstorff, *Until Justice and Peace Embrace* (Grand Rapids: William B. Eerdmans Publishing Company, 1983), 68-69.

472 Rayan, "Peace: Biblical Perspectives," 112, 118.

473 John R. Donahue, *The Gospel in Parable: Metaphor, Narrative, and Theology in the Synoptic Gospels* (Philadelphia: Fortress, 1988), 175. cf. Sang Chang "Justice of Jubilee in Luke: Bible Study," *Reformed World* 45/1 and 2 (March-June 1995), 3-6, http://www.warc.ch/dp/rw9512/12.html (15 March 2003).

excellence.[474] Failing this, God's justice means judgment, for God's peace and justice confront and overcome evil.

The whole issue of justice/righteousness is the core concern of God that continues with the prophets and is fulfilled in Jesus in the New Testament. God himself was just to the people of Israel and acted with love and mercy liberating and redeeming them from all sort of oppressions and at such time of their exodus. God is seen as restorer of broken covenant between him and human beings and the rest of the creation. Different scholars have varied opinion on understanding the term justice, however the basic commonality in their meaning centres on both vertical and horizontal relationship. Justice is a paradoxical in meaning which concerns wrath of God upholding integral restoration and conversion of an individual or community. It seeks a rightful and faithful conduct to society leading to deliverance (saving) and victory. This then, is the righteousness equally found in covenantal fellowship with God and people, and human to human. Righteousness confirms and preserves the norms or order at the given situation. Relationship is the implication of freedom, sustenance, power, love, and caring of humanity that promotes harmony in the society. Of all of these the state of being in peace/*shalom* precedes justice meaning without peace no justice.

Therefore, true religious faith on God is qualified when justice is practiced and known. Justice is not a claim for equality of resources or status in strict sense (which could be a misunderstood idea in today's context) rather a restoration of right relationships. In Jesus the new righteousness and greater justice is revealed through God's love to humanity. Accordingly an individual's capacity and ability is demanded in working towards restoration and transformation of better reality. Injustice and social evils against humanity were condemned not because the covenant was broken but God is just and people were hurt from various forms. They were oppressed, deprived of rights, murdered and neglected. As a result the spiritual plight of the people was lost.

474 Gennadios Limouris ed., *Justice, Peace and the Integrity of Creation* (Geneva: WCC Publications, 1990), 121.

The researcher believes that it is imperative for the Sumi Baptist Church to reconsider this issue of justice in the context of Nagaland. The situation is so severe that people at all levels are in need of justice. Nagas are socio-politically corrupted and divided, divided in religious matters and among the church leaders, ethnic clashes and tribalism, economically crushed, mentally tortured and affected, and the moral disintegration and consequence of social evils. The Church needs to work for Justice of God to intervene in Naga context. This will bring theological relevance to the mission of the Church to participate in response to the biblical teaching bringing into light the problems and prospect of Nagas in future. It would also help the Nagas to pull together and become a community of justice.

III. The Significance of Communal Living

The most significant symbolic example of communal living can be drawn from Sabbatical year (e.g., God's concern for the poor and injustice) mentioned both in Exodus and Deuteronomic law code. The well-known texts are Exodus 21 and 23 and Deuteronomy 15 (on the sabbatical year) and in Leviticus 25 (on the sabbatical year and Jubilee) stem from different stages of development. For instances, (1) the most original notion seems to be of a Sabbath rest for the land and its people. In the sabbatical year the land must be left fallow (Ex. 23:10-11; Lev. 25:11). (2) Israelites reduced to poverty who had sold themselves as slaves to their countrymen must be released in the seventh year (Ex. 21:2; Lev 25: 40f). (3) In the Sabbath year debts must be remitted (Deu.15: 2). (4) Finally, the jubilee law in Leviticus 25:23-28 adds to all this that land which had to be sold in bad times must be returned to its original owner. Indeed no land was to be sold outright, because the land is the Lord's (Lev. 25:3).[475]

The jubilee law includes clarifications which amount to economic reorganization and the assignment of different economic values to means of production.[476] Doing so, would blunt the sharpness of the economic extremes. The jubilee law may therefore be

475 Th. Marius Van Leeuwen, "The Jubilee challenge," *The Ecumenical Review* 50/2 (April, 1998), 245. cf. Takatemjen, 86.

476 Yairah Amit, "The Jubilee Law - An Attempt at Institution Social Justice," in *Justice and Righteousness: Biblical Themes and their Influence,* edited by Henning

described as having fundamentally socialistic characteristics. Further, its purpose was to prevent injustice and oppression from taking root in Israel (Deut.15: 4; Lev. 19:33; Exo. 22:21), to maintain harmony in the community, and to prevent accumulation of wealth in a few hands. The giving of such legislation was to prevent any improper accumulation of wealth and lands. The Old Testament insists that the Jews must have special care for the strangers and foreigners who live among them.[477]

In other words, a society in which the competitive race for achievement is arrested after every 50 years, so that each member gains a new cycle of opportunities.[478] It also imposed society's own will to ensure the right of every one of its members to live honourably, with a guaranteed minimum of economic means. In the same way both biblical symbols of the Sabbath and the Jubilee have served as signposts or markings generating "a sense of communion."[479]

Jewish tradition wrestled with the problem of how to preserve the dignity of recipients of charity. The rabbis based much of their discussion on the commandment, "If there be among you a needy man... thou shall surely open thy hand unto him, and shall surely lend him sufficient for his need in that which he wanted" (Dt 15:7,8).[480] This verse became the basis for a highly developed system of loans. "Thou shall open thy hand... and shall surely lend him." Through rabbinic literature, a loan is emphasized as the finest form

---

Graft Reventlow and Yair Hoffman (England: Journal for the Study of the Old Testament, 1992), 52.

477 Takatemjen, *Studies on Theology and Naga Culture* (Delhi:ISPCK, 1998), 85-86.

478 D' Abreo. *Turning the Tide of Injust*, 7.

479 Konrad Raiser, *For a Culture of life: Transforming Globalization and Violence* (Geneva: World Council of Churches, 2002), 163.

480 Richard G. Hirsch, "Judaism in Pursuit of Economic Justice," in *Contemporary Religion and Social Responsibility*, edited by Norbert Brockman (New York: ALBA House, 1973), 291. The phrase "that which he wanted" was interpreted to mean that if a man did not have sufficient funds to marry; the community should assume responsibility for providing him with the means to support a wife. The phrase "sufficient for his need" became the peg on which to hang the concept that a man was entitled to be sustained at a standard of living to which he had become accustomed.

of charity. "Greater is he who lends than he who gives, and greater still is he who lends, and with the loan, helps the poor man to help himself."[481]

According to the medieval philosopher Maimonides, the highest degree of charity is to enable a man to become self-supporting.[482] The task is never finished until the condition of one become dependence to the state of self-reliance and self-support. Thus, a Jew looks upon poverty as the responsibility of the entire community. This system of social welfare became the means of restoring integrity to the community. All members of the community were expected to contribute, even those who were themselves recipients of charity which shows the principle that no person was free from the responsibility of the welfare of all.

Characteristic of all strands of Israel's traditions is concern for the widow, the orphan, the poor and the sojourner in the land. It also underscores not to pervert the justice due to the sojourner or to the fatherless, or take a widow's garment in pledge (Dt. 24: 17, 24).[483] For instance; in the legal traditions as represented by the covenant code and the Deuteronomic legislation we find the following texts Ex. 22:21-22; Dt. 14:29. Cf. Dt. 15:7. These concerns are rooted in the nature of Yahweh himself who is defender of the oppressed (Dt. 10:18; Ps. 83:3-4; Ps. 103:6 cf. Ps. 140:12; 146:7; Ex. 3:7-8).[484] The spirit of the Hebrew Bible lies in the fact that the relationship to the divine takes place through the relationship to people and coincides with social justice.[485]

---

481 Hirsch, "Judaism in Pursuit of Economic Justice," 292.

482 Ibid. The organization of charity became so specialized that numerous societies were established in order to keep pace with all the needs. Each of the following functions was assumed by a different society on behalf of the community at large: visiting the sick, burying the dead, furnishing dowries to poor girls, providing clothing, ransoming captives, supplying maternity needs, and providing special foods and ritual objects for holidays. Caring for the poor became a matter of civic pride.

483 Scara K, "Social Justice in the Old Testament," 177.

484 Donahue, "Biblical Perspectives on Justice," 73-74.

485 Roelf Haan, *The Economics of Honour: Biblical Reflections on Money and Prophecy,* translated by Nancy Forest Filer (Geneva: WCC Publications, 1988), 42.

It is Yahweh's concern to be the guardian of the oppressed class in all respects. Moved by this concern he makes stipulations about measures of length, weight and quantity (Lev. 19:35-37). The use of two kinds of measures, i.e., one for buying and another for selling, is strictly forbidden (Dt. 25: 13-16); Prophets accuses both Jews (Mic. 6: 10-11) and Gentiles (Hos. 12: 8) for using fraudulent scales. Amos warns of doom because Israel had "sold the righteous for silver and the needy for a pair of shoes", and had "trampled the head of the poor into the dust of the earth" (2:6-7). In the same way, Isaiah condemns "him who builds his house by righteousness, and his upper rooms by injustice; who makes his neighbour serve him for nothing and does not give him his wages" (22:13).[486]

The New Testament has a continued significant teaching on community life apart from Old Testament discussion. Sunil Caleb writes that Jesus' teaching about economic life centers around the foundation of a community of believers who share their life together, depending upon God and with a thrust towards equality, seeing that the needs of each person are met. He further quotes Douglas E. Oakman saying that Jesus points to a community based upon loving service to the least (Mk. 10.44) and the worship of God alone (Mk.12.29-31).[487]

This kind of a community began with Jesus himself, who with his disciples, shared a common purse as can be seen in John 12.6 and 13.29, where we are told that Judas held the common purse. It seems that the community consisted of the twelve and other disciples including some women who seem to have provided most of the finance (Luke 8.1-3). Jesus' reaching out to those marginalized by mainstream Jewish society (such as the tax collectors, prostitutes and Samaritans), was motivated by a desire to 'rebuild community between socio-economically alienated groups'.[488]

---

486 *Christian Faith and the World Economy Today: A Study Document from the World Council of Churches* (Geneva: WCC Publications, 1992), 8.

487 Sunil Caleb, "An Ethical Evaluation of Indian Economic Development, 1947-1997," (Ph. D. Dissertation, University of Kent at Canterbury, UK, 2000), 24.

488 Ched Myers, "Jesus' New Economy of Grace," *Sojourners* (July-August 1998), 3. http://www.sojourners.com/soj9807/980723.htm (12 April 2003).

Takatemjen observes that the real New Testament concept of the new social order is based on relationships. He gives the whole idea of *Koinonia* that leads to the theology of rich and poor. This *koinonia* as the revolutionary concept in the New Testament has the way of answering the community's problem, such as, social (slaves and master), ethnic (Jews and Gentiles), and sexist (male and female).[489] Justo L. Gonzalez defines *koinonia* not only as the feeling of fellowship, but also essentially as the sharing of material goods.[490] Both Takatemjen and Gonzalez agree that probably what Luke was describing (Acts 2:41-42 and 4:32-37) was the enacted parable of the Christian *koinonia* that had been at the very heart of Paul's ministry' (Gal. 28).[491] This practical aspect of the Christian fellowship/ *koinonia* is also spoken of in Romans 15:16: " Collection for the poor saints in Jerusalem." The word *koinonia* is used thrice in connection with the collection Paul took from the Gentile churches for the poor saints at Jerusalem (II Cor. 8:4; 9:13).[492] The reference to the concept of *koinonia* was highly significant for the early church, which goes beyond the programmatic statement of Galatians 3:28.[493]

The Gospel of Luke emphasizes on the question of sharing food and relationship between the rich and the poor (Lk. 14:7-14; 15-24). Luke corrects his Hellenistic society in which reciprocity was among the equals. Indeed the Table Fellowship should be enhancing the social relationship between the two groups than for the purpose of self-serving ends. Luke recognizes the presence of the poor community in a situation where making friendship and inviting them would be rewarded (14:14 cf. 16:9). Luke shows Jesus' love

---

489 Takatemjen, *Studies on Theology and Naga Culture,* 90. He points out that probably Acts (2:41-47; 4:32-35) could be the enacted parable of Galatians 28.

490 Justo L. Gonzalez, *Faith and Wealth: A History of Early Christian Ideas on the Origin, Significance, and the Use of Money* (San Francisco: Harper & Row, 1990), 83.

491 Takatemjen, *Studies on Theology and Naga Culture,* 90. cf. Gonzalez, *Faith and Wealth*.

492 M. J. Joseph, "Paul's Understanding of "Economics" in Social relations," *NCCR*. (October, 1996), 636.

493 Gerhard Lohfink, *Jesus and Community: The Social Dimension of Christian Faith*, translated by John P. Galvin (Philadelphia: Fortress Press, 1984), 99.

towards poor, sinners and the tax collectors by associating with them. Doing so would become a sign of the outworking of the mystery of God, which his community should be emulating (Lk. 5:27-32; 7:36-50; 10:38-42; 19:1-10).[494]

Paul in I Corinthians 11:17ff marks the Eucharistic vision in relationships very carefully. This Eucharist embraces all aspects of life including the rich poor divide. For Paul, the believers are called to be responsible householders "for themselves and for all human beings" especially who are of the household of the faith" (Gal. 6:10).[495] Both Jesus and Paul demonstrated that people from different backgrounds could come together to form a community. They continued to belong to a particular class, but their commitment to sharing with others led to the formation of a community of people, which did away with the damnable divisions between people and classes.[496]

For Conrad Boerma, all these suggest that the mutual solidarity of Christ's community began to exercise a powerful influence on social structures. It is clear that society did not have to be ruled by force or by exploitation. The community proved otherwise. It represented an alternative, a new life-style. Love, togetherness, brotherhood still seemed possible. For instance, Paul seeks urgently a brotherly love, which requires equality (II Cor. 8:14ff.). He refers back to the Old Testament: 'He that gathered much had nothing over, and he that gathered little had no lack' (Ex. 16:18).[497] Paul sees on a matter of plain justice. This ideal of equality and principle of justice were given a new dimension by the love of Christ and the grace of God.

The remarkable value of giving away the whole self and wealth in terms of almsgiving occupies a very important place in the Christian community. Examples can be drawn from Luke's parable about the unjust steward (16:9). Failures of almsgiving is condemned and judged (Lk. 12:16-21) as in the parable of the rich man with a farm. Thus, in this way the social injustices were eradicated. The emphasis on good works especially in the story of the Samaritan points out the

---

494 Takatemjen, *Studies on Theology and Naga Culture,* 90-91.

495 Joseph, "Paul's Understanding of "Economics" , 636.

496 Conrad *Rich man, Poor Man and the Bible* (London: SCM Press, 1979), 73.

497 Boerma, 74-75.

failure of the 'righteous' to do right. Instead the Samaritan becomes a model for reaching out to people with physical needs, which extends to one's enemy (cf. 6:27-36).[498]

In summarizing the discussion we could find the significance of Jubilee law and Sabbatical year provision aiming at the harmony of a community preventing unjust accumulation of wealth from poor. The land is seen as a gift of God's provision and Israel's responsibility to execute their obligations towards poor, widows, strangers & slaves, and to the rest of the community. Thus, Jubilee law points to basic social welfare involving God's ownership and covenant supporting to reduce social conflicts and induces relationship. Another aspect of community is charity of the given loans supporting individual till he/she becomes self-supportive. Any poverty in a community is considered as a responsible obligation of the whole community. This is worked out for restoring the integrity and dignity of the community by defending the dignity of a recipient. This obligation is extended to the recipients and poor who contribute to the charity work in their capacity for the welfare of a community.

Jesus' concern of community building is seen in his sharing of the purse with his disciples; accommodating the outcasts and marginalized is the core redeeming idea of lifting community from any socio-economic alienation. Jesus' community concerns women and others who were alienated from the community. The early Christian community bounded themselves for unity and management of building the household. Paul's implication of *koinonia* gives a strong understanding of sharing, which has social indication, based on relationships to enhance social order, such as enhancing social relationship between poor and rich, equality among people of different status in the community, and supporting financially and materially. This certainly uplifted the commitment and sharing of the community showing new dimension of brotherly love in God, the Christ that paved the way to social justice.

Our view of Jewish tradition has been brief, but sufficient to demonstrate it's relevance to the issues of Naga people. Sumi Baptist Church must understand their vocation as a responsibility to not only

---

498 Takatemjen, *Studies on Theology and Naga Culture*, 90-92, 94.

take spiritual matters seriously, but also issues regarding property, employment, consumption and poverty. Therefore, stewards of creation are not owners of it thereby manipulating it for personal wealth and advantage, but they need to state what they are if not owners, for the sustenance of livelihood and the benefit of those who are marginalized: the widow, the poor and the stranger. Thus, the Sumi Church's life and character should be encouraged to become integral and essential to its witness in the context. As the new spirit and practice of selfless sharing (*koinonia*) was central in the early church community, that spirit should make the church participate in this new social reality created by the Spirit of Christ and offered to the world.[499]

IV. The Importance of Kingdom Teaching

The revelation of God and His salvific intervention begun in the Old Covenant reaches its fulfilment in Jesus and the Kingdom announced by Him. In his Nazareth manifesto, Jesus presents his life and mission as bringing the Good News to the poor, of proclaiming liberty to the captives and of making justice reign (Lk. 4:18-19).

The phrase "Kingdom of God/ Heaven" is found largely in the synoptic Gospels, where it is attributed to Jesus himself. Punnapadam explains that the term Kingdom of God for Jesus and the Synoptists in general, is a synonym for the New Covenant.[500] Luke continues to use the phrase in Acts when he reports Paul's sermons, and there are scattered references in the Pauline letters and the general epistles. Norman Kraus writes that the Kingdom of God means God's saving, governing presence.[501] The Kingdom of God is understood as a symbol and Jesus himself portrayed as presuming that his hearers know enough about the kingdom. It means more "the act of reigning than the place of reign."[502]

499 C. Norman Kraus, *The Community of the Spirit: How the Church is in the World* (Scottdale: Herald Press, 1993), 91.

500 Punnapadam, "*Justice as Spirituality*," 159.

501 Kraus, The Community of the Spirit, 87.

502 Soares, G, "The Social Implications of the Message of Jesus," in *The Church in India in the Struggle for a New Society*, edited by Amalorpavadoss (Bangalore: National Biblical, Catechetical and Liturgical Center, 1981), 225.

This rule has both present and future dimensions. God is present in saving power; where His authority is acknowledged and His will is done on earth, there His kingdom becomes present.[503] God's act, the saving event is the coming into being of a community, a social reality capable of representing to an unwilling world the order to come.[504] On the other hand, the future aspect of the Kingdom of God relieves us of the impossible challenge to create the Kingdom of God in all its fullness here and now. For instance, the parable of the mustard seed and yeast (Matt.13: 31-3) show that "the present realization of the Kingdom of God can only be described in the category of small beginnings. Euphoric expectations are thereby prevented, as is the temptation to force through the consummation of Kingdom of God in an authoritarian system."[505]

The relation of Kingdom to justice may not be immediately apparent, but a connection is suggested by the observation of Norman Perrin that, in the New Testament, Kingdom is a "symbol."[506] For instance, Jesus manifested the meaning of God's kingdom by his close association and table fellowship with sinners and toll collectors, the ritual and legal outcasts of his time (Mk. 2:17).[507] In associating with these groups Jesus is a parable of God's justice where mercy (*hesed*) and justice *(tsedaqah)* are not in opposition, but in paradoxical agreement.

The kingdom is the power of God active in the world, transforming it and confronting the power of the world. It is to find

---

503 Kraus, The Community of the Spirit, 84-85.

504 Lewis S. Mudge, *Rethinking the Beloved Community: Ecclesiology, Hermeneutics, Social Theory* (Geneva: WCC Publications, 2001), 55-56.

505 Duchrow & Liedke, *Shalom*, 131.

506 Donahue, "Biblical Perspectives on Justice," 86.

507 Cf. John Riches, *The World of Jesus: First-Century Judiasm in Crisis* (New York: Cambridge University Press, 1990), 17; Bruce J. Malina, *The New Testament World: Insights from Cultural Anthropolgy* (Atlanta: John Knox Press, 1981), 71; Gerd Theissen, *Social Reality and the Early Christians: Theology, Ethics, and the World of the New Testament*, translated by Margaret Kohl (Edinburgh: T& T Clark, 1993), 221. Jesus' social world had crucial distinction between gentile and Jews, and Jews with Samaritans. The first-century was thoroughly patriarchal where birth determined one's position in the hierarchy of family, first born males ranking above subsequent male offspring.

a home among the poor (Mt. 5:3) and the persecuted (Mt. 5:4); and only with difficulty will the rich enter it (Mk. 10: 23). The person who can summarize the whole Law as love of God and neighbour, is not far from the Kingdom of God (Mk. 12: 34). The exorcisms of Jesus represent Jesus' confrontation with and victory over the powers of evil and are signs that "the kingdom of heaven has come upon you" (Lk.11: 20).[508]

By identifying the advent of God's Kingdom with His ministry and teaching, Jesus proclaims the advent of God's justice (Mk. 1:15; Mt. 4:17). Jesus as the eschatological proclaimer of God's Kingdom and God's justice shows that this Kingdom is to have effect in everyday life. Nevertheless, the future-oriented dimension that peace acquired in the Old Testament is not lost.

Therefore, the Kingdom and the justice of God, His fidelity and His call to fidelity are manifested in Jesus' incarnation in history. The Beatitudes presuppose the concept of the Kingdom and of its justice in the whole of biblical revelation, particularly in Deutero-Isaiah. The poor are blessed because through Jesus, God intervenes on their behalf as their liberator. The liberation of Jesus' salvation benefits primarily not "God's own" but those outside the boundaries set up by "God's own" in order to keep themselves "pure" for God. It in concretised in Jesus' command to "love your enemies and pray for those who persecute you (5:43-48)."[509] He clearly presents the Kingdom of God, about to be realized in his own person, as fulfilment of God's justice for the needy and helpless.[510]

In Luke, the Beatitudes are proclaimed in the Sermon on the Plain, as opposed to the Sermon on the Mount in Matthew. Modern exegesis recognizes that the text of the Beatitudes in Luke offers the original version, whereas the rendering of Matthew includes a later addition. This is particularly true of the first and second Beatitudes as presented by Luke, to which Matthew has added 'in spirit' and 'righteousness'. The text clearly alludes to the words of Isaiah (61:

---

508 Donahue, "Biblical Perspectives on Justice," 87.

509 Willard M. Swartley, *Israel's Scripture Traditions and the Synoptic Gospel: Story Shaping Story* (Peabody: Hendrickson, 1994), 263.

510 Punnapadam, "*Justice as Spirituality*," 161.

1-2).[511] In Matt. 5: 21-48 examples of this "greater righteousness" are given which actually define the term *dikaiosunē*.[512]

We note the parallel expression between Matthew and Luke "the way of righteousness" in Matt. 21:32 to "the purpose of God" in Lk. 7:30. The two are similar in meaning where righteousness refers to the will of God. Those who reject the demands of *dikaiosunē* will not enter the *basileia (*cf; parable of wicked tenants 21:33-46). Entering into the kingdom is open to those who produce the fruit of it (21:43). It appears as the inner substance and the fruit of salvation in God's kingdom (Mt 5: 6, 10).[513] Thus, righteousness within this framework of chapter 21 refers to right conduct demanded of human beings by God and to God's gift.[514]

The discussion on the Kingdom of God gives a clear implication of the present and future rule of God in which the act of His rule is marked important. The relational aspect is seen from God's saving act and governing presence in humankind. The significant pointers to the Kingdom of God are seen in core manifestation of God in Christ and being in association with outcasts and marginalized. This power of the kingdom is seen as active in transforming the world. The whole aspect of Jesus' ministry and miracles performed confirmed the active presence of the Kingdom of God. Jesus is the greater righteousness transforming the tradition fulfilling the Old Testament vision and justice of God to humanity in blessing and defending the poor, and liberating them. The Kingdom of God in response demands to be righteous in religious ordinances and moral

---

511 Punnapadam, "*Justice as Spirituality*," 160.

512 "Righteousness In Matthew's Gospel: Its Social Implications," *Bible Bhashyam an Indian Quarterly*, Vol. 13, No. 3, (Sept, 1987), 152. For Matthew, righteousness refers to that human conduct based on the new interpretation of the law by Jesus, which represents God's will. It is much faceted term involving concrete acts and including: goodwill, reconciliation, purity of heart and motive, forgiveness, truthfulness, non-retaliation, mercy, love, almsgiving, prayer and fasting.

513 "The Righteousness Required of the followers of Christ (Mt Ch. 7)," *Bible Bhashyam an Indian Biblical Quarterly* 10/2 (June, 1984), 132.

514 "Righteousness In Matthew's Gospel: Its Social Implications," *Bible Bhashyam an Indian Quarterly*, Vol. 13, No. 3, (Sept, 1987), 159.

conduct to others. Since, righteousness is a gift of God which is an intrinsic substance of salvation in God's kingdom.

Sumi Baptist Church has an ample challenge to participate in the continuous transformation of the Naga society as Jesus demonstrated in his time. Kingdom of God continues to call for liberation and justice/righteousness in the society. Its implication has a strong hold on religious ordinances and moral conduct in response to the Kingdom of God. Therefore, Sumi Church mission is a failure without fulfilling its requisite discharged in the kingdom message making its presence known to the Nagas. It is imperative for Sumi Church to look into the context and realize things that oppose the rule of God on Nagas and allow His rule to intervene on them.

V. Teaching on Wealth

A royal ideology of the land was promoted in Israel's history, which was considered a major function. It provided a justification for the control of power and strategic resources and proclaimed that the deities of the state guaranteed the king's right to rule. A heavy emphasis was placed on the benefits of peace, scrutiny and wealth for the population of the state, which flowed from the king's position in the cosmic scheme of things.[515]

To this, the basic concept of the land ideology was land as the source of wealth, the divine right of the monarch to appropriate that wealth and the entitlement of the monarch as God's representative to have dominion over the whole earth as an empire (Psalm 8:6-8).[516] But if the rule of the king was in some way the model for human 'dominion' over creation, therein lies a very important clue as to the meaning of this term. Two principles determined how the king should rule: "neither exalting himself above other members of the community nor turning aside from the commandment (of God)", Deuteronomy 17:20.

In terms of social organisation, the king was to be a leader among equals, not a despot; while on an ideological level, everything

---

515 Keith Whitelam, "Israelite Kingship: The Royal Ideology and Its Opponents," in *The World of Ancient Israel,* edited by Ronald Clements (Cambridge: Cambridge University Press, 1989), 12.

516 Drane, "Defining A Biblical Theology of Creation," *Transformation* 10/2, 8.

he did was to be rooted in devotion to God. In practice this means that the king should be just, loving and merciful in dealing with his subjects, just as God had been with the nation (Psalm 72:12-14).[517]

As a matter of fact, the Old Testament fundamental criterion of a Ruler or King was judged against his responsibility whether he was "Shepherd of his flock, Father to the fatherless and Protector of the protectionless."[518] The stranger and foreigner are seen as neighbour. Though this is an ancient norm, it contains no element of close-up communalism or antagonism to those who do not belong to one's race or group, which is growing and becoming so widespread in our country today.[519]

Basically the biblical texts from 1 Kings 3-10 and royal Psalms especially 2 and 27 give the portrayal of the wealth, the image of land as empire, the locus of the power in the social order, the location of God, and the rights of diverse groups to land in the perceived implementation of the ideology.[520] For example "to possess the land," means to participate in the salvation of the age to come.[521] According to the Old Testament the inheritance was primarily applied to Israel's privilege of inheriting the land of promise, which is understood as a gift of God. The power and wealth need not be in the hands of some elite group; resulting in the impoverishment of the masses rather it should be under the mutual care (mutuality), and not individual possession.[522]

The prophets also denounce injustice at the level of social structure- for example, an unjust legal system. According to Brian

---

517 Drane, "Defining A Biblical Theology of Creation," *Transformation* 10/2, 8.

518 D' Abreo. *Turning the Tide of Injust*, 7.

519 In the New Testament, this antagonism was contradicted by Christ in the parable of the Good Samaritan through which he answered the question, 'Who is my neighbour?'

520 Norman C. Habel, *The Land is Mine* (Minneapolis: Fortress Press, 1995), 17-18.

521 Daniel J. Louw, "International Economy and International Communication within the Network of Cyberspace: Pastoral Care to Cyber Punks," *Bangalore Theological Forum* 36/1 (June, 2004), 60.

522 This points the researcher to draw out the parallel understanding of the Naga context in the later part of the chapter although it is also discussed in the preceding the chapter.

Griffths, the Old Testament prophets point the root cause of the trouble as spiritual because the nation departed from God and economic injustice occurs as one of the results.[523]

In line with the Old Testament prophets, the New Testament teaching on charity and one's attitude to wealth is derived from the life and teachings of Jesus Christ. Jesus warned his disciples of the dangers of riches, the coming judgement and commands them to divest themselves of their wealth and use their possessions in a right way. Jesus saw nothing inherently evil in money, wealth, or private ownership. However, Jesus certainly condemned materialism and the compulsive quest for wealth. In other words, Takatemjen puts it as 'lust for wealth.'[524] Jesus did not teach that being rich means necessarily being evil. Jesus did not see anything sinful in the ownership of houses, clothes and other economic goods. He had wealthy friends and followers (Luke 14:1); he stayed in the homes of wealthy people; he ate at their tables (Luke 11:37).

A number of Jesus' parables provide insights into views on wealth. In Luke 16:9 and the accompanying parable, Jesus taught his followers to use their resources with the same dedication and keen judgement as the unjust steward. In the parable of the rich farmer (Luke 12:16-21), Jesus did not condemn the farmer for making money but rather for his single-minded concern with his own wealth and happiness. He was considered a fool because he was a self-centred materialist who had forgotten God.

The parable of Lazarus and the rich man (Luke 16:19-31) does not teach that a person's eternal destiny is determined by the amount of possessions he acquires in life. On the other hand, any interpretation of the parable that suggests the poor man entered heaven simply because he was poor would contradict everything the New Testament teaches about regeneration.[525]

Jesus often spoke about wealth without condemning it (Matt. 13:44-46; 21:33-46). Jesus admonishes the rich to live trusting in

523 Nash, Ronald H. *Poverty and Wealth: Why Socialism Doesn't Work* (Westchester: Crossway Books, 1986), 168.This point will be discussed later in the context of Nagaland.

524 Takatemjen, *Studies on Theology*, 86.

525 Nash, Ronald H. *Poverty and Wealth: Why Socialism Doesn't Work*, 163.

God as means of securing one's soul (Lk. 12:22-32; 33-34).[526] When he did call on people to renounce their possessions, his statements reflected special conditions; in one instance, for example, he made this demand in a situation where people had made their possessions into a god (Luke 18:22-24). Thus, wealth that is accumulated dishonestly or that becomes a controlling principle in one's life falls under God's judgement.

In Lk. 16:13, wealth is equivalent to a master. It stands like a god in opposition to God himself. Jesus makes the point that if a person is trusting in money then it is impossible to be trusting in God as he talks on serving God and mammon. Further he mentions the impossibility of the rich entering the Kingdom of God (Lk.18: 24-25). He warns the rich of the danger of losing the values of the Kingdom of God because of the inherent danger in the rich becoming lovers of money or greedy in Luke 12:15; 16:14. This particularly leads to separation from God, which affects the losing of poor neighbours from their sight (Lk. 16:19-31).[527]

Brian Griffiths explains that God placed human beings in His world to cultivate it, improve it and harness its resources for their own use. Human beings have been created to have dominion in this world. The urge to control, direct and manage the resources of this world is part and parcel of human nature and vocation. Idleness is at root alien to human personality.[528] The researcher believes that the word dominion would mean not only taking overtly for individual benefit or monopoly but creating and sustaining the whole creation, as is in God's purpose for human beings.

Jesus' teaching also stresses on human obligations that cannot be fulfilled unless one first has certain financial resources. For example, passages that oblige believers to use their resources for God's purposes

526 Takatemjen, *Studies on Theology*, 88.

527 Takatemjen, *Studies on Theology*, 89. Cf. Waldron Scott, *Bring Forth Justice: A Contemporary Perspective on Mission* (Grand Rapids: William B. Eerdmans Publishing Company, 1980), 91. The Palestine of Jesus' time was like many other eastern countries, a land polarized between the rich and the poor. Furthermore, under the pretext of piety the Pharisees exploited the common people.

528 Nash, Ronald H. *Poverty and Wealth: Why Socialism Doesn't Work,* 164.

presuppose the legitimacy of private ownership.[529] Jesus taught that children have an obligation to take care of their parents (Matt.15: 3-9) and that his followers ought to be generous in their support of worthy causes (Matt 6:2-4).

In summarizing the whole teaching of wealth it could be understood from the strict sense as gift with responsibility. Israel's kings were responsible to ensure peace, security and wealth to members of the state. They were expected to be appropriate in utilizing the land as resource of wealth, power and authority in the community. The foremost responsibility of the king is to be devoted to God in submission to justice extending protection to foreigners and strangers, and other races. The whole idea was that a few elite in community should not accumulate the wealth but leave at mutual care. This reveals God's willingness for justice economically, to which He condemns the abuse of power and economic injustices, and exploitation of the weak and powerless. Jesus was concerned that wealth should be utilized in rightful ways where he warns of the attitude and motivation to wealth and riches in letting it substitute God. We see the clear indication of Jesus condemning of the rich becoming self-centered and materialistic and losing trust in God.

Therefore, wealth is not a problem in itself but when one who possess it becomes obsessed, Jesus condemns it. Jesus warns the rich reminding the danger of trusting in their wealth, which stands in opposition to God. Finally, Jesus also gave the importance of possessing wealth without which the obligation towards others or neighbors is not possible. All this discussion could be summed up that neither poor nor rich is exceptional for their status, rather the message focuses to right utilization and motivation of wealth in devotion to God as His gift.

The researcher sees a similarity in the context discussed with the Naga society. Sumi Baptist Church has not taken any prophetical stand against the issue of wealth and its accumulation through different forms, and the emergence of unjust social structure and

529 Private ownership does not necessarily mean at the cost of others rather it implies ownership with proper obligations towards others, which at same time fulfils God's purpose.

systems. The rich poor divide is not a strange thing found in Naga society at present but it could be seen in every society in the world, which the researcher believes cannot be rectified in terms of equality. However, the church can move forward to bring transformation in their functions and management of wealth to accommodate every individual giving their due right within the given structure. This responsibility could be extended even to the migrants/outsiders living in Nagaland. The church has a greater mission challenge, which could be carried out in future.

VI. Concerns on Human Rights

Shimreingam Shimray writes that there is no phrase Human Rights as such employed in classical sources of the Jewish religious tradition, which means the Bible does not speak of it in the sense of modern understandings. However, one system of values and ideas, which constitutes the concept "Human Rights", is hardly absent from the Jewish worldview. On the contrary, those values and ideas are among the beliefs, which constitute the very core of Jewish sacred Scripture and the tradition of ideas, and practices, which flows from it.[530]

The Bible shows how one should try to respond to the demands of God in the very heart of the human condition, in real flesh and blood situations; it does not provide ready-made prescriptions but it does pose the question of human rights. Right from the very beginning of the Bible; the most ancient creation story of human beings and their way of life in this world; affirms that God created humankind to enjoy fullness of life. The creation account speaks of humanity's primordial place among all living creatures. Every human being has a right to live and also have rights over the rest of creation.[531]

A Christian perspective of human rights begins with a definition of 'human' that requires God. Shimray writes that for Christians, the whole doctrine of creature-hood is the landmark to understand the dignity of human beings and their relationship with God and other creatures. In line with this framework, the concept of human

530 Shimreingam Shimray, *Theology of Human Rights: A Critique on Politics* (Ukhrul: Ruth Shimray and CESAC, 2002), 185-186.

531 Jean-Francois Six, *Church and Human Rights.* Translated by Susan Leslie (London: St Paul Publications, 1992), 36.

beings created in the Image of God is one of the basic grounds to understand the biblical idea of Human Rights.[532] Gen 1:26 describe that God created human beings in His own image. The Psalmist (Ps.8) stated that human is just a little less than God. Therefore, he or she has to be respected, taking away someone's life is not only a violation of human rights, but it is a destruction of God's image. The Bible disapproves murder (Gen. 4:1-16); Cain murdered his brother Abel when they were in the field. The blood of the innocent brother cried to God. Thus, God punished him and he was destined to be a wanderer. Likewise the Sixth commandment says, "You shall not kill" (Exod. 20:13).[533]

In this respect, Nagas have bypassed divine teaching on human rights. The distorted image of an individual is the outcome of the present socio-political scene. In contrast to what was just mentioned, Lasuh substantiates this point further that in the past if anyone committed murder he was exiled for seven years. However this is not true in the present context.[534] The freedom of individual rights has deteriorated somehow by the powerful in all spheres of life.

The other aspect of human rights is liberty of conscience. Every one has freedom to decide for oneself. For instance, through Moses God had given different laws of Israel. Yet, they are given freedom to choose, either life or death (Deut. 30:15-20). K. Lasuh cites Owen Thomas who gives a precise statement on human freedom where he said that human freedom is to be exercised in carrying out dominion over the earth as God's stewards and God's law.[535] Further in the book of Acts the Apostles refused to obey Jewish leaders but decided to obey God. Jesus also encouraged his disciples not to fear those who kill body, yet cannot kill the soul (Matt. 10:28).

---

532 Shimray, Theology of Human Rights, 186.

533 K. Lasuh, "The Biblical Concept of Human Rights," in *Crusade on Naga Morality*, compiled by V. K. Nuh (Kohima: Council of Naga Baptist Churches, 1996), 62-63.

534 K. Lasuh, "The Biblical Concept of Human Rights," in *Crusade on Naga Morality*, 63. This point of discussion will be taken further in a later chapter.

535 K. Lasuh, "The Biblical Concept of Human Rights," in *Crusade on Naga Morality*, 64.

In relation to the discussion made every human being has the right to possess property. The story of the parting of Abraham and Lot in Genesis 13 involved issues of property rights and the vital access to cultivatable land and to supplies of fresh water. Such concern must have been central to the lives of the groups who joined together to form the tribal confederation. God's involvement in this question underlines its importance- God gave Promised Land to Abraham and His descendants (Gen. 15:18; 17:8). The divine sanction of the right of possession and of access to its fruits are central, for example, to the covenant language of Genesis (13, 15, and 28).[536]

The lands, which were once freely held by the peasants, went into the hands of rich landowners. One concrete example is the story of king Ahab and Naboth.[537] I Kings 21:1-29 talks about the murder of Naboth by king Ahab and his wife who were in want of their land. They had to bear the consequence as God was against their forcible grabbing of land and property.[538] Hence, every individual's right to possess property or any possessions was no longer seen as a possession of the community. It was treated as private property to be sold and bought due to a few wealthy landowners who were depriving poor peasants.

Thanzuava writes that a human right in the tribal community is seen as the responsibility of human beings to contribute to the common good.[539] In other words, it is a community right, part of what it means to exist authentically. It is further an affirmation that land is the gift of God to all. People's perception of land as the gift of and owned by God is the basis of the community's claim of a legitimate ownership of land, because God is the God of the people.[540]

---

536 Ceresko, *The Old Testament*, 408-409.

537 K. Thanzauva, *Transforming Theology: A Theological Basis for Social Transformation* (Bangalore: Asian Trading Corporation, 2002), 143.

538 Lasuh, 64-65.

539 K. Thanzauva, *Theology of Community: Tribal Theology in the Making* (Bangalore: Asian Trading Corporation, 2004), 227.

540 Thanzauva, *Theology of Community*, 225.

This exclusive ownership of God implies, for the tribal people, that land equally belongs to all with equal rights and freedom to live in it. Therefore, no human being can claim it exclusively for himself nor can he sell it as if it is his own property. It may sound redundant to the Nagas at present to act upon as it is. However, the cultural ethos and significant values, which is inherent, could be preserved and maintained.[541]

The Gospel message is meant to be universal and cannot bear fruit unless it is proclaimed to beings who are themselves open to the universal; the radical invitation to practice the Beatitudes presupposes that every human being is able to receive and respond to this message; all human beings are equally able to do this and the God of the Gospel has no favourites. The significance of Jesus' death in the context is the death of an innocent man who has been condemned with a total disregard for human rights. The Christian faith shows, in the resurrection of Jesus, how God rises up against injustice and manifests Himself as the God of the living, the one who will not allow people to deny a person's rights.

Accordingly, God appears as the one who is firmly on the side of the oppressed; for Him, a future promise of 'supreme good' to be achieved can in no way justify the sacrifice of human beings to a cause.[542] God constantly protects the rights of human beings over against those who trample on these rights. He has an unceasing programme to restore the dignity of the violated people, which signifies the unfailing obligation of the covenantal relationship that is justice. Shimray points out the clear reference to human rights in Deuteronomy 16:19-20 where 'Human Rights' is God's will and concern.[543] God's concern covers to the extent of not showing

541 The researcher means to say that ownership by God applies to everyone, which is also equally true in the tribal setting of the Nagas. Therefore, be it individual or community ownership it should be allowed to be utilized and freedom to live and possess because it is the gift of God to humanity. Today the Nagas have gone to the extent of rich and poor divide.

542 Jean-Francois Six, *Church and Human Rights.* Translated by Susan Leslie (London: St Paul Publications, 1992), 36-37.

543 Shimreingam Shimray, *Theology of Human Rights: A Critique on Politics* (Ukhrul: Ruth Shimray and CESAC, 2002), 204. The accounts of Sabbath

partiality, not taking bribe, as bribe blinds the eyes of the wise and subverts the cause of the righteous. The focus on justice is made that one may live and inherit the land the Lord gives.

The implication of human rights depicts the individual's right to life and human being as dignified being in the image of God. Therefore, any violation and destruction of human beings is violating God's image in human being. Accordingly, human beings are given freedom to decide and carry out responsibility in God's will. All human beings are given rights to property and possessions particularly the importance of land as resource of wealth is seen as gift of God. This was strictly given as a community possession and therefore restricted from any private ownership of a few. The gospel message of Beatitudes demands the response from every human being. Finally, God's siding towards oppressed focusing on justice in all human relationships and God's covenantal relationships justifies human rights.

The message has come through from the discussion above that God affirms the rights of the people and this challenges the Naga situation at present. Politically and economically people are deprived of their rights and ownership in varied forms, physically afflicted and psychologically disturbed. The power and money is misused & manipulated, and people are exploited. Thus, Sumi Baptist Church can play a vital prophetic role in this situation if it affirms God's mission as their obligation.

Summary

Whatever the researcher has discussed on biblical and theological aspects of the socio-economic study is not to be taken as a complete study because the research has been done within the limited focus. This chapter implies God as the managing creator who holds together all His creation: human beings and natural environment; and to the extent of creatures, living and non-living things. What the human

---

perspective and teaching on Jubilee year which reaffirms and renders God's justice and protection on his people. The discussion to these references can be referred back from the section 'The Significance of Communal Living' as discussed earlier. Moreover Jesus' attitudes and action towards the people whom he interacts gives a clear clue of what Jesus was up to.

being possesses is only the responsibility transferred to act like God, as stewards. Just as the Creator is the manager or steward over His creation sustaining and liberating, human beings are called to be co-creators. In this sense, the whole concept of divine 'economy' of God in order to provide a holistic salvation to human being is to become a community of God just as we see in the Trinitarian relationships.

For these aspects 'work' has a special role in the management of God's world. The God of righteousness and justice extends His love particularly to the poor (physical, materially and psychologically) and the history of Israel exodus is the best example in history of human kind. Besides, the legal provisions granted to them specifically during the Sabbath and Jubilee year where the poor get their share to enjoy under divine economy signify the inclusion of all in God's community. In the same way, Jesus' relationship with the gentiles (his demonstration of the Kingdom of God in the ethical and moral sense), the ministry of early church and St. Paul elaborated a concept of what it means to be a community. The relationship among the people and the significance of sharing and caring in justice and righteousness; teaching on wealth and obligations who is entrusted to be a responsible steward and the extension of human freedom and right to existence. All these teach humankind to execute perfect stewardship as the co creator with Him.

From this chapter, the researcher formulates a mission model and the challenges that the Sumi Baptist Church need to carry out in their socio-economic context of Nagaland such as corruption, hatred, division, lost of social values and the rights of the people. Therefore issues of stewardship, justice, wealth, Kingdom and community, and human rights are considered as a pertinent message for the quest of Naga spirituality and transformation of the society. Sumi Church has responsibility to seriously look into biblical teaching, and reflect theologically on the problems, all this can help the church to come up with certain changes in the situation.

The following final chapter would present transformational development and explain why it is needed in the Naga context. It will also bring out the biblical and theological reflections as discussed from the present chapter to form a model for the mission of the

Sumi Baptist Church in the socio-economic context of Nagaland. Such issues like, stewardship, justice vs. injustice and Naga spirituality, liberative perspective vs. Naga liberation, and Kingdom community vs. Naga community will be taken into consideration for the transformational development of the Naga society. Finally, a few practical suggestions made will be helpful for the Sumi Baptist Church in future.

Chapter 7

TRANSFORMATIONAL DEVELOPMENT FOR THE MISSION OF THE SUMI BAPTIST CHURCH

Introduction

In this concluding chapter, the researcher proposes the introduction of transformational development, which she believes will improve the quality of life of the Nagas and bring wholesome spirituality that includes material, psychological, mental, physical, spiritual and moral integrity.

Mission as transformation should show that Christian faith is translatable as context shapes the very understanding of the Bible. Whatever change is attempted it cannot be done without reference and relation to what Christ offers to people. Mission must be seen as an integral relationship between evangelism and social change. Vinay Samuel defines the components of mission as relationship between evangelism and social action neither of which should stand on its own.[544] To this, 'transformational development,' the Sumi Church is called for total commitment to the Naga social community, to build and bring change.

The researcher believes that transformational development is better than other material development because it allows God's

---

544 Cited in, Chris Sugden, *Gospel, Culture and Transformation* (New Delhi: Regnum Books International, 2000), 23.

intended will to be established in human society and in the rest of the creation. Therefore, any developmental concept without looking into the benefits of the whole creation shatters God's purpose. This challenge comes as an urgent task for the Sumi Baptist Church to set its mission perspective looking into the socio-economic context of Nagaland.

Today in the name of human rights and freedom one can claim what is actually not. The researcher argues that human rights in correct perspective are when one directs oneself towards common goodness in exercising one's freedom. Today development means growth that is: materialistic; competitive; individualistic; where there is money there is development. In fact the question remains- what does development means?

This research proposes development as the holistic approach of human hood as individual and community without the divergence of spiritual quest for total life. In other words, each person should have freedom to enjoy the fullness of life as the prior criterion, which simply means that development takes place from within and gradually to the outside of the person. For M. M. Thomas[545] and Charles Elliot[546] development would mean humanization. M. M. Thomas has developed a theology of humanization and interprets salvation in this term. He says that it is in Christ Jesus we find our true humanness.[547]

Liberation in a true sense is liberation from oppression, exploitation, negligence, social injustice, war and poverty. This idea is timely and contextual, because we are exactly confronting such issues in Northeast India. The Nagas are not exempted from this sort of situation, where political and economic corruption, injustices, exploitations and malpractice are at higher degree. However, the researcher goes beyond where development brings the process of constant redeeming of a human situation ethically, environmentally

545 M. M. Thomas, *The Church's Mission and Post-Modern Humanism: Collection of Essays and Talks 1992-1996* (Delhi: CSS and ISPCK, 1996), 131 and 143.

546 Charles Elliott, *The Development Debate* (London: SCM Press, 1971), 59-68.

547 Cited in Renthy Keitzar, *In Search of a Gospel Message: Introducing a Contextual Christian Theology for North East India* (Guwahati: Christian Literature Center, 1995), 79.

and spiritually. Therefore, development becomes important for renewal and transformation of human society.

Amartya Sen says that development is when freedom is enhanced and a person is committed to that freedom.[548] In line with Sen's thought the researcher agrees that for development to take place in the Naga society commitment to individual's freedom is a must, which is barely seen among the Naga community. As a result it has brought a great failure in taking up responsibility, thrust and stewardship in the community. In this context it is imperative for the Sumi Baptist Church to rethink its spirituality for the transformational development of Nagaland.

Returning back to early Naga society reveals an element of egalitarian social conditions community orientated political structure. Community development was the core concern which forms a need base for community well being and naturally through an individual's motivation and pro-active cooperation it worked well. This common platform prevents any entrance to distinction among the people. The traditional community and village structure with chiefs, clan representatives, rich and royals, enabled these people to be seen as security and help in times of any crisis unlike the situation today.

The activities and functions were manifested in the interest of others and then the self. The provisions were set apart of common welfare and particularly for the poor in crisis. The potential and skill development programmes (in a cultural and traditional way in morung) were simultaneously carried out and taken care of in a community, preparing the young generation to face the responsibility shouldered upon them as men and women. This gave them a moral and ethical value of living, developing human resource potential, which became an instrument for wider Naga community.

The network of each tribal organisation was based on more or less communal and corporate nature. In the same way, every Naga individual was under well-knit and organised system of community, bounded by the social customs and discipline. Thus, considering such social fabric, an effective traditional socio-political administration,

---

548 Amartya Sen, *Development as Freedom* (New York: Anchor Books, 1999), 13-14.

economic sustenance and the whole social ethos of life of the Nagas could be befitting values in any transformational development concerns.

Thus, these reflections lead the researcher to propose a model of transformational development for mission of the Sumi Baptist Church, since, there is a need of re-organising the Naga community and church towards spiritual maturity and wholesome socio-economic growth. One can take advantage of the past Naga system in improving socio-economic situation. This may be possible only when a community's protection is ensured through community control and an active co-operation is lived out.

The following are the approaches for future mission developments of the Sumi Baptist Church for the transformational development of the Naga society. The researcher believes that the Sumi Church through participating in God's stewardship and development, confronting injustices and division, advocating God's justice, defending the rights of the people and liberating them from all kinds of oppressions, and upholding kingdom community and values among the Nagas would fulfil God's intention and purpose among the Naga Church and community.

I. Missiological Implications for the Mission of the Sumi Baptist Church in the Socio-Economic Context of Nagaland

1. Stewardship vs Naga Socio-Economic Developments

A sense of God's economy is understood in various ways- sometimes God is revealed as spiritual manager and sometimes God becomes human as an earthly economist. The whole universe is under the control of God who manages and unfolds His programmes to all His creations. The three sense of God- as creator, sustainer and liberator and the relationships of Trinity in God's character and nature imply the thrust and management to His people. This deliberate mandatory concern is to show through the act of justice/righteousness and peace that is relational to the bound of love and relationships, and total commitment to life. It reveals the concept of stewardship and levels of work that persistently produce and invest in His creation, in His graciousness.

The continuous resounding of God's activities in the life of His creation is then progressive, wherein God becomes a constructive developmentalist for the harmony of His creation creating, sustaining and liberating. The place of poor, oppressed & widows; and the strangers and foreigners are well noticed in dealing with God's careful providence for them, most importantly God's identification with His people in a needful situation. On the other hand there are ample teachings on the rich and the exploiters, and against infidelity, which degraded God's stewardship bestowed upon them.

Thus, the Biblical dictum calls for God's economy and appropriate management of the household of all creation, taking the responsibility and commitment to continued development of the resources and gift of life for wholeness and fulfillment of the purpose of God in creation. The Sumi Baptist Church as a body of Christ and representing God in the creation needs to undergird this principle of development in earthly and heavenly realms. The foremost change needed in the Christian society will begin with the body of Christ and that is Church. The church has to grapple with the down realities of human situation.

Nagas have lost motivation in maintaining cultural and traditional values of being honest, sincere, responsible, community building, commitment and relationships among the community. The essence of genuine hard work and developing skills within themselves are only a reminder of the past. The mismanagement of riches and wealth, be it a few who are in political leadership and in power or equally the middle person or opportunist, have manipulated the common wealth and security. Any socio-economic development in the state is at stake. The government grants and funds for development remain in the hands of a few which is utilized for self-purpose. The negligence of putting people's needs at the first place is hardly observed. Any government or public programmes and properties are destroyed without any expression of responsibility and commitment. There are always uncertainties in the hearts of the Naga people. This feeling of fear and insecurity from freedom of development probably sums up the Naga situation.

The Naga socio-political leaders and partly religious leaders, while much engrossed for the peace initiation, must scrutinize the increase of immorality and social evil in the land. A few people in an interview expressed that the political issue in Nagaland is the core burning issue and unless it is settled there will be no economic development.

However, the researcher is of the opinion that creation of socio-economic stability in the State is rather crucial than the political problem. This means that the proposed model of development when established through various approaches will help solve both political and economic problems in future. In the name of political investment the economy of the common people is relinquish by the powerful for their selfish purposes. Inspite of the development projects, facilitations and opportunities granted by the National and State government it is unfortunate that those are orally communicated and sometimes hold back.

Therefore, development never happens, rather the common or poor people are denied of their rights to property and ownership for survival. The grievous and sinful situation as such could be rectified by the participation of the church. God was willing to do that for the sake of poor and every bit of injustice that prevailed in the past in Israel. Jesus himself was engaged in reforming all the infrastructures that hit the poor, widows, orphans, sinners and outcasts of his day.

Many Nagas are uncomfortable and uneasy to accept the clear truth that they bear major responsibility for the present state of affairs. They recoil when people question the economic and developmental disaster for personal interests. The "law and order" is filled with tribalistic overtones and organized oppression and suppression under the pretext of maintaining peace and tranquility.

Therefore, in this context the Sumi Baptist Church can develop theological vision and mission basically to build a just, sustainable, free, progressive and peaceful society. A theology of development can be defined as an articulation of a Christian understanding of God's intention for human beings from the faith experience of human suffering in order to strengthen the commitment of the Church and individual believers to build a just, participatory, progressive, sustainable and *shalomic* society in this world. [549]

The Sumi Church has not touched widely the social concern in its mission endeavor. What the church is doing is only a few counts of awareness and socio-economic upliftment programmes. The general resource generating programmes and development under WSBAK is done within and for the association and mission outreach as discussed earlier. The occasional call for government official and socio-religious leaders for awareness and strengthening their responsibility in the government and religious life is helpful. There are times when WSBAK participate in rallies and peace marches when the situation calls for it. Apart from these few participation WSBAK is burdened for evangelism within and outside the association. In this sense WSBAK has to look within its social context, which cannot be bypassed. It is imperative that the Sumi Church can truly become committed to the commandment of God in Jesus Christ fulfilling and following Jesus' way of doing mission.

Unlike the Naga community and church, God was interested in human community development as we witnessed from Israel's history, by providing them food, liberating them from the wilderness, acknowledging the poor, widow, stranger and foreigner in community. God himself was engaged in human development work as creator blessing them to multiply and fill the earth bestowing such commitment and responsibility on human beings. The church has to be blamed because it has failed to look beyond church institution and church structure. Sumi Church belonging to Christian Naga commitment is part of the context to uphold and improve the situation through pushing and confronting the community, upgrading resources and utilizing human resources and potentiality to act as human and safeguarding stewardship in all socio-economic and political spheres. Church itself needs to reexamine its mission towards the problem of stewardship.

Christian involvement in social life and development is one part of the holistic approaches to mission. Evangelization or bearing

549 K. Thanzauva, "Theology of Human Development," *NCCR* 110/7 (August, 1990), 407.

witness to Christ by word, lifestyle and action is a liberating process in response to human needs. The Sumi Church as a steward of God's creation should be encouraged to lead people to be responsible in their use of resources. The church has to participate in total commitment to God's justice in which men and women becomes responsible stewards of God's creation. Participation can lead to transformation on both the personal and the societal level. Participating in the cause of the people is not only means to change their material base but also to bring them closer to God.[550]

Therefore, the Sumi Church in its attempt to bring about a just and peaceful society has to address both. Inspite of taking State government as solely responsible for development and eradication of poverty in meeting basic human needs the church need to perceive its role as part of the reality of the Kingdom of God. As Melba Padilla Maggay advocates 'Kingdom-keeping strategies,' believing that development is a task of the church that may be rooted in the spiritual resources if it is to remain vibrant and tap into the transforming powers of the Kingdom.[551] Thus, the Sumi Church should be made responsible to confront the socio-economic situation of Nagaland by committing itself to the call of God's stewardship.

2. Justice/Righteousness vs Injustice and Division in Naga Community

Nagas are socio-religiously divided at many instances. Sumis are emphatically divided among the religious leaders and Baptist churches. In the beginning they had a mutual understanding to locate different church organizations at different places because of geographical difficulty. However, the Sumi Baptist Church could not come together for the celebration of 100 years of Christianity in 2003. The researcher sees this as a great failure and crisis of unity and peace among the religious leaders and churches.

550 John Jashva Raja, *Facing the Reality of Communication, Culture, Church and Communication* (Delhi: ISPCK, 2000), 66.

551 Melba Padilla Maggay, *Transforming Society* (Quezon, Philippines: Institute for Studies in Asia Church and Culture, 1996), 72.

There was no such system existed in the past looking into the hierarchical structure of the Naga society today. It takes different forms such as gap between the rich & poor, wealthy & common people, political leaders & public, and religious leaders & social activists. The Sumi Church has to examine the need of the Naga people and attempt to rectify the situation through continuous working with all these groups and seek for justice and peace.

Jesus' life and ministry was in a similar situation as the Nagas of Nagaland today. Jesus challenged the power structure of his time. Socially, he was aligned with the poor, outcasts and sinners surprising and arousing anger in the minds of the people and religious leaders. He challenged the religious leaders who bound themselves with law yet created divisions among the people. Jesus' ministry in his context was a socio-religious revolutionary and prophetic act, which could be an example to the Naga churches today in the context of division and injustices.

In Lesslie Newbigin's assertion of the slogan "Let the Church be the Church,"[552] he recognizes God's unique ordained reality of the church as standing over the state to call it to account in the name of God. Newbigin sees the church as the only alternative body for renewal and the prevention of increasing moral anarchy and social disintegration.[553] Thus, the church has to make a difference to the society becoming the salt of the earth and light to the world. Jesus was devoted to the cause of the people by healing and nurturing both spiritual and physical needs, but as a prophet he condemned the evil practices of his days and challenged injustice outrightly (Luke 11: 43-47). Therefore, the church that represents the body of Christ on earth must be willing to carry on her prophetic ministry. The church cannot be neutral in the face of poverty, suppression and injustice.

The Naga church is eventually realizing and acting upon the prevailing situation; moving behind the curtain of rich and strong people, it lies in a neutral position not prepared to face the social world, remaining aloof and traditional. God's truthfulness is what

552 Lesslie Newbigin, "Can a Modern Society Be Christian" in *Christian Witness in Society*, edited by K. C. Abraham (BTE-SSC Publications, 1998), 97.

553 Ibid., 105.

justice demands. *Shalom* as we have discussed earlier shows a close connection with righteousness and truth on the one hand, and sharp opposition with falsehood and wickedness on the other.

The gospels talk about God's righteousness, justice, peace, reconciliation and the restoration of broken relationships between human with human; human with God; and the whole creation. Thus, the obligation on humanity in not less important than what God has done for humanity. Within God's boundary human being is given a choice to exercise God's undivided freedom, which could only lead them to enjoy the fullness of life in fulfilling God's ultimate purpose.

The implications of this for the church are obvious for the establishment of true *shalom.* There must be concern for truth and righteousness, and rejection of falsehood and wickedness. This biblical view of *shalom* teaches us that harmony and prosperity depend upon a proper balance between a concern for individual and a concern for the community.[554] But the Naga churches today have withdrawn from the issues of social justice and justified in their stand.

The separation of religious activity from social involvement has led to what Ron Sider calls "lopsided Christianity."[555] This "lopsided Christianity" is a product not just of ecclesiastical history, but of incomplete understanding of the Church's mission. This has limited the understanding relative to the Biblical concept of justice, which includes right relationships between humans, God and each other, and the physical world.

Thus, the Sumi Church has to struggle for the restoration of the broken relationship with individual, God, fellow human beings and the world. Until the Nagas build this relationship and exhibit 'love,' the basis of the Christ's justice, nothing will work outrightly. The biblical and theological reflection gives the clear understanding

---

554 Anil D. Solanki, "The Implication of Shalom in The Old Testament for Evangelism and Justice Today," in *Mission as Witness and Justice: An Indian Perspective,* edited by Nicholls, Bruce J. and Raj, Christopher S. (Delhi: The Theological Research and Communication Institute, 1991), 130.

555 Cited in, Bruce Wilkinson, "Justice in Christian Relief and Development: A Community-Centered Approach," 9-10 cieurope.net/justice/justice%20 christian%20Relief/20ad%20development.pdf (12 October 2004).

that Christian witness and social actions are of equal importance to God and that the two are inseparably intertwined.

The dreadful fact that the Nagas face today is a great divide among the tribes and communities both in social and spiritual spheres of life. The tribal communities are awakened to a new sense of identity, political consciousness, nationalism and ethnic consolidation within larger kinship groups. Ethnicity, an amalgam for race and culture including language, religion and the tribal way of life has come to be defined by tribals as "Us" and "Them" as V. K. Nuh has stated.[556] The levels of divide are clearly indicated in Naga political movement and in religious break ups. This leads us to wonder where is the justice we preach? Where is the repentance and reconciliation we witness? Which God/god do we serve? Theologically as we reflect upon 'justice/righteousness,' it would rather mean going forth and accomplishing the truth in our word and action. It means to reunite, reconcile, forgiving individuals and whole communities even to the extent of the whole creation. Further it is a very concrete action based concept.

The church cannot work towards justice without the Christian virtues of love and hope. The God of love through Jesus Christ has inaugurated God's reign of justice/righteousness and peace. It is already present among humanity and is continually unfolding. Therefore at the foundational level, the Christian attitude and commitment towards justice is based on and shaped by the love they have experienced from God. And so justice is to be understood as an expression of human love in social institutions and structures. Further the commitment for justice/righteousness calls for undergirding with holistic spirituality.

The researcher believes that the church is, essentially, a prophetic community. Every church could be a prophetic community fulfilling its appointed mission in society.[557] The church is playing a prophetic role only when it identifies injustices prevailing in the

556 V. K. Nuh, *Struggle for Identity in Northeast India: A Theological Response* (Delhi: Spectrum Publications, 2001), 100.

557 Jack Corbett & Elizabeth Smith, *Becoming a Prophetic Community* (Georgia: John Knox Press, 1980), 17.

society. A community of justice and peace rejects anything that prevents people from becoming fully human, such as the barriers of caste, race, class and gender. Sumi Church can help in the liberation of the people from the grip of power holders and manipulation. It supports and respects culture by redefining people's basic cultural identities, human dignity and religious values. The Sumi Church has to foster the truth that challenges falsehood. Prophetic acts should uncover the injustice of the present order and try to convert those who maintain it and aim at solidarity with victims of oppression, injustice and exploitation. It could change sinful structures to build an order, which is just and humane.

Therefore, the Naga religious and social leaders have no other option than to turn to the truth. The Naga context calls for honest and responsible individuals to exhibit discipline and integrity in moral and spiritual life. It calls for alignment with peace than divisions and conflicts. Naga Christianity needs integration of the traditional understanding of God and theology to our situation today. Thus, V. K. Nuh pertinently states that our theology need to first realize people's needs and be able to change our situation.[558] Thus, Sumi Church can be strengthened to claim and propagate justice in the context of broken relationships in all spheres of life, which will lead them to accomplish God's intended mission task.

3. Liberative Perspective vs Naga Politics and Human Rights Violations

The liberative perspective demonstrates the bible itself and its interpretation in the context of struggle for liberation. The Naga context challenges the church to examine the reality of their solidarity with those who are involved in the struggle for building the Naga society. The Church could be the appropriate body to call for the full participation of the women, race and tribes for promoting liberative community. A Christian view of the foundation of human rights starts from God as the creator of all things (Gen. 1:26-27). This truth

558 V. K. Nuk, "Christian Mission in the Socio-Political Life," in *In Search of Praxis Theology for the Nagas,* edited by V. K. Nuk, (New Delhi: Regency Publications, 2003), 102.

reveals to us fundamentals concerning every human being having special position in the creation because of their creation in God's image. The creation of human being in God's image and likeness has important moral implications. It makes clear why we have to recognise the dignity of each and every individual human being as such. Every individual is created with a purpose and he or she is a responsible person called to live in communication with God and respond to His demands, to reflect His glory. Therefore, humans are called to preserve and develop the earth and have freedom to make decisions, to choose a path of life as moral beings.

The creation of people in the image and likeness of God is also the basis for the equal worth and dignity of all human beings. Louis Pojman says that secular egalitarian arguments for equal rights have not offered plausible reasons for the equal worth of human beings. In his view this doctrine can only be based on the Judeo-Christian tradition.[559] Christians are called to assert the equality and dignity given by God and the authority of the Bible. This does not mean that all humans are excluded from all differences in treatment of human beings. Distinctions are seen in a moral and legal sense, corresponding to different responsibilities concerned, yet not conflicting with the fundamental concept of the equal worth of all human beings.[560]

Today the question of the equal worth of all human beings is a crucial issue which the church needs to tackle without delay. The growing manifestations of inequality between Nagas and non-Nagas residing in Nagaland, tribalism, superior social and political structure over above other human beings are the issues that require attention without any delay. Church has not raised any prophetic voice to denounce the existing situation. However, the Church needs to find the equal worth of human dignity in its expression materially for peoples' sustenance and development ensuring a just society. Thus, not condemning the private property but respecting and affirming one's obligations to social security and common good.

---

559 Cited in, Paul R. Beaumont ed., *Christian Perspectives on Human Rights and Legal Philosophy* (Cumbria: Paternoster Press, 1998), 19.

560 Ibid., 20.

A human being is created as a responsible creature. He or she is called to respond to the creator and to develop a living and joyful relationship with God and His or Her fellow human beings. This fact does not diminish the strong biblical arguments in favour of the recognition of freedom, both in physical and mental sense. Human beings should have the possibility to decide, to make choices about the way they live. Therefore, the Sumi Church could be recommended to promote this biblical view of the rights of the citizenship, their decision, relationships between individual and society. The church in Nagaland has the potential to transform the Naga society into a new liberating prophetic praxis.

The political situation in Jesus' day is comparable in important respects to the unjust political order of Naga in present context. The political situation of Nagaland is not stable and corrupted from two sides, i.e., government policies & their implementation, and the Naga political movement.

Biblical scholars see Jesus as an agent of radical social change and many acknowledge him as such. Some writers conclude that at the very least, "the movement of Jesus and that of the Zealots converged in revolutionary action in Jerusalem."[561] Jesus confronted the institutionalised socio-politico-economic system of his day.[562] His attacks on the moneychangers in the temple confirm this in the gospels (Jn. 2: 13-16, Mk. 10: 15-17 cf. Mt. 12: 1-16). Jesus' identification with the poor, and his readiness to defend their interests against their oppressors and ruling parties was seen as a real threat to the establishment. One can thus see how was the socio-politico-economic structure of Palestine in Jesus' day and the extent to which religion has undergirded and interpenetrated into the social system.[563] The Sumi Baptist Church has obligation to take up the movement similar to Jesus. Unlike Jesus' revolutionary action, the Sumi Church has been calm and non-prophetic.

Jesus' revolutionary act can be compared to the Naga church in a small way where the church apex body has tried its best to touch

561 Cited in Waldron Scott, *Bring Forth Justice,* 91.

562 Malina, *The New Testament World*, 73.

563 Scott, *Bring Forth Justice,* 94.

the lives of the people in the situation of divide especially at the political level. This same trend has to be implemented in each tribal church and community not simply pushing everything to happen at the top level. What Nagaland Baptist Council of Churches (NBCC) does is a less effort in bringing political consciousness and economic participation so as to promote peace and justice/righteousness in Nagaland. Council of Naga Baptist Churches (CNBC) is also involved in political peace process.

However, over all Naga churches have made their peace with the established institutionalized system. Naga churches have lost fine cutting edge of theology by justifying the pretense and counterfeit of the State. The church pulpits are devoid of theology, which calls for allegiance to the claims of the Gospel and living it out in the socio-political and economic arena of life.

Its message is harmless and non-prophetic to the corrupt status quo and its agents. Wati Aier considers the Church as guilty of misplaced allegiance and failed to distinguish the gods of civil religion and the God of the Bible revealed in Jesus Christ.[564] The prophetic announcement of spiritual and moral message has to be brought out on behalf of the common good and call to question the function of the socio-political and economic systems. Thus, "We must obey God rather than human beings"(Acts. 5:29).

John Yoder insightfully says, "Jesus was not just a moralist whose teachings had some political implications; he was not primarily a teacher of spirituality whose public ministry unfortunately was seen in a political light... Jesus was, in his divine mandate (i.e., promised, anointed, messianic) prophethood, priesthood, and Kingship, the bearer of a new possibility of human, social, and therefore political relationship."[565] Jesus challenged the people, bringing transformation in the context of a plurality of the people in all spheres of life, political power, economic and social differences, Hellenistic cultural influence and domination. "The attraction of the wealth and power associated with Hellenistic life and culture would have been great for those who are in a position to take advantage of it. The difficulties of making

564 Aier, "The Nagas at Present," in *From Darkness to Light,* 171.

565 Cited in Scott, *Bring Forth Justice*, 94.

a living must have put different kind of pressures on rural Jews who strove to be true to their traditions."[566]

Thus, we see the Naga situation similar to Jesus' social world where the Sumi Church has to revive their total commitment to the social surroundings apart from the regular religious responsibilities. Power and money manipulation, and the whole structure of political rule come under certain elite or family and clan. The opportunity then flow only in line to those who are favoured and the majority of the people is left oppressed.

Many of the Christians are reportedly involved in canvassing and taking money from the politicians against an unwise involvement of the people in election. The political leaders and their agents create their vote banks by using their power and money to manipulate particularly the migrants and outsiders stationed in Nagaland. Further, the innocent public are enticed with money and false promises, which they sideline after the election is over. This indicates a severe issue of taking away one's voting right and decision; and denial of their conscience. This results with crisis in proper political leadership in the State leading to corruption, injustice and other social evils.

V. K. Nuh laments that, today, "State election teaches innocent people to accept all kinds of corruption. The beautiful fabric of the Naga society has been torn into pieces."[567] As a result there are divisions politically among the political leaders. The Naga political movement has made people money and power maniacs induced by easy money. Psychologically, people are affected with fear and many innocent lives have been taken away in the name of factional divide and enmity. In this context, in the name of church, only a few interested leaders are involved in the political integration, but the mass of Christian believers and church have not been educated to become a motivated body to push forward peace and freedom of movement and development in Nagaland.

566 Norman Perrin, *The New Testament: An Introduction* (New York: Harcourt Brace Jovanovich, 1974), 311.

567 V. K. Nuh, *My Country, My People*, 8.

The Naga Hoho works to safeguard and promote Naga family, culturally , economically & politically; and uphold Naga solidarity. Similar bodies function among the different Naga tribes and one of them is Naga Council, Dimapur. They work politically with the different factions and concerned people in the form of appeals, seminars, rallies and awareness for peace process and other social awareness showing solidarity among the people. It needs strengthening from all sides of the Naga tribal groups in Nagaland. The Naga Students Federations (NSF), Naga People's Movement for Human Rights (NPMHR) and Naga Mothers' Association (NMA) attempt the upliftment of the socio-economic and political situation in Nagaland. However, the result is hardly noticeable. Despite the leaders and volunteers of these organizations the whole population could be motivated and educated towards Naga peace and development. For this to happen the Sumi Church along with Naga Baptist churches needs to become a transformational body to the socio-political and economic context of Nagaland.

The church has no political mission of its own, yet its mission is not fulfilled apart from the political struggle. Nial Mac Dermott states, 'The struggle for Human Rights is inevitably a political activity.'[568] Human beings are tortured, imprisoned without trial, discriminated against, kept in permanent poverty. It is necessary to assert rights in order to protect human persons from this cruel and degrading treatment and therefore human dignity is denied.

The Sumi Church cannot remain silent in political matters after witnessing tortures, tensions, fear and unrest. The power of Christ needs to inspire the Naga church to reflect on the present political situation. The church has to critically participate in liberative mission. It is true that many social organisations and leaders truly participate for the Naga political struggles but there is a flow of emotional hurt and pressure that often pushes them to the situation. However, the researcher here warns the political and church leaders to produce

568 Cited in, Shimreingam Shimray, *Theology of Human Rights,* 267. Cf. quoted from "Human Rights in a Theological Perspective: A Contribution from the German Democratic Republic" by Gunter Krusche, *Lutheran World,* 1977, 65.

God's ways of liberative prospects and development based on the word of God.

In the context of political conflicts the Sumi Church need to re-examine their understanding of participation in politics. The political task of the Sumi Church in the present context of peace process becomes more challenging and crucial at the same time. The Sumi Church could recall the spirit of the Church's concern for human rights in the past and strengthen their productive faith towards creative participation in the peace process. The church may motivate people on Christian concerns of Human Rights. The Nagas need to understand the essence of dignity and the recognition of relationship that can move them towards peaceful political development. Until it is improved the political failure would continue to threaten the stability of the socio-economic situation and also religious growth in a State.

Human Rights violations in Nagaland are an integral part of the political contexts. Christians can establish a practical way to understand human rights. The Naga Christian must develop a theological-ethical approach relevant to their situation. In that context of conflicts, it is necessary to suggest that they should overcome their tribal exclusivism and become open to the people around, without whom their existence would have no meaning. The issue is how one deals with the other and otherness. One easily indulges in judging, classifying, ignoring or ruling over the other according to one's convenience and ability. The question arises how one can best deal with the other. To this Lalsangkima Pachuau suggests that re-adjustment of the self can bring about restructuring how one perceives the other and otherness.[569] The church may educate the Naga Christians to develop a positive perception of otherness to overcome conflict situations caused by a depreciative perception of otherness, which turns to violence and threat to each other.

Hunter P. Mabry, in his ethical discussion emphatically proposes an ethical discourse of responsibility-relationality, which is concerned

569 Lalsangkima Pachuau, "Towards Overcoming Violence in North East India: A Perspective Drawn from Minority Experience," in *Overcoming Violence*, edited by Samson Prabhakar (Bangalore: South Asia Theological Research Institute, 2004), 43.

primarily not with what law is to be obeyed or what end of life is to be pursued, but with what is most fitting. It has great value in the context of plurality of human communities. He emphasizes responsible action in living with other people.[570] Christian faith has to be realized in the production of intrinsic human relationship. God has no religion and Jesus did not come to establish a religion but a community. In this case, Nagas need to extend concern and protection to the outsiders and different religious groups established in Nagaland. The Sumi Church may raise its voice against any manipulation for the political purpose and domestication of resources but treat them as human in the community's participation and development of the State.

The Church's mission in the world and Human Rights is like the separation of faith and works, words and deeds, theology and sociology, theory and practice. There is no biblical basis for these separations, since freedom and liberation for all men and women for the struggles of Human Rights is basic to the Church and its mission.[571] Thus, the Church in its overall mission to the world cannot sideline the reality of human issues. The Church's unchangeable and undeniable task could be to create a society, which accepts the dignity of every person. Thus, the Christian role of liberation is to liberate the poor and oppressed from economic and political exploitation. Luke 4:18-19 advocates liberation from all sorts of injustices even from political domination.[572]

Hence, Sumi Church's preaching and teaching must be in terms of our contemporary realities. Our theology should be characterized by constant reference to actual conditions. As John Perkins says a passion for reality is element realism.[573] It also means starting from within to move outward; that is, through a process

570 Hunter P. Mabry, *Christian Ethics: An Introductory Reader* (Kottayam: Indian Theological Library, 1987), 7-9.

571 John Perkins, "What it Means to be the Church: Reflections on Mission and Human Rights," *International Review of Mission*, Vol. 66/ 263 (July, 1997), 244.

572 V. K. Nuh, *Nagaland Church and Politics* (Kohima: V. Nuh and bro., 1986). 11-39.

573 Cited in, Pongsing Konyak, " Theological Concept of Human Development," in *In Search of Praxis Theology for the Nagas*, edited by V. K. Nuh, 141.

of conscientisation, seeking the self-propelled development of persons and the community, not an authoritarian, imposed coercive development from outside. In order to make Christianity practical and meaningfully applicable to the Naga people the Sumi Church has to take the social, religious, economic and political life of the people seriously, and transform them by the message of the gospel. The Christian theology for Nagaland should be more of traditions and thought forms, realities of present situations and struggles of the people to transform the society towards the life and the Kingdom of God as envisaged in the Bible.

4. Kingdom Community vs Naga Community

The reign of the Kingdom of God is highlighted through the Old Testament, Isaiah 40:1-9 and 52:7 which was not lost on the Gospel writers, demonstrate the rule of God, God's action. Vinay Samuel says that the Kingdom of God provides the vision for setting goals for community development work.[574] Further, Jesus mission was the proclamation and demonstration of the Kingdom of God in human society, in individual lives and the communities. Those who respond to the kingdom community experience full humanity as stewards of creation and servants of one another in a new community.

The Kingdom of God is also a source of values that we must expect to emerge in any Christian work as outcomes of mission attempted as an activity of the Kingdom of God. These include God's righteousness, the right relations he established between God and people, among people and in all His creation. It is closely related to the purpose of Christ's incarnation, death and resurrection in reconciliation, support and solidarity with His people. The church as the body of Christ could model such reconciliation and work for it in the whole of the community.

The act of redemption is another aspect of the kingdom where Jesus is worshipped and his Lordship and Kingdom activity continues for those who consciously accept his rule.[575] The Church kingdom

574 Cited in, Chris Sugden, *Gospel, Culture and Transformation* (New Delhi: Regnum Books International, 2000), 28.

575 Ibid., 30.

activity is not to convert the present Naga society into the Kingdom of God but simply to witness to the reality of the kingdom and God's intention for humanity against the distorting witness of evil.

The Bible reveals the cost of being in a community and its impelling concerns: the art of provision and providence; sharing and fellowship, and the commitment of every individual to another. The concept of *koinonia* in the Pauline though extends even more to ethnic concern of gentiles and Jews; male and female; any kinds of class and background distinctions that include fellowship, partnership, sharing, participation and a sense of belongingness. *Koinonia* is to bring back that lost peace into present reality and the church's desire for redress and remedy.[576] Jesus' ultimate example is revealed concretely in the gospels that Jesus dealt with each problem very distinctively within the inclusion of his salvific economy.[577]

To the rich and wealthy he condemned their selfish gain and accumulation of wealth, to the poor provision he was set apart, to sinners he helped them to discover themselves. According to Joachim Jeremias Jesus' meals with the publicans and sinners were not only an event on a social level or unusual expression of humanity and social generosity, and his sympathy with those who were despised, rather they were an expression of the mission and message of Jesus (Mk. 2: 17), which is eschatological meals, anticipatory celebrations of the feast in the end time (Lk. 13:28f; Mt. 8:11-12), the community of the saints already being represented (Mk. 2:19).[578]

The sick experienced complete healing according to their illness (psychological, physical, mental, material poverty and spiritual). God's reign arrives wherever Jesus overcomes the power of evil (evil takes many forms: pain, sickness, death, demon-possession, personal

576 Prechard B. M. Basaiawmoit, "Koinonia: A True Community" in *Hope in Action: Essay in Honour of Dr. Mathai Zachariah,* edited by Aruna Gnanadason, (Nagpur: National Council of Churches in India, 1990), 43-44.

577 Cf. Francis X. D'Sa ed., *Theology of Liberation: An Indian Biblical Perspective* (Collected Writings of George M. Soares Prabhu, Vol. 4), (Pune: Jnana-Deepa Vidyapeeth, 2001), 225; V. V. John, "The Role of the State in Jesus' View: A Synoptic Perspective," *Bangalore Theological Forum* 36/1 (June, 2004), 7.

578 Cited in, Takatemjen, *The Banquet is Ready: Rich and Poor in the Parables of Luke* (Delhi: ISPCK, 2003), 315-316.

sin and immorality, the loveless self-righteousness of those who claim to know God, the maintaining of special class privileges, the brokenness of human relationships).[579]

The Sumi Church can become a kingdom catalyst for social change and transformation in preaching, teaching and reforming anti social evils in the society. The Sumi Church can be strengthened to promote kingdom values by being an integral part of the society in the existing context of various social evils, such as moral disintegration, lostness of Naga cultural values of life and work, hatred and despair, socio-religious bankruptcy, injustice and division at political and religious levels, fear and doubts psychologically, and insecurity in the State. Thus, it demands the Sumi Church to understand greater prophetic challenges in mission activities and struggles.

The Sumi Church needs to scrutinize its spirituality since at present spirituality is understood as personal faith in God. Churches tend to differentiate between spiritual and secular as two opposite poles with no meeting point. The word secular is attributed to those people who do not belong to the church. Therefore, any social, development is often judged as pertaining to material needs, which is the opposite of the life of the spirit, i.e., non-material. K. M. George states that spirituality is understood as the totality of Christian faith and life in community as guided by the Holy Spirit of God.[580] The point is that spirituality is to be exercised in relationship with others in doing so it would extend the community of God on earth.

There are a few social organizations and NGOs that are attempting to uplift the socio-economic and political situation of Nagaland as discussed earlier. Akimbo society works especially among the commercial sex workers, HIV/AIDS, STD victims and drug users. It also rescues women and young people from the trap of social evils and helps them to have a better life. Sisterhood Network (SN) is actively involved in empowering and training women for vocational help for economic survival and also forming self-help groups (SHGs).

---

579 David Bosch, *Transforming Mission*, 32-33.

580 K. M. George, "Towards a Spirituality of Development" in *Christian Witness in Society*, edited by K. C. Abraham (Bangalore: BTE-SSC Publications, 1998), 218.

Morung looks for indigenous ways of learning together with different groups of young people in different professions. Mother's Hope (MH) works with unwed mothers (socially they are outcasts, rebuked and looked down upon) and infants giving hope and life under certain family's care and sometimes the mothers themselves. The church can join their efforts with these organizations to bring social transformation in Naga community. If the Sumi Church believes that its mission comes from God then it need to be encouraged to allow God's redemptive rule over the Naga community through its participation in upholding kingdom community.

Thus, community development could start with the people to strengthen their relationships in the community and solve the social evils such as violence, corruption and tribalism. In other words, the Sumi Church must see to it that people's spiritual and physical needs are met first. Having realized such needs, the church not only becomes a guardian of faith but also a facilitator for the growth of the people by fulfilling and fostering transformation and becoming leaven for change in society at large.

To be a Christian is to adopt Jesus' praxis of emptying oneself in the service of others. It is action through involvement rather than exercising power or command. The mission of the Sumi Church then may start with her own struggling members and with all those in distress rather than distancing herself from social reality. The church could become a facilitator in upholding and sustaining the community for its well-being and peaceful co-existence. The task of the church is to raise living standard and facilitate a process of adopting Kingdom values, such as equality with justice and peace as core values of the community. Thus, Sumi Church is expected to be a witnessing community through her praxis of love and care. The model before us is the kind of love Jesus showed, that is, sacrifice and service in the face of oppression and suffering.

In upholding kingdom community and values in Naga community the Sumi Church need to demonstrate the communal life of equality, freedom of expression, respect of elders, collective decision-making and the spirit of work culture. The traditional community bonds rooted in culture, religion and socio-economic development could raise every individual to be committed to work for a better quality of life for all. Litteral believes that in a proper Christian perspective the task of the church in the process should be to become a catalyst of people's development, and all other activities should be means to enable them to grow toward their potential. The basic problem of development is lack of hope, rather than lack of wealth.[581]

As Kingdom of God implies a culturally rooted Gospel, Naga cultural values can be a base of transformational development interpreting the Gospel into Naga culture, which demonstrates kingdom community as it took place and developed in its Jewish social culture. For instance, Jesus was conscious of their cultural enslavement therefore his attention was turned to unveiling their cultural propensities for liberation. Jesus spoke of the lilies of the field, the birds of the air, salt of the earth, the light of the world and so on. All symbols are taken from their situation drawing out elemental realities of life – affirming people's situation.[582]

Sumi Church in proclaiming the Kingdom of God in Naga context can take seriously the cultural and religious symbols and tradition, which embody their vision of life and wholeness. Sumi Church needs a spirituality that provides a basis for meaningful involvement in society and the struggles of people. This spirituality demands, reading the biblical materials in terms of a dominant concern for our times removing the oppressive structures, social evils and moral disintegration in various forms. The Sumi Church should be encouraged to move beyond traditional spirituality of reading the word of God, prayer, meditation, fellowship, meetings and conferences, and other regular religious activities although these are all valid provided they have new orientation and new meanings to the context and scriptures in its cultural setting.

The Sumi Church needs to recommend the issue of stewardship at all levels as a prophetical community confronting the situation of the people, social involvement as part of the mission of word

581 Robert L. Litteral, *Community Partnership in Communication Ministry* (Wheaton: The Billy Graham Center, 1988), 41.

582 K. C. Abraham, *Liberative Solidarity: Contemporary Perspective On Mission* (Thiruvalla: Christava Sahitya Samithy, 2001), 93.

and deed, becoming a liberator tackling injustice in Naga society politically, economically and religiously. In doing all this, the Sumi Church will uphold kingdom community among the Nagas.

II. Practical Suggestions

The Sumi Church can develop appropriate approaches for the transformational development of the Naga community in the emerging socio-economic context of Nagaland. There are many ways to envision the process by which individual and communities can promote self-reliance and sustainable economy; moral and cultural values; and as such the development and integration of the whole creation through the transforming action of the Sumi Church. In this case 'work' becomes an important aspect that embrace all kinds of work: ranging from lower to higher level, domestic, office, agriculture, business. Respect for work would add dignity and life to an individual. The need is more raised on the attitude towards work, and how faithful and sincere is an individual Naga towards work.

The concern of work is both on moral and economic basis. All work has a threefold moral significance. First, it is the principal way that people exercise the distinctive human capacity for self-expression and self-realization. Second, it is the ordinary way for human beings to fulfill their material needs. Finally, work enables people to contribute to the well being of the larger community. Work is not only for one's self. It is for one's family, for the nation, and indeed for the benefit of the entire human family.[583] Thus, the Sumi Church can work through the following approaches -

1. Strengthen Naga Traditional Institution of Customary Laws and Acts

There is a need for new development to affirm a real continuity with traditional patterns of life and ethos. The researcher in no way proposes the Nagas to return to the old ways of life rather he suggests to uphold and develop their values in the society. These developments can become human and promote human potential

583 "Economic Justice For All," Tenth Anniversary Edition of National Conference of Catholic Bishops: Untied State Catholic Conference, 1998, 50.

without disintegration.[584] It is possible only if the traditional society, its institutions, codes, and values are transformed by the gradual assimilation of the forces and values of modernity. Development as a transformation and expansion of the indigenous patterns is still a possibility and it is necessary for social health.

This may not be a new approach because it is a repetition of what was already there in the past. However, it could be brought out to help the present system from falling short in responding to the people's need and security. The researcher also recognizes the existing organizations such as Hohos, Naga tribal councils (at local level) and village councils. The Sumi Church may raise awareness and encourage the people to develop more of these representations in every local area, village and town. The reason for strengthening this institution has many objectives-

First, it will hold responsibility in selecting the appropriate person to stand as a candidate during election who could be responsible for the Naga people. For instance, as in the traditional way the clan sends representative on behalf of the particular clan in carrying out the necessary responsibility for the cause of the people. By doing so, the wealth, possessions, and power monopoly will not have a chance to be manipulated by a handful of people.

Second, the social evils and loose functioning of the law have allowed many young people to fall out of place. The special concerns can be taken care of, such as, drugs, rape cases, divorce, prostitution and others, which were rare in the past. In the case of prostitution the findings from the study shows, that the involvement of young single girls in this profession is due to economic poverty. However, the researcher believes there are other options for any Naga to work, eat and survive. Hence in this kind of case the Council or Hohos can look into their own respective area helping to reduce the problem and promote social and moral integrity in the Naga society.

Third, this institution should guard any development projects received from the government or NGOs or other social organizations to implement according to the needs and situation of the people.

---

584 Thomas, *The Nagas Towards, A.D. 2000.* 41.

Finally the researcher does not propose the present governmental system to be eliminated but clarifies that the enforcement of the traditional institutions could be able to assist the law and governing body making it easier to solve the existing flaws in Nagaland. However, any Council or Hoho may constitute enough people (inclusion of tribes and women representatives) to delegate their rightful responsibility.

2. Co-operative Community Development[585]

Co-operative Community Development is a process of vigorous involvement in bringing improvement in socio-economic areas of life. It is an opening of the individual's freedom and rights that assures opportunity for optimum development, equality of status and opportunity. It could be a multipurpose program with over-all improvement progressively and continuously in areas like education, health, general public services and so on.

The Sumi Church has a role to play in co-operative community development of the Naga people since the church is in a community with the purpose to fulfill God's will for His children. Though it may not directly involve in the situation; calling for joint efforts and networking with villages and town communities, would be worthwhile.

Right now in Nagaland we have co-operative offices particularly located in Dimapur. An individual may register and apply for loans for fishery, commercial purposes, building and housing loans, farming, and others. The Sumi Church could network with the co-operative offices with the help of village development board making it accessible to the people even in the rural areas.

Therefore, the advantages of new forms of informal planning especially for those people with no income of their own underemployed and unemployed would be appropriate. The young

---

585 Cf. Thangadurai Thangaraj, *Community Development* (Malaysia: University of Malaya Co-Operative Bookshop Ltd., 1969), 106, 108-109. Its principles have in them some significant, basic and far-reaching implications, which constitute some of the very foundations for community development concept. Co-operatives are free group enterprises for public benefit and profit sharing instead of private profit-motivated individual or corporation enterprises.

people may be motivated at the first place to utilize their available talents and skills. Church may encourage and introduce a co-operative system for community development to the people in both rural and urban settings. Church also needs the participation of the people themselves to improve the standard of living on their own initiatives. Church may provide technical provision and other services which may encourage them to initiate self-help for effective living.[586]

3. Reviving Community Work Culture

The Sumi Church can initiate to form a community work and utilize human power and resources within the jurisdiction of the community. This will motivate people to work and arouse work culture in the community, which is non-existent today. Community work such as, maintenance, welfare, sanitary system, roads and house construction, farming and others would be effective.

The value of work is to be revived in the present Naga society. The essence and importance of work is misunderstood and commonly, 'work' is attached with an attitude of 'shame and shyness' amongst the younger generation. This contrasting ethos from the past needs a very serious review. Work was the core objective of people's life and survival. Therefore, everybody was expected to work hard and eat from his or her sweat.

In the same way, the Bible has similar insights for the Nagas from the creation narratives and the stewardship bestowed on the human beings to carry out God's creativity in developing and fulfilling His purpose in creation. The researcher believes that the Sumi Church may persuade and cooperate with the Naga Christian community to enforce the work culture in terms of being responsible and productive which will fulfill God's stewardship bestowed upon them. The orientation can be given through pulpit preaching, teaching and involving practically at all levels of appointed work division and responsibilities.

---

586 Paul Henderson and David N. Thomas, *Readings in Community Work* (London: George Allen and Unwin, 1981), 7.

4. Human Potential - Resource Development

The Sumi Church has a vital role to play as stewards of God's economy and most importantly, to develop human potentiality in order to bring out God's creativity in human beings as created in His image.

Thus, development could be given priority to produce maximum human resources. While emphasizing on human potential, it is necessary to guard against the danger of valuing human beings merely as means for economic development.[587] The church could affirm the development of personhood in freedom and justice to human beings in community as the goal of development itself.

The position of skilled labour is very poor. The immediate need is to acquire skills and technology and develop the local talents for various development programmes that the State may plan. Training for human power, which is human capital, has not been taken into account. It is unfortunate that Nagas have begun to depend fully on the outside market for food and clothing inspite of their traditional arts and skills for living.[588] In this case, the Sumi Church may come out from depending upon the government of the state to tackle these problems and being in the forefront by educating the masses at different levels to work, value and produce what is their own.

Nagaland has great potential for development in horticulture and animal husbandry. [589] Therefore, fruit and vegetables, poultry, duckery, piggery, sheep breeding, cattle breeding, fodder cultivation can do well. Village industries based on locally available materials like cane, bamboo, wood, and handloom textiles, tanning of leather, soap making, bee keeping and pottery can be established and encouraged. In fact there must be determined efforts to use the local resources to produce goods that can compete in the national and international markets.

---

587 Thomas, *The Nagas Towards, A.D. 2000.* 40.

588 'Arts and Skills' are important parts of Naga life. It is a must 'course' in modern terms because every young individual is taught naturally the traditional trend. The 'dormitory' system in Naga tradition provides informal education to be active and professional in their ability and talents which helps them to become dignified, hard working and self-reliant, etc.

589 Sema, *Emergence of Nagaland,* 175.

The Sumi Church may also persuade the people to continue the agricultural and industrial tools and practices, which can be modernized to increase productivity since agriculture is the only source of livelihood for the majority of the people.

At present, a few of the social organizations and NGOs such as Naga Mothers' Association and Nagaland Development Outreach are engaged in these self-reliance and other socio-economic development projects. Thus, the church could carry out awareness for individuals, families and groups on these approaches.

5. Education for Development

Education is the process by which a person is formed or forms himself according to the truth. It works on the basis of the developmental urge and in line with it to achieve the developmental goal. Therefore, development is the urge inherent in the person where its goal is prescribed for the person and the task is set up on behalf of the person.[590]

Education is value-bound, not value free. Academic value is integrated with social, economic, material, moral and spiritual values. [591] It is building a network of these values in the chosen order of priority within the curricula of an educational system that we seek to give it a natural identity of its own besides making it helpfully purposeful.

According to M. M. Thomas "education is always training for participation in the larger society."[592] The alienation of educated youth from the age-old cultural tradition of hard work and earning a living by the sweat of their brow is so deep and widespread. Therefore it is necessary to relate education to the work ethic without which no society can develop.[593]

---

590 Cornelius Jaarsma, *Human Development, Learning and Teaching: A Christian Approach to Education Psychology* (Grand rapids: Wm. B. Eerdmans Publishing Company, 1961), 73.

591 J. T. K. Daniel and Nirmal Selvamony, *Value Education Today: Explorations in Social Ethic* (Jointly published by Madras: Madras Christian College; New Delhi: All India Association for Christian Higher Education, 1990), 17.

592 Thomas, *The Nagas Towards, A.D. 2000,* 57.

593 It is discussed in the above heading "developing and reviving work culture".

Thus, the educational system of the State has to be employment-oriented with prior emphasis on technical and vocational institutions because education in a true sense prepares a man for life and livelihood. It must be encouraged to inculcate work ethic that would lead to self-confidence and self-reliance. The educational aim than must be to prepare the youth to stand on their feet by engaging them in productive activities. For such, an appropriate curriculum of community-oriented education could be introduced. Until this happens the present guise of our system as a foster mother feeding appetites of careerism will remain unchanged.

The government schools established in main centers of the areas and villages, are manipulated by replacing proxy teachers, neglection of students and denial of their right to quality education. In this case Nagas do not see any future leaders in the next generation. Therefore, Sumi Church can intervene through awareness programmes for strengthening the educational system, which would be helpful to motivate the people to execute their responsibility faithfully and be good citizens and leaders of Naga society.

The researcher suggests that Sumi Church may take initiatives to motivate those people who are involved in the educational institutions, heads of the departments and the government through networking with the Naga Students Federation and other traditional institutions for improvement of the educational systems according to the taste of the people. The church may move forward for systems like Morung sort of educational learning along with modern education.

The researcher acknowledges that there are several other people, who discuss and propose the same at the National level, and State levels but so far nothing has been worked out seriously. One must use one's psychological capacity and potentiality giving choices to learn and educate as the priority in developing good citizens and leaders, thus reducing poverty and social evils that distort the image of Naga society.

6. Job Creation Project Development

A Latin American Mission Job creation project provides an example for the Nagas to consider.[594] The statement of the Apostle Paul being its theological basis: "Make it your ambition to lead a quiet life, to mind your own business and work with your hands, just as we told you, so that your daily life may win the respect of outsiders and so you will not be dependent on anybody" (1 Thes 4:11-12).

The response in the squatter town of Chapulines, Costa Rica was a project to make beanbag furniture, based on sewing that could be done within the home. The majority of them were women, unemployed, sole supporters of their families and in many cases unable to leave their homes. Many of them started to make other products that they sold on their own. Gradually, the management of all the business activity was transferred to the women, without outside support.[595]

It is relevant to the Nagas since the Naga women are committed in taking advantage of the opportunity. It may start with women's groups then gradually pass on to the young people especially those unemployed and underemployed. Women groups at some places have already introduced this form of self-help groups.

The question is how do we create jobs and help the people? It could be lending funds or loans to start with some project. Sometimes it could be by way of supplying raw materials and articles according to the needs of the projects. Help people to involve in regular agricultural work, traditional arts and crafts, weaving, sewing works and carpentry. People may get engaged in these categories of work and labour if provided with opportunities through community projects. Further, Sumi Church can introduce community farming, building and housing projects, which can be a great help in the context. Thus, Sumi Church has a multiple role to play to develop the resource income for management of the church maintenance, development

594 Max L. Stockhouse, at el., *The Local Church in a Global Era: Reflections for a New Century* (Michigan: William E. Eerdman Publishing Company, 2000), 51.

595 Stockhouse, *The Local Church in a Global Era*, 51.

and other regular activities. Church can become a facilitator in providing productive growth for the church community.

Therefore, the church has its share of benefits in generating cycles of resources supporting and accommodating people for socio-economic survival. Church can activate this system directly or through the help of government, NGOs or other social organizations of the same kind. This may serve a new kind of approach among the Naga churches particularly Sumi Church, however, the community nature of working together is an intrinsic old age doing in Naga society which can be adopted by the church today in motivating the wider community.

Conclusion

The Naga socio-economic context challenges the church to focus on Christian education, which would aim for change both at individual and social structural levels. Christian educational ministry should aim at "becoming and not on knowing" as stated by Akheto Sema.[596] He further says that Christian education calls for a paradigm shift from 'content –centered' to 'life –centred' education; from 'ecclesio-oriented' to 'social-oriented' therefore, addressing the context of the society and extending individual concern to community welfare which becomes the agenda of the Christian educational mission of the church.

The researcher is of the opinion that the Sumi Church has to look into the aspect of Christian educational mission. At present, the church is mostly engaged in outreach mission besides other activities within the mission center. It is imperative for the Sumi Church to give a serious reflection on theological vision of mission and broaden also its horizon towards socio-economic context of Nagaland.

However, the researcher's main concern is why Christian education is important for all. It is because the Nagas have broken their moral and spiritual integrity. They have misused the God given freedom for their selfish ends. Therefore, the need of the hour is to

596 Akheto Sema, "A Study of Paulo Freire's Educational Thoughts in the Context of Nagaland" (D.Th Thesis, United Theological College; SATHRI, Bangalore, 2000), 216.

rebuild their personal dimension for developing character, morality, and a sense of the responsibility towards nature and human being and harmony of the whole creation. Strengthening this will impact each individual and community for transformational development of the Naga society. Sumi Church as prophetic church may involve in educational ministry directing towards liberating and transforming society.

As Freire believes, the churches are not abstract entities; they are institutions involved in history. Therefore, the church needs to understand their educational role taking into consideration the concrete situation in which it exists.[597] The church in its educational mission is challenged to take a prophetic posture by denouncing what is wrong and announcing God's will for the world that is to be more humane, just and loving.

Hence, the goal of Christian education is to enable the church and its members to be faithful to the calling of the Kingdom of God and to enable them to respond to the social realities creatively.[598] In doing so, the researcher believes that Sumi Church can build people's critical consciousness of the socio-economic and political realities of Nagaland and will help to act critically and responsibly towards social injustices creating awareness and making all human beings enjoy the fullness of life.

The discussion in this chapter has thrown light on the transformational development of church mission seeking to achieve wholesome spiritual maturity. Transformational development is fulfilled in God's intended purpose in human beings, which demands a continual process of development of a human situation ethically, environmentally and spiritually. In other words, a holistic understanding of transformation, in turn will motivate people to act and shoulder the responsibility fulfilling God's purpose in creation.

The biblical and theological developmental approach dealt with in this book has a lot of potential for enriching the socio-

597 Paulo Freire, "Education, Liberation and the Church," in *Religious Education,* 79/4 (Fall, 1984), 106.

598 Samson Prabhkar, "Towards a Christian Education for an Inclusive Community," *A Seminar Paper* at U.T.C. June 21, 1996, 3.

economic prospects for the Sumi Church to practically involve in the context. Development of humanity should be encouraged to take into consideration in our concern for development. Thus, the Sumi Church may attempt to promote the socio-economic situation of the people in a creative and helpful way as co-creators with God sustaining and liberating the people. In doing so, the church would fulfil God's stewardship bestowed upon it.

Further depending on these points the author has drawn the implications for the mission of the Sumi Church. The four main issues relevant to the Naga context where the Sumi Church is called for mission in the transformational development of the Naga people are pointed out. The reflection on biblical and theological basis has paved the way for the mission of the Sumi Church appropriate in the context. The aspects of stewardship and socio-economic development of the Naga people are discussed where the Sumi Church is called for commitment, love and responsibility in establishing God's stewardship in the Naga community. Sumi Church is called to confront the whole issue of justice in the midst of injustice and division in the Naga community. The Sumi Church is called for liberative mission to address all sort of oppressive structures, socio-economically and politically, which delimit the rights of the people. Finally, the Sumi Church is called for upholding kingdom community, admitting that in Naga community the social and moral values are corrupted and spirituality bankrupt.

Further, relevance of the concept of traditional community life from the past has been brought forth in approach to transformational development through practical suggestions of a seven point approach- Reviving Community Work culture; To Strengthen Naga traditional Institution of customary laws and act; Co-operative Community Development; Human Potential - Resource Development; Education for Development; and Job Creation Project Development.

Thus, the discussion above leads the Church to realize its special ability to promote socio-economic activity that is 'development oriented', by connecting economic programmes and other community projects. The strategic vision must now emerge for economic development as a worthy programme in its own right, a ministry that is allowed to grow in meeting the needs of the people to obtain their daily bread by working with their own hands. If Sumi Church claims that its mission is "to follow our Lord and Saviour Jesus Christ in working with the poor…" church would seek to have the mind of Christ in God in discovering constructive roles to promote and fulfil his purpose (Hebrews 4: 15).

BIBLIOGRAPHY

Books:

A Brief Account on Nagaland. Prepared by Federal Government of Nagaland Kohima: Nagaland, June 2000.

Abraham, K. C. *Liberative Solidarity: Contemporary Perspective on Mission*. Thiruvalla: Christava Sahitya Samithy, 2001.

Abreo, Desmond A. D.' *Turning the Tide of Injustice*. Mangalore: Margaret D'Abreo, 1991.

Agrell, Goran. *Work, Toil and Sustenance*. Sweden: Verbum Hakam Ohlssons, 1976.

Aier, Wati. "Nagas at Present: From a Theological Perspective." In *From Darkness to Light.* Edited by Alongla P. Aier. Kohima: NBCC, 1997.

Amit, Yairah. "The Jubilee Law - An Attempt at Institution Social Justice." In *Justice and Righteousness: Biblical Themes and their Influence*. Edited by Henning Graft Reventlow and Yair Hoffman. England: Journal for the Study of the Old Testament, 1992.

Ao, Bendangyabang A. *History of Christianity in Nagaland: The Ao Naga Tribal Christian Missionaries, 1872-1972*. Mokokchung: Shalom Ministry Publication, 2002.

Ao, N. Toshi. *Mission to the Nagas: A Tryst with the Aos*. NP: 1995.

Ateek, Naim Stifan. *Justice, and Only Justice: A Palestinian Theology of Liberation*. Maryknoll: Orbis Books, 2001.

Bag, G. N. *Rural Transformation in Tribal Areas*. New Delhi: Akansha Publishing House, 2001.

Barua, P. C. "Employment Survey: Need for Changed Emphasis." In *Development Planning of North East India*. Edited by P. C. Barua. New Delhi: Mittal Publications, 1990.

Basaiawmoit, Prechard B. M. "Koinonia: A True Community." In *Hope in Action: Essay in Honour of Dr. Mathai Zachariah*. Edited by Aruna Gnanadason. Nagpur: National Council of Churches in India, 1990.

Beaumont, Paul R. ed. *Christian Perspectives on Human Rights and Legal Philosophy*. Cumbria: Paternoster Press, 1998.

Befus, David. "Discovering a Role in God's Provision: Sustainable Economic Development for the Church and Poor People." In *The Local Church in a Global Era: Reflections for a New Century*. Edited by Max L. Stockhouse, et al. Michigan: William E. Eerdman Publishing Company, 2000.

Bosch, David. *Transforming Mission*. Mary knoll: Orbis Books, 1991.

Ceresko, Anthony R. *The Old Testament: A Liberative Perspective*. Mumbhai: St. Pauls, 2001.

Christian Faith and the World Economy Today: A Study Document from the World Council of Churches. Geneva: WCC Publications, 1992.

Conrad. *Rich Man, Poor Man and The Bible*. London: SCM Press, 1979.

Corbett, Jack and Elizabeth, Smith. *Becoming a Prophetic Community*. Georgia: John Knox Press, 1980.

D'Abreo, Desmond. *A Voice to the People: Communication for Social Change*. Madras: Culture and Communication, 1990.

Daniel, J. T. K. and Nirmal Selvamony. *Value Education Today: Explorations in Social Ethic*. Jointly published by Madras: Madras Christian College; New Delhi: All India Association for Christian Higher Education, 1990.

D. D. Mali. "TRYSEM and Development of Rural Entrepreneurship in North-Eastern Region." In *Development Planning of North East*

India. Edited by P. C. Barua. New Delhi: Mittal Publications, 1990.

Donahue, John R. "Biblical Perspectives on Justice." In *The Faith that Does Justice*, edited by John C. Haughey. New York: Paulist Press, 1977.

Donahue, John R. *The Gospel in Parable: Metaphor, Narrative, and Theology in the Synoptic Gospels*. Philadelphia: Fortress, 1988.

D'Sa, Francis X. ed. *Theology of Liberation: An Indian Biblical Perspective.* Collected Writings of George M. Soares Prabhu, Vol. 4. Pune: Jnana-Deepa Vidyapeeth, 2001.

Duchrow, Ulrich & Gerhard Liedke. *Shalom: Biblical Perspective on Creation, Justice and Peace.* Geneva: WCC Publications, 1989.

"Economic Justice for All". In *Tenth Anniversary Edition of National Conference of Catholic Bishops: New York, Untied State Catholic Conference.* 1998.

Elliott, Charles. *The Development Debate.* London: SCM Press, 1971.

Elwin, Verrier. *Nagaland.* Shillong: P. Dutta for the Research Development, 1961.

Fernandes, Angelo. *Towards Peace with Justice: The Role of Religion Today.* New Delhi: Indian Social Institute, 1991.

Fowler, H. W., et al. *The Concise Oxford Dictionary of Current English.* 3rd Edition. Oxford: Oxford University, 1934.

G. Soares. "The Social Implications of the Message of Jesus." In *The Church in India in the Struggle for a New Society.* Edited by Amalorpavadoss. Bangalore: National Biblical, Catechetical and Liturgical Center, 1981.

Ganguli, Milada. *A Pilgrimage to the Nagas.* New Delhi: Mohan Primlani, 1984

George, K. M. "Towards a Spirituality of Development." In *Christian Witness in Society*. Edited by K. C. Abraham. Bangalore: BTE-SSC Publications, 1998.

Ghosh, B. B. "Emergence and Role of Middle Class in Nagaland." In *The Emergence and Role of Middle Class in Northeast India.*

Edited by B. Datta Ray. New Delhi: Uppal Publishing House, 1983.

Ghosh, G. K. *Tribals and their Culture in Manipur and Nagaland.* Vol. 3. New Delhi: Ashish Publishing House, 1999.

Gnana Robinson. "Justice in the Old Testament." In *Where is Justice?* Edited by Frenz Albrecht. Madurai: Tamilnadu Theological seminary, 1976.

Gnanakan, Richard S. *Work in God's World: Insights into a Theology of Work.* Bangalore: Theological Book Trust, 2003.

Goulet, Denis. *The Cruel Choice: A New Concept in the Theory of Development.* Cambridge: Center for the Study of Development and Social Change, 1973.

Gutierrez, Gustavo. *A Theology of Liberation.* New York: Orbis Books, 1973.

Haan, Roelf. *The Economics of Honour: Biblical Reflections on Money and Prophecy.* Translated by Nancy Forest Filer. Geneva: WCC Publications, 1988.

Habel, Norman C. *The Land is Mine.* Minneapolis: Fortress Press. 1995.

Hay, Donald A. *Economics Today: A Christian Critique.* Leicester: Intervarsity press, 1991.

Henderson, Paul and David N.Thomas eds. *Readings in Community Work.* London: George Allen and Unwin, 1981.

Hill, Lewis E. "*Economic History as a Source of Socioeconomic Normative Value.*" In *Social Economics: Premise, Finding, and Policies.* Edited by J. O' Boyle. London: Routledge, 1996.

Hirsch, Richard G. "Judaism in Pursuit of Economic Justice." In *Contemporary Religion and Social Responsibility.* Edited by Norbert Brockman. New York: ALBA House, 1973.

Hutton, J. H. *The Sema Nagas.* London: Oxford University Press, 1968.

Imnayongdang. *Levels of Rural Development in Nagaland: A Spatial Analysis.* Meerut: S. K. Mittal, 1990.

Iralu, Kaka D. *How Then Shall We Live?* Kohima: Kaka D. Iralu, 2001.

Jaarsma, Cornelius. *Human Development, Learning and Teaching: A Christian Approach to Education Psychology*. Grand Rapids: Wm. B. Eerdmans Publishing Company, 1961.

Jayakumar, Samuel. *Mission Reader: Historical Models for Wholistic Mission in the Indian Context*. Delhi: ISPCK, 2002.

Justo, L. *Faith and Wealth: A History of Early Christian Ideas on the Origin, Significance, and the Use of Money.* San Francisco: Harper & Row, 1990.

Kantonen, T. A. *A Theology for Christian Stewardship*. Philadelphia: Fortress Press, 1956.

Keitzar, Renthy. *In Search of a Gospel Message: Introducing a Contextual Christian Theology for North East India.* Guwahati: Christian Literature Center, 1995.

Khutsoh, Wezote. *Tourism Scenario and Its Potentiality in Nagaland.* Guwahati: Marg Advertising, 2000.

Kirk J. Andrew. *What is Mission? Theological Explorations*. Minneapolis: Fortress Press, 2000.

Konyak, Phola W. *Sample Survey on Consumption of Imported Meat, Fish and Eggs in Kohima Town 2003*. State Institute of Rural Development, Nagaland: Kohima, 2003.

Konyak, Pongsing. "Theological Concept of Human Development." In *In Search of Praxis Theology for the Nagas.* Edited by V. K. Nuh. New Delhi: Regency Publications, 2003.

Kumar, Keval J. "Communication Approaches to Participation and Development: Challenging the Assumptions and Perspectives." In *Participatory Communication: Working for Change and Development.* Edited by Shirly A. White. New Delhi: Sage Publication, 1994.

Land, Philip. *Justice in the World: An Overview*. Vatican City: Pontifical Commission Justice & Peace, 1972.

Lasuh, K. "The Biblical Concept of Human Rights." In *Crusade on Naga Morality.* Compiled by V. K. Nuh. Kohima: Council of Naga Baptist Churches, 1996.

Limouris, Gennadios ed. *Justice, Peace and the Integrity of Creation.* Geneva: WCC Publications, 1990.

Litteral, Robert L. *Community Partnership in Communication Ministry*. Wheaton: The Billy Graham Center, 1988.

Lohfink, Gerhard. *Jesus and Community: The Social Dimension of Christian Faith*. Translated by John P. Galvin. Philadelphia: Fortress Press, 1984.

Longchar, A. Wati. *The Tribal Religion in Northeast India: An Introduction*. Jorhat: Eastern Theological College, 2000.

Mabry, Hunter P. *Christian Ethics: An Introductory Reader*. Kottayam: Indian Theological Library, 1987.

Maggay, Melba Padilla. *Transforming Society*. Quezon, Philippines: Institute for Studies in Asian Church and Culture, 1996.

Malina, Bruce J. *The New Testament World: Insights from Cultural Anthropology.* Atlanta: John Knox Press, 1981.

McFague, Sallie. *Life Abundant: Rethinking Theology and Economy for a Planet in Peril.* Minneapolis: Fortress Press, 2000.

Meeks, M. Douglas. *God the Economist: The Doctrine of God and Political Economy*. Minneapolis: Fortress Press, 1989.

Myers, Bryant. *Walking With the Poor: Principles and Practices of Transformational Development.* New York: Orbis Books, 1999.

Meyer Carl S. and Herbert T. Meyer, eds. *The Caring God: Perspectives on Providence*. London: Concordia, 1973.

Mudge, Lewis S. *Rethinking the Beloved Community: Ecclesiology, Hermeneutics, Social Theory*. Geneva: WCC Publications, 2001.

Nash, Ronald H. *Poverty and Wealth: Why Socialism Doesn't Work.* Westchester: Crossway Books, 1986.

.... *New Webster's Dictionary of the English Language.* 6th edition. New Delhi: Surjeet Publications, 1995.

Norman, Kraus, C. *The Community of the Spirit: How the Church is in the World.* Scottdale: Herald Press, 1993.

Noulezhalie, Ricky Medom. *The Relevance of the Theological Motif of Exile to the Naga's Struggle for Sovereignty as a People.* Delhi: ISPCK, 2002.

Nuh, V. K. *My Native Country: The Land of the Nagas*. Delhi: Spectrum Publications, 2002.

Nuh, V. K. *Struggle for Identity in Northeast India: A Theological Response*. Delhi: Spectrum Publications, 2001.

Nuh, V. K. "Christian Mission in the Socio-Political Life." In *In Search of Praxis Theology for the Nagas* Edited by V. K. Nuh. New Delhi: Regency Publications, 2003.

Nuh, V. K. *Nagaland Church and Politics*. Kohima: V. Nuh and Bro., 1986.

Pachuau, Lalsangkima. "Towards Overcoming Violence in North East India: A Perspective Drawn from Minority Experience," In *Overcoming Violence*. Edited by Samson Prabhakar. Bangalore: South Asia Theological Research Institute, 2004.

"Past and Present Status of Training Conducted by SIRD, Nagaland." In *Action Plan of Panchayati Raj Training for The State of Nagaland for Chairman, DRDAs/Ex-Officio Chairman, VDBs and Village Council Members/VDB Members/ G. Bs.* Kohima: State Institute of Rural Development, 2003.

Perrin, Norman. *The New Testament: An Introduction*. New York: Harcourt Brace Jovanovich, 1974.

Philip, P. T. *The Growth of Baptist Churches in Nagaland*. Assam: CLC, 1976.

Potter, Philip. "The Global Economic System in Biblical Perspective." In *The Ecumenical Movement Tomorrow*. Edited by Mac Reuver, et al. Geneva: WCC, 1993.

Punnapadam, Thomas. *Justice as Spirituality: The Challenge Posed by the Synodal Document Justice in the World*. Bangalore: Kristu Jyoti Publications, 1991.

Puthenpurakhal. *Baptist Missions in Nagaland*. Shillong: Vendrame Missiological Institute, 1984.

Raiser, Konrad. *For a Culture of Life: Transforming Globalization and Violence*. Geneva: World Council of Churches, 2002.

Raja, John Jashva, *Facing the Reality of Communication: Culture, Church and Communication*. Delhi: ISPCK, 2000.

Ramunny, Murkot. *The World of Nagas*. New Delhi: Northern Book Center, 1988.

Rao, O. M. ed. *Longri Ao; A Biography*. Calcutta: Swapna Printing Work, 1986.

Ray, B. Datta. *Tribal Identity and Tension in Northeast India.* New Delhi: Omsons Publications, NY.

Ray, B. Datta. *The Emergenc and Role of Middle Class in North-East India.* New Delhi: Uppal Publishing House, 1983.

"Repercussion of the Indo-Nagas Cease Fire." In *The Nagas: Truth and Hope for the Living*. Kohima: NPMHR.

Reumann, John. *Stewardship and the Economy of God.* Grand Rapids: William B. Eerdmans Publishing Company, 1992.

Riches, John. *The World of Jesus: First – Century Judaism in Crisis.* New York: Cambridge University Press, 1990.

Robinson. "A New Economic Order: The Challenge of the Biblical Jubilee." In *A Vision for Man.* Edited by S. Amirtham. Madras: CLS, 1978.

Rodrigues, Clarissa. *The Social and Political Thought of Dr. S. Radhakhrisnan: An Evaluation*. New Delhi: Sterling Publishers, 1992.

Rongsen, M. *Development and Ecology.* Delhi: Cambridge Press, 1999.

Saikia, Jogamaya. "People's Participation in Rural Development: A Study in Nagaland." In *Rural Development in North-East India: Perspectives, Issues and Experiences*. Edited by Samanta, R. K. New Delhi: Uppal Publishing House, 1991.

Scott, Waldron. *Bring Forth Justice: A Contemporary Perspective on Mission*. Grand Rapids: William B. Eerdmans Publishing Company, 1980.

Sema, Hokishe. *Emegence of Nagaland: Socio-economic and Political Transformation and the Future.* Uttar Pradesh: Vikas Publishing House, 1986.

Sen, Amartya. *Development as Freedom*. New York: Anchor Books, 1999.

Shimray, Shimreingam. *Theology on Human Rights: A Critique on Politics*. Ukhrul: Ruth Shimray and CESAC, 2002.

Singh, B. P. *The Problem of Change: A Study of Northeast India*. Delhi: Oxford University Press, 1987.

Singh, K. S. ed. *Tribal Situation in India.* Shimla: Indian Institute of Advanced Study, 1972.

Six, Jean-Francois. *Church and Human Rights.* Translated by Susan Leslie. United Kingdom: St Paul Publications, 1992.

Solanki, Anil D. "The Implication of Shalom in The Old Testament for Evangelism and Justice Today." In *Mission as Witness and Justice: An Indian Perspective*. Edited by Bruce J. Nicholls and Christopher S. Raj. Delhi: The Theological Research and Communication Institute, 1991.

.... *Statistical Hand Book of Nagaland 2001*. Kohima: Directorate of Economics & Statistics Government of Nagaland, 2002.

Stockhouse, Max L. et al. *The Local Church in a Global Era: Reflections for a New Century.* Michigan: William B. Eerdman Publishing Company, 2000.

Stott, John. *Christian Mission in the Modern World.* Bombay: Gospel Literature Service, 1975.

Sugden, Chris. *Gospel, Culture and Transformation*. New Delhi: Regnum Books International, 2000.

Swartley, Willard M. *Israel's Scripture Traditions and the Synoptic Gospels: Story Shaping Story.* Peabody: Hendrickson, 1994.

Takatemjen, *Studies on Theology and Naga Culture*. Delhi: ISPCK, 1998.

Takatemjen. *The Banquet is Ready: Rich and Poor in the Parables of Luke*. Delhi: ISPCK, 2003.

Theissen, Gerd. *Social Reality and the Early Christians: Theology, Ethics, and the World of the New Testament.* Translated by Margaret Kohl. Edinburgh: T&T Clark, 1993.

Thangaraj, Thangadurai. *Community Development*. Malaysia: University of Malaya Co-Operative Bookshop, 1969.

Thanzauva, K. "Tribal Ecclesiology: 'Community House' as the Basis of Tribal Ecclesiology." In *Tribal Theology: A Reader*. Edited by Shimreingam Shimray. Jorhat: Tribal Study Center, 2003.

Thanzauva, K. *Theology of Community: Tribal Theology in the Making*. Bangalore: Asian Trading Corporation, 2004.

Thanzauva, K. *Transforming Theology: A Theological Basis for Social Transformation*. Bangalore: Asian Trading Corporation, 2002.

.... *The Naga Foundation: Towards Fulfillment of a People' Unwavering Aspiration*. Kohima: Naga Students Federation, 2002.

"The Formation of Nagaland Baptist Church Council." In *From Darkness to Light*. Edited by P. Alongla Aier. Kohima: NBCC, 1997.

.... *A Brief Account on Nagaland.* Kohima: Federal Government of Nagaland, June 2000.

Thomas, M. M. *The Nagas Towards 2000 A. D*. Madras: Center for Research on International Economic Order, 1992.

Thomas, M. M. *Tribal Awakening*. Bangalore: Christian Institution for the Study of Religion and Society, 1965.

"Training of the Members of Village Councils and Village Development Boards (VDBs)," *Reading Materials*. Kohima: SIRD 1999.

Vamuzo, *Develop Your Own Village: An Approach to Grass Root Planning and Development*, (Kohima: Author),1978.

Vasum, R. *Nagas' Right to Self-Determination: An Anthropological Historical Perspective*. New Delhi: Mittal Publications, 2000.

Vizo, Kiyasetuo. *A Case Study of Cattle Rearing in Kohima Village Kohima R. D. Block Nagaland: A Socio-economic Perspective*. Kohima: State Institute of Rural Development, 2003.

Vizo, Kiyasetuo. *Self Sustainable Integrated Farming: An Alternative for Sustainable Agricultural Development in Nagaland.* Kohima: State Institute of Rural Development, 2003.

Von Rad, Gerhard. *Old Testament Theology*. Vol. 1. New York: Harper & Row, 1962.

Wenham, David. *Paul Follower of Jesus or Founder of Christianity?* Grand Rapids: William B. Eerdmans Publishing Company, 1995.

Westerhoff, John. *Will Our Children Have Faith?* New York: Seabury Press, 1976.

Whitelam, Keith. "Israelite Kingship: The Royal Ideology and Its Opponents." In *The World of Ancient Israel.* Edited by Ronald Clements. Cambridge: Cambridge University Press, 1989.

Wolterstorff, Nicholas. *Until Justice and Peace Embrace.* Grand Rapids: William B. Eerdmans Publishing Company, 1983.

Wren, Brian A. *Education for Justice.* Mary knoll: Orbis Books, 1977.

Yepthomi, Najekhu. "Early History of the Nagas." In *From Darkness to Light.* Edited by P. Alongla Aier. Publication of the Nagaland Baptist Church Council on the Occasion of the Celebration of 125 years of Christianity in Nagaland, 1997.

Yongdang. Impact of Topography on the Activities of Rural Life in Nagaland. Kohima: State Institute of Rural Development, 2003.

Souvenirs:

"Human Rights Week in Nagaland 10-15 December 1978: A Report." 25 years of Naga Peoples Movement for Human Right, *Souvenir.*

Lhotohe Ayemi. "Nagami Yeghilo Eno Sumi Gholo Ayehkulu Ighikeu." *Souvenir* (Sumi Christian Centenary-WSBAK 1904-2003).

Longkumer, N. T. " Naga Council-Its Achievements." Naga Council Golden Jubilee, 1949-1999, *Souvenir.*

Loucu, Lhoutuo. "Back-ground of Naga Club, Naga Youth Club and Naga Council." Naga Council Golden Jubilee, 1949-1999, *Souvenir.*

Sumi Aphuyemi Baptist Akukuhou Kuqhakulu (Association) Diamond Jubilee Xulhe, 1912-1987, *Souvenir.*

Sumi Baptist Diamond Jubilee Vesulho Eno Xughili, 1904-1978. *Souvenir.*

Swu, Vitoshe. "WSBAK Mission Ghili." Sumi Christian Centenary-WSBAK, 1904-2003), *Souvenir.*

"Recent Activities of Naga Peoples Movement for Human Rights." NPMHR 25 years, *Souvenir.*

"The Nagas: Truth and Hope for the Living." NPMHR 25 years, *Souvenir.*

"The Achievements and Failures of NSF." Naga Students Federation Golden Jubilee, 1947-1997, *Souvenir.*

Reports:

A Brief Report on the People to People Dialogue on the Indo-Naga Conflict at Vishwa Yuvak Kendra, New Delhi on 29 January 2000.

A Report of NBCC, Submitted to the CBCNEI 39th Annual Council, Jorhat February 15-19, 1889.

A Report on Naga Peoples Movement for Human Rights (NPMHR): One Step Back Two Steps Forward 1999-2000.

A Report on Peace Conference organized by CBCNEI/NCCI/MBC/ CASA on 12-14 October 2001 at MBC Center Church.

A Short Report of URF Outreach Mission to Adiland, Arunachal Pradesh, From 1985-2000. Presented by Rev. I. Khala, Director, United Revival Fellowship.

"A Strategy of Hope! No matter how long the night the day is sure to come." *A Paper* produced by NPMHR. NY.

Annual Administrative Report of SIRD, 2004-2005. By Government of India.

Annual Report of NDO, Submitted at Triennial Convention Nagaland Baptist Church Council, CBLT on 30 January-1 February 2004

Annual Report of the New Life Ministry, NBCC, October 2001.

Ayemi, Phoghoto. "Executive Kumla Yepithi/ Report, 1995-2004", *A Report*, (46th Western Sumi Baptist Akukuhou Kuqhakulu 2004 Yepithi at Nikhekhu Baptist Akukuhou on 3rd-5th, December 2004).

Kapfo, K. *A Brief Report of the NBCC Women's Department Secretary from October 2003 to September 2004* at T. Chekri, Pfutsero During its 22nd Annual Meeting on 8-9 October 2004.

"Naga Hoho reaffirmed its political stand to work for integration of all the Naga areas." 7th General assembly of the Naga Hoho, May 20-22 2000. *A Report.*

Nuh, V. K. *Statistical Report 2005 of CNBC.*

Pongsing. *Annual Report of 2004 Nagaland Development Outreach Towards Fuller Life.*

Pongsing. *Annual Report of Nagaland Development Outreach.* Submitted at 16th Triennial Convention Nagaland Baptist Church Council on 30 January - 1February 2004.

"Summary report on the conditions of the Internally Displaced Persons (IDPs) from the Imphal Valley to the Naga Hill as areas of Manipur." *Naga Peoples Movement for Human Rights (NPMHR),* 2001.

Sumi Christian Centenary (WSBAK) Cum 45th Western Sumi Baptist Akukuhou Kuqhakulu 2003 Yepithi/*Report,* 4th - 7th December 2003.

Swu, Vitoshe. "WSBAK Mission Kumla Yepithi 2004." A *Report* (46th Western Sumi Baptist Akukuhou Kuqhakulu 2004 Yepithi at Nikhekhu Baptist Akukuhou on 3rd – 5th, December 2004).

Teruja, Zhabu. *The Nagaland Baptist Church Council in 2004: A Brief Report Presented at the Annual General Meeting of the Council of Baptist Churches in North East India* at Sivasgar on 21-24 April 2005.

Trinity Theological College 1st Annual Report, 1993-94 presented by Principal, Trinity Theological College on 24th April 1994.

"WSBAK Women Department Kumla Yepithi", *A Report* (46th Western Sumi Baptist Akukuhou Kuqhakulu 2004 Yepithi at Nikhekhu Baptist Akukuhou on 3rd-5th, December 2004).

Newspapers:

Eastern Mirror, 19 August 2003.

Eastern Mirror, 21 August 2003.

Eastern Mirror, 8 August 2003.

Nagaland Post, 1 October 2004.

Nagaland Post, 14 December 1999.

Nagaland Post, 15 December 1999.
Nagaland Post, 17 April 2005.
Nagaland Post, 2 May 2005.
Nagaland Post, 25 March 2005.
Nagaland Post, 27 April 2005.
Nagaland Post, 27 September 2004.
Nagaland Post, 5 May 2005.
Nagaland Post, 5 May 2005.
Nagaland Post, 6 March 2005.
Nagaland Post, 9 April 2005.
Times of India, 16 July 2003.

Theses:

Lotha, Myanbemo Kikon. "Social and Cultural Implications of Agricultural Development.

A Case Study of Two Villages in Wokha District." M.Phil. Thesis, North East Hill University, 1987.

Achumi, Hevukhu. "Revival Movement in Nagaland and its Impact on the Nagas." M.Th. Thesis, New Zealand, 2000.

Aier, I. Lanu. "The Emerging Middle Class in Naga Society." M.Phil Thesis, North East Hill University, 1982.

Ao, Sashinungla. "A Study of the Role of the Nagaland Baptist Church Council in the Socio-Political Life of the Nagas in Nagaland from 1947-1997." M.Th. Thesis, Easter Theological College; Senate of Serampore College, 2000.

Kape, Loli "A Christian Ethical Analysis of and Response to Contemporary Economic Trend in Dimapur." M.Th. Thesis, United Theological College, 1999.

Sema, Akheto. "A Study of Paulo Freire's Educational Thoughts in the Context of Nagaland." D.Th. Thesis, United Theological College, 2000.

Swu, Hetoni. "A Study of The Holistic Concept of Mission Found in Luke's Gospel in Relation to the Concept of Mission of the Sumi Naga Churches." BD Thesis, Bishop's College, 1997.

Swu, Inaho G. "A Study of the Growth of the Baptist Churches Among the Sumis with Special Reference to Southern Baptist Churches." BD Thesis, Clark Theological College, 1996.

Tali, Rongsenrenla. "A Study of the Problems Faced by High School Teachers and their Attitudes Towards Teachings Profession in Nagaland." Ph.D. Dissertation, North East Hill University, 1984.

Zhimomi, V. H. "British Policy and Administration in Nagaland." M.Phil. Dissertation, 1981.

Interviews:

Achumi, Hekhevi. Finance Secretary, Naga Hoho and Chairman Sumi Council. Interview, 5 April 2005.

Aier, Alongla. Convenor/Director, Sisterhood Network. Interview, 14 April 2005.

Angami, Bandi. One of founding Members of Morung. Interview, 14 April 2005.

Arenla Imsong. Office Adminstrator, EA, Interview, 27April 2005.

Awomi, Pushika. President, NSF. Interview, 16th May 2005.

Awomi, Tovishe. Evangelist, WSBAK. Interview, 7 September 2004.

Aye, Kanili. Women Secretary, WSBAK. Interview, 6 October 2004.

Aye, Phughoto. Executive Secretary, WSBAK. Interview, 6 September 2004.

Ayemi, Hekuto. Deacon Chairman of Dimapur Church. Interview, 2 September 2004.

Chishi, Hukhali. President, WSTH. Interview, 8 April 2005.

Chishi, Khesheli. President, NMM. Interview, 16 May 2005.

Kiho, Nohozu. Missionary, Arunachal Pradesh. Interview, 9 September 2004.

Aye, Khevili. Associate Women Pastor of Dimapur Church. Interview, 6 September 2004.

Chophy, Ahoto. Asst. Pastor of Dimapur Church. Interview, 27 September 2004.

Doulo, Neichute. Secretary, EA. Interview, 22 April 2004.

Hekali. Deputy Commissioner of Dimapur. Interview, 4 May 2005.

James, Pheuba. Director, Akimbo Society. Interview, 14 April 2005.

Ligse, Savi. President, Naga Council. Interview, 4 April 2005.

Longkumar, Akum. One of the Founding members of Morung. Interview, 12 April 2005.

Ao, Moamenla. Founder of Hope Center, Interview, 14 April 2005.

Naro. Women Secretary, NBCC. Interview, 26 April 2005.

Peku, Nepuni. Convenor of Nagaland, NPMHR. Interview, 12 April 2005.

Pongsing. Director of Nagaland Development Outreach. Interview, 14 April 2005.

Sasu, Lanu. Lecturer, Nagaland University. Interview, 29 March 2005.

Swu, Heniho. Ex-chairman Deacon Board of Dimapur Church. Interview, 26 September 2004.

Swu, Inaho. Pastor of Dimapur Church. Interview, 27 September 2004.

Swu, Vitoshe. Mission and Evangelism Director of WSBAK. Interview, 7 September 2004.

Terhuja, Zhabu. Executive Secretary, NBCC. Interview, 28 April 2005.

V. K. Nuh, General Secretary, CNBC. Interview, 26 April 2005.

Velu-o-swuro, Deputy Director of SIRD. Interview 27 April 2005.

Awomi, Vikheho. Chairman, Municipal Dimapur. Interview 4 April 2005.

Zeito, Former President, SKK. Interview, 8 April 2005.

Zhimomi, H. K. Assembly Secretary, Naga Hoho. Interview, 6 April 2005.

Papers/Booklets/Pamphlets/Newspapers and Participatory Records:

A Profile of Nagaland Development Outreach. Prepared by NDO Office, Chumukedima: Nagaland, 2003.

Ayemi, Hetovi. Development Officer, WSBAK , Letter to the author, 4 January 2005.

Constitution of Sumi Baptist Convention (now changed into SBCC) 2nd edition, 1995.

"Declaration of the Naga People's Movement for Human Rights." *A Leaflet.* By NPMHR.

Develop Your Own Village: An Approach to Grass Root Planning and Development. Produced by Vamuzo in 1978.

Doulo, Neichute. Lecture on Entrepreneurs Associates at UBS, Pune on 22 April 2004 organized by Center for North East Studies and Policy Research.

"Education from Christian Point of View." A paper presented V. K. Nuh, 2005.

NMPHR. "A Journey Continues… a Call to all Nagas." *Pamphlet.*

Prabhkar, Samson. "Towards a Christian Education for an Inclusive Community." A Seminar Paper at United Theological College. June 21, 1996.

Prospectus 1998 Rev. Inache Memorial Mission School, WSBAK Centre.

School Policy/ Guideline, Baptist School: Kuhuboto, Nagaland.

"Sisterhood Network (SN): A Profile." *A Paper* produced by Alongla Aier, Consultant /Director, SN. 1.

Swu, Hetoni "A Missiological Study on the Mission Application of the Western Sumi Baptist Church Association." A Seminar Paper Submitted to Consortium for Indian Missiological Education in October 2004.

The 19th Annual Assembly Council of Naga Baptist Churches 18-20 March 2005 at Zeme Baptist Churches Dimapur. A Paper Presented by V. K. Nuh, General Secretary, CNBC, 2003.

The Main/Important Festivals of Sema Naga. *A Booklet* produced by K. David Sema, 2001.

V. K. Nuh, "Liberty in Socio-Political Transformation." *A Paper* presented at Sumi Baptist Centenary on 4-7 December, Zunheboto.

White Paper on Naga Integration. Compiled by the Naga Hoho, 2002.

Workshop on "Self Help", "Horticulture", "Health and Cookery" organized on 20th May at Dimapur Town Church, 2004.

WSBAK Mission Sutsa/News. July-August 2004.

WSBAK Mission Sutsa/News. Mission Department, Akuvuto, Thahekhu, 2004.

Brochures:

"Akimbo Society." *A Brochure.*

"Entrepreneurs Associates Micro Finance." *A Brochure.*

"Introducing NEICORD." *A Brochure.*

"Morung: for indigenous affairs and just peace." *A Brochure.*

"Nagaland Development Outreach." *A Brochure.*

"Nagas are What Nagas were." *A Brochure.* NMA/ NPMHR/ NSF.

"Nagas Towards our Rightful Place Through Healing of our Spirit." *A Brochure.* NPMHR.

"Samaritan Home Project: WSBAK Women Department." *Brochure.*

Journals/Newsletters/Quarterly-Occasional Publications:

Arenla Longchar, "Education and Communication." *NBCC Newsletter* IV/4 (July-September, 2004), 9.

Arputhamurthy, J. E. M. "Ecology, Economics and Ecumenics." *TBT Journal* 2/1 (2000), 39-48.

"Awareness Programme for HIV/AIDS." *Vanguard* 1 (May-July 2003), 35.

Beisner, C. Calvin. "Justice and Poverty: Two Views Contrasted." *Transformation* 10/1 (January-April, 1993), 12-16.

Belho, Nezokhotuo. "To The Hon'ble Chief Minsiter, Nagaland." *Vanguard* 1 (May-July, 2003), 49.

Belshaw, Deryke. "Socio-economic Theology and Ethical Choices in Contemporary Development Policy: An Outline of Biblical Approaches to Social Justice and Poverty Alleviation." *Transformation* 14/1 (January-March, 1997), 6.

"Church Consultation on Drugs Abuse, HIV/AIDS." *Baptist News* 53/1 (January-March, 2002), 35-40.

Drane, John. "Defining A Biblical Theology of Creation." *Transformation* 10/2 (April-July, 1993), 8-11.

Getu, Makonen. "Measuring Transformation: Conceptual framework and indicators." *Transformation* 19/2 (April, 2002), 92-97.

Freire, Paulo. "Education, Liberation and the Church." *Religious Education* 79/4 (Fall, 1984), 106.

Holder-rich. "Cynthia: Development as Freedom or Freedom as development?" *Journal of Theology for Southern Africa* 110 (July, 2001), 89-96.

In Touch, 2 (October 2004).

John, V. V. "The Role of the State in Jesus' View: A Synoptic Perspective." *Bangalore Theological Forum* 36/1 (June, 2004), 1-18.

Joseph, M. J. "Paul's Understanding of "Economics" in Social Relations." *NCCR*. (October, 1996), 633-644.

Scara, K. J. "Social Justice in the Old Testament." *Biblebhashyam* 1/3 (September, 1978), 163-192.

Katalyst. A bi-monthly newsletter of the Entrepreneurs Associates. 1/4 (March-April 2003), 1.

Katalyst. A bi-monthly newsletter of the Entrepreneurs Associates. 1/3 (January-February 2003), 1.

Katalyst. A bi-monthly newsletter of the Entrepreneurs Associates. 2 (November-December, 2002).

Katalyst. A bi-monthly newsletter of the Entrepreneurs Associates. 1/5 (May-June, 2003).

Katalyst. A bi-monthly newsletter of the Entrepreneurs Associates. 2/1 (January-February, 2000).

Katalyst. A bi-monthly newsletter of the Entrepreneurs Associates. 1/4 (July-August, 2004).

Keikung, Anjo "Nagaland Missionary Movement Mission Week May 1-7, 2005." *NBCC NewsLetter* V/2 (Janaury-March, 2005), 4.

Van Leeuwen, Th. Marius. "The Jubilee Challenge." *The Ecumenical Review* 50/2 (April, 1998), 244-249.

Louw, Daniel J. "International Economy and International Communication within the Network of Cyberspace: Pastoral Care to Cyber Punks." *Bangalore Theological Forum* 36/1 (June, 2004), 53-69.

Luithui, Shimreichon. "Indigenous Women." *Indigenous Affairs.* (July-September 2000), 24-27.

Mayori, R. S. "Naga Talks Enter a New Phase." *Indian Currents* 13 (February 2005), 46.

Minutes and Resolutions of the First Federal Assembly, Camp at Tamenglong on 27 June 2003." *Vanguard* 1 (May-July 2003), 33.

Mott, Stephen and Ronald J. Sider. "Economic Justice: A Biblical Paradigm." *Transformation* 17/2 (April, 2000), 50-62.

Mott, Stephen Charles. "The Partiality of Biblical Justice." *Transformation* 10/1 (January, 1993), 23-29.

NBCC NewsLetter V/1(October-December, 2000), 3-4.

NDO. "HIV/AIDS: A Development Issue." *NBCC NewsLetter* 5/1 (October-December, 2004), 10.

NPMHR. *Journal* (April 2004).

NPMHR. *Journal* (April 2004).

NPMHR's Occasional Publication. (February 2000), 2.

Vipopal Kinsto. "Presidential Address Delivered on the 20th General Conference of the Naga Students' Federation at Niuland on 23rd April 2003." *Vanguard* 1 (May-July 2003), 10.

Perkins, John. "What it means to be the Church: Reflections on Mission and Human Rights," *International Review of Mission,* Vol. 66/ 263 (July, 1997), 244.

Rayan, Samuel. "Peace: Biblical Perspectives." *Jnanadeepa Pune Journal of Religious Studies* 4/2 (2002), 104-119.

"Righteousness In Matthew's Gospel: Its Social Implications." *Bible Bhashyam an Indian Quarterly*. 13/3 (September 1987), 151-178.

"Seminar on The Impact of Transmigration on the Nagas organized by the Naga Students Federation at Dimapur, 4th-5th April 2002." *Vanguard* 1 (May-July 2003), 25.

Shangkham, Gins. "Naga Women and Peace Process." *NPMHR's Occasional Publication*. (2000-2001), 8.

Shekatkar, D. B. "Resolving Conflict in North East." *The North East Frontier Magazine* (Feb. 2004), 9-14.

Thanzauva, K. "Theology of Human Development." *NCCR*, 110/7 (August, 1990), 394-411.

The Righteousness Required of the Followers of Christ (Mt Ch. VII)." *Bible Bhashyam an Indian Biblical Quarterly* 10/2 (June, 1984), 132-139.

"Tenure 2001-2003 at a Glance: Brief Report of the General Secretary of the NSF." *Vanguard* 1 (May-July 2003), 13-19.

Warangal. "Andhra Pradesh on 5-7 October 2000." *NPMHR's Occasional Publication*, (Winter, 2000-2001), 5.

"Women for Peace in Nagalim." *NPMHR's Occasional Publication*. (2000-2001), 3.

Websites:

Chang, Sang. "Justice of Jubilee in Luke: Bible Study." *Reformed World* 45/1 and 2 (March- June 1995). http://www.warc.ch/dp/rw9512/12.html (15 March 2003).

"Christian Socialism in the Naga Context." In *Manifesto of the National Socialist Council of Nagalim: National Socialism*. www.nscnonline.org/webpage/manifesto/national-socialism.htm (15 March 2003).

"Church, Naga Unhappy with poll process." (20 February 2003) http://newsarchives.indianfo.com/spotlight/election2003/21nagapoll.html (2 March 2003).

Myers, Ched. 'Jesus' New Economy of Grace', *Sojourners* (July-August 1998), http://www.sojourners.com/soj9807/980723.htm (12 April 2003).

"Nagaland a profile and map." www.mapsofindia.com/stateprofiles/nagaland/ (25 March 2003).

Nayar, Kuldip. "Nagaland: Too Distant and Too Alienated." www.radicalparty.org//humanrights/nagaland.htm (24 October 2004).

"Two Apex Naga Church Groups Call for Reconciliation." (10 August 2001) http://www.rediff.com/news/2001/aug/10naga.htm (2 March 2003). Wilkinson, Bruce. "Justice in Christian Relief and Development: A Community-Centered Approach." cieurope.net/justice/justice%20christian%20Relief/20ad%20development.pdf (12 October 2004).

To,

....

....

Dear Sir / Madam
Greetings to you

I am Hetoni Swu doing my Ph. D Research in Missiology under Consortium for Indian Missiological Education (CIME), Bangalore. At Present working as faculty in Union Biblical Seminary from 2002 till date. My interest area is on **"The Church Role of the Sumi Baptist Church in the Emerging Socio-Economic Situation of Nagaland."** Therefore, for this reason, I would like to request you to kindly help me in filling the questionnaire. Your contribution and help towards my research would be of great help and valued. Thus, information received from you will be kept confidential.

Thanking you,

Hetoni swu
UBS,
Bibvewadi, Pune – 37
Maharastra
Phone: 09823825231
020 24211747 (Extn 314)
Email: hetoni_swus@yahoo.co.in

Note: Please refer the necessary instructions given on each question
Expected date for return: on or before 14 May 2005.

Appendix I

QUESTIONNAIRE

Let us look into the emerging socio-economic situation of the people in Nagaland.

1. What is the size of your family? Tick the appropriate one.
   1 2 3 4 5 6 and above
2. Give their age ranges, specifying male or female.
   ....
3. What is your family's monthly average income? Tick the appropriate one.
   (a) Below 500 (b) 500-1000
   (c) 1500-2000 (d) 2500-3000
   (e) 3500-4000 (f) 4500 and above.
4. How many of you are employed in the Government sector?
   ....
5. Who are they? ....
6. How many of you are employed in private sector?
   ....
7. Who are they? ....
8. How many of you are self-employed?
   ....

9. Who are they? ....

10. Mention the types of work under these three types of employment structures you and your family members are involved in.

    ....

    ....

    ....

11. Could you please give some reasons from your perspective why the people remain unemployed (inclusive of all the above structures)?

    ....

    ....

12. If you are not employed in any of these employment structures discussed above, what do you do for a living? Tick the appropriate one.

    (a) Rent house　　　　　　(b) Own commercial buildings
    (c) Collect from others　　　(b) Depend on relatives
    (e) Occasional visit to wealthy homes
    (f) Own a farm
    (g) Any other? ....

13. What is your average daily working hour? Tick the appropriate one.

    2-3hrs　　4-5hrs　　6-8hrs　　9hrs and above　　Not working

14. How do the young people in your home (those not engaged in study) spend their time?

    ....

    ....

15. What do the young people in your home usually do after they return from School/college?

    ....

    ....

16. According to your observation, how is the educational system in Nagaland helping the people for economic survival? Your comment on positive and negative sides.

    ....

    ....

17. How would you like the educational system to improve? Your comments.

....

....

Could you please indicate your observation on the young people's attitude to work by grading them accordingly in the column below?

	Very rare	**Mostly**	**Commonly**	**Not at all**
(18) Feel embarrass				
(19) Afraid				
(20) Lazy				
(21) Active				
(22) Not motivated				
(23) Energetic				
(24) Sincere				
(25)Do not give importance				
(26) Ignorant about work				
(27) Find hard				
(28) Graceful				
(29) Keep distant				
(30) Not bothered				

31. Do (the parents today) you encourage (their) your children to work hard apart from studies? Tick the appropriate one.

    (a) No/ Yes (b) Very little / mostly (c) Commonly / rarely
    (d) Any other? ....

32. Could you mention your observation on the present Naga community life? Tick one option in each code ( ).
    (a) Common decision / only the rich takes decisions
    (b) Interdependent / Independent
    (c) Clan system / class system
    (d) Rich and poor divide / sharing of resources

(e) Community orientated (Family orientated)/ Individualistic
(f) Tribalism/ anti-tribalism
(g) Justice community / corruption
(h) Traditional/ Westernisation
(i) Dependence/ independence
(h) Any other? ....

33. Could you please indicate the percentage of the following according to your own observation?
the percentage of the poor people ....
the percentage of the rich people ....

34. Do you think the present Naga community have provision for the poor, orphans and widows? Comment.
....
....
Could you please indicate the most dreadful social evils that exist in our society by grading them according to order of importance.

	Very Serious	Serious	A little serious	Not a problem
(35) Drug addiction				
(36) HIV/AIDS				
(37) Intoxicating drinks				
(38) Division/clashes				
(39) Illegal marriage				
(40) Prostitution				
(41) Divorce				
(42) Infidelity				
(43) Abortion				
(44) Killing/murder				
(45)I ndulge in criminal cases				
(46) Theft				
(47) Easy money				
(48) Threat				
(49) Injustice				

50. What according to you are the causes of the emergence of these social evils?

 ....

 ....

51. From your point of view comment on the Sumi (Naga) marriage pattern from socio-economic perspective.

 ....

 ....

52. Do you agree to the statement that Naga community life has changed from better to worse? Your comment please.

 ....

 ....

53. Can you please comment from your perspective on the present socio-economic situation?

 ....

 ....

54. What is the people's attitude to each other today? Tick one option in each code ( ).
 (a) Loving and peaceful/ Enmity
 (b) Insecure/secure
 (c) Sharing/ Injustice
 (d) Faithful/unfaithful
 (e) Sensitive/ Insensitive
 (f) Caring/Cruel
 (g) Any other? ....

55. How do you feel about the influx of the outsiders in Nagaland? Your comment please.

 ....

 ....

56. Do you think to some extent they have taken over the economic income resources and products from the local people? Your comment.

 ....

 ....

57. How do you feel about the intermarriage of the local people to the outsiders from the socio-economic perspectives? Your comment.

    ....

    ....

58. Has the government taken any steps to control the influx of the outsiders to the state?

    ....

    ....

59. Is the government of our state effective? Yes/ No and give your reason why?

    ....

    ....

    We shall now look into the roles of the NGOs, social organisations and government for the upliftment of the socio-economic situation.

    ....

    ....

60. Are you aware of any NGOs or social organisations working for the upliftment of the society? Yes/ no. Comment.

    ....

    ....

61. What kind of work are they involved in?

    ....

    ....

62. Do you feel the above type of work helps the people?

    ....

    ....

63. Give your comment on the present NGOs/Social organisations; what are their positive and negative sides.

64. Naga Mother's Association is a visible wing that initiates the social upliftment of the society. Yes/No comment.

    ....

    ....

Could you please indicate their main contributions by grading the following according to order of importance in each column?

	Usually	More	Not at all	Sometimes
(65) Awareness towards social evils				
(66) Social and legal action taken				
(67) Not sure				
(68) Socio-political involvement				
(69) Socio-economic upliftment				

Any other? ....

70. Comment on the role of the Naga Hoho from the socio-economic perspective.

....

....

71. Do you have any idea on Nagaland Development Outreach -NDO (NGO based at Chumukedima)? Comment.

....

....

72. Comment on the role of the Naga Students Federation from the socio-economic perspective.

....

....

73. Do you have any idea of Entrepreneurs Associates (NGO based at Kohima)? Comment.

....

....

74. Do you have any idea of NICORD (NGO based at Shillong)? Comment.

....

....

75. What would you suggest further for these organisations to be effective and relevant for the socio-economic development of the society?

    ....

    ....

76. Can you please point out some of the pros and cons of the Naga political movement from the present socio-economic perspectives?

77. How do you feel about the government's role on the present socio-economic prospect of the people? Tick the appropriate one.
    (a) Satisfactory (b) Not satisfactory
    (c) Unaware of situation

78. If (a) why? ....

79. If (b) why? ....

80. Do you support the continuing insurgency in the state? Will it ever stop? How?

    ....

    ....

81. Can you point out the opportunities the government provides for the upliftment of the socio-economic situation?

    ....

    ....

82. Do you feel these opportunities are made known to the common people? Your comment please.

    ....

    ....

83. What do you feel has been the government's approaches for the socio-economic upliftment of the society?

    ....

    ....

84. How according to you are these programmes implemented? Please comment.

    ....

    ....

85. Have you benefited from the government's socio-economic programmes? If so how? Please elaborate.
86. Who normally benefits from the government's programmes? Tick the appropriate one.
    (a) The party workers (b) The rich
    (c) There is no partiality, all according to availability of funds
    (d) Any other ....
87. Comment on the strengths and weaknesses of the government in implementing these programmes.
    ....
    ....
88. In what ways has the government taken steps to stop social evils in the state? Comment.
    ....
    ....
89. What are your aspirations for the future role of the government in the socio-economic development of the state?
    ....
    ....

    Let us look into the role of the church (it implies the Sumi in particular and Naga churches as a whole) in the present socio-economic context.
90. What are the roles played by the churches in the present socio-economic context?
    ....
    ....
91. Comment on the church's impact in the life of the people.
    ....
    ....
92. How effective is the church's mission and evangelism within and outside the mission field?
    (a) Satisfactory (b) Unsatisfactory (c) Not sure
93. Your comment please. ....
    ....

94. Is it appropriate for the church to involve in socio-economic and political spheres of life? Yes/ No. Why?

....

....

95. Could you suggest the role of the church in the present socio-economic and political context of Nagaland?

96. Could you please indicate your expectation of the church's role in a society by grading them according to order of importance.

	Very Important	Important	Not Important
(96) To set social awareness			
(97) To be creative agent in all social spheres of life			
(98) To Involve in nation building			
(99) To Work for social action			
(100) To preach			
(101) To transform			
(102) To promote Christian education for all stages of people			
(103) To teach			
(104) To train and provide skills for survival			
(105) To evangelise			
(106) To provide tools and facility for survival			
(107) To promote opportunities for survival			
(108) To work for human rights and dignity of all people			
(109) To work to promote relevant education			

110. Should the Sumi Baptist Church have any concern for the outsiders working in the state?

....

....

Appendix II

INTERVIEW GUIDE FOR GOVERNMENT OFFICIALS

1. How would describe the present situation of the common Naga people and their quest for survival?
2. Do you feel that the present management of state resources adequately meets the needs of the common people, or do you see a need for change?
3. Could you point out some examples of the emerging socio-economic situation of the people?
4. Among the changes you have seen (or mention), how do you feel this is influencing the cultural values and traditions of the Naga people?
5. Could you mention some of the opportunities the government provides for the unemployment and underemployment youths and adults?
6. How are children and women reached out socio-economically? Is there any specific programme meted out for them?
7. May I know your contributions and failures towards the cause of the people?
8. How would you respond to the socio-economic exploitation of the people?
9. There seems to be an uneven economic growth among different groups of people in Nagaland. Why do you think this is so?
10. What according to you leads to the weakening of socio-economic life of the people?
11. How does the government feel about the influx of outsiders in Nagaland?

12. Do you feel the government has a role to play in this situation?
13. Comment your observations on the influx of the outsiders in Nagaland.
14. From your perspective, would you be able to point out the failures and success in socio-economic governance of Nagaland at present?
15. Can you describe any further socio-economic development programmes that the State government has taken up for the upliftment of the people? If, how are they going to help the people?
16. I would also like to ask about the role of the church. What role would you like to see the church play in the upliftment of the people's socio-economic situation?

INTERVIEW GUIDE FOR NAGA POLITICAL LEADERS

1. How would you describe the present situation of the common Naga people and their quest for survival?
2. Do you feel there is a gap between the rich and the poor? Why? Comment.
3. Would you please comment on what specifically hinders the socio-economic development of Nagaland?
4. Could you mention the socio-economic role of the Naga political movement leaders in the society?
5. How would you describe the future of the Nagas from your own perspective?
6. What are your expectations towards the common people in your struggles?
7. From your perspective would you be able to point out your contributions and failures towards the upliftment of socio-economic situation of the people?
8. In what ways do you think that present Naga political movement will bring solution to socio-economic situation of the Nagas?
9. The long periods of political struggles and pains have caused many break ups among the brethrens to the extent of taking people's life and emotions, in a situation like this, how would you plea for hope on the Naga sovereignty and regaining the Naga communal ethos?

10. Please comment on the present socio-economic situation of the people.
11. What role would you like the church to play in the Naga political movement?
12. Could you please mention your observation on the church role at present?

INTERVIEW GUIDE FOR THE NON GOVERNMENTAL ORGANISATIONS

1. Could you state the beginnings of your organisation?
2. Could you mention your motivation behind it? Or what prompted you to start the organisation?
3. How is your organisation functioned?
4. Could you please mention the central focus of your organisation?
5. Could you describe the sort of programme you have on the socio-economic development of the people?
6. Could you please mention whether you network with any other NGOs?
7. From your perspective would you point out the success and failures of your organisation?
8. Could you please mention in what ways your work benefits the people?
9. How do you feel about your organisation does it promotes socio-economic growth?
10. Do you think that the Naga churches through linking with the NGOs would bring successful result in uplifting the people's socio-economic living?
11. What are your future projects and goal in the development of socio-economic perspectives in Nagaland?
12. What type of people are involved in your organisation? Is there any set parameter in regard to religions, qualifications, Man/ women etc.?
13. Would you agree that they faithfully execute the works in a given situation?
14. Are the reports reviewed occasionally and improved accordingly to the needs of the people?

15. Could you mention your observation on the present socio-economic situation of the people?
16. Do you feel the church has a role to play in the society? Suggest.
17. What is your observation towards church conduct on present situation?

INTERVIEW GUIDE FOR OTHER SOCIAL ORGANISATIONS

1. Could you mention what motivated you to form your organisation?
2. Would you please highlight the programmes that your organisation is involved in?
3. Could you please mention the central focus of your organisation?
4. I would like to know about the type of work you are particularly involved in. Could you mention few examples?
5. Who are the people involved in the organisation?
6. How do feel about the people involve in this responsibility? Comment.
7. Could you please bring out the areas in which your organisation has helped the people?
8. How do you feel about the influx of the outsiders in the land?
9. Do you feel these people as helpful in our socio-economic setting? Or are they threat to our socio-economic growth?
10. As there is gradual increase in marriage with the outsiders, what would be your opinion towards the intercultural marriage?
11. How do you feel about the influx of the outsiders in our land?
12. Do you feel the outsiders have right to work, run a business, job opportunities and property, and to some extent they have taken over the rights of the local people?
13. Would you please mention what will be the rights and opportunities for the local people?
14. From your perspective what would be your concern on this issue for the future of Nagas?
15. Could you mention the failures and success of your organisational work particularly towards socio-economic development?

16. Would you point out the specific achievements?
17. Would you mention the future of your organisational work if you have planned out?
18. Please mention your observation on the present socio-economic situation of the people.
19. What is your observation towards the present church role in a society?
20. What would you suggest the church to play in socio-economic developments of the people?

INTERVIEW GUIDE FOR THE CHURCH LEADERS

1. Could you mention the basis of your mission work?
2. Would you mention your mission focus?
3. According to your perspective what would be the church role in a society?
4. Would you agree that mission should focus only on the spiritual realms of the people? Your comment please.
5. What is your interpretation of the gospel towards community building?
6. Will it be appropriate for the church work for the upliftment of the socio-economic development of the people? Comment.
7. Would you mention your awareness and participation towards socio-political situation of Nagaland?
8. Could you mention the mission achievements and failures of the church particularly in the socio-economic context of Nagaland?
9. Would you briefly mention what the church aspires to do in future?
10. How do you feel about the role of the other Social organisation and NGOs in the upliftment of the society?
11. Would you mention your observation in what ways these could be link together with the church and work for the betterment of our society?